April 29, 199_

Daris Swindler: You are
one of my oldest friends.
We meet all too
rarely, but it is a
great pleasure when
we do and I look
forward to these
occasions.
Best wishes,
Garret Parker

Happenings
and
Hearsay

Happenings
and
Hearsay

Experiences of a
Biological Anthropologist

Gabriel Ward Lasker

With a foreword by
Michael A. Little

SAVOYARD BOOKS   Detroit, Michigan   1999

Library of Congress Catalog Card Number
99-70808

Jacket design by Robert Lasker.
Text design by Elizabeth Hanson.

Contents

Foreword

*G*abriel Lasker is a biological anthropologist who has contributed to the profession of anthropology in many ways for more than five decades. He retired in 1982 from the Department of Anatomy of Wayne State University in Detroit after more than thirty-five years of teaching, research, and journal editing. For other, more conventional academics, this transition might have led to a somewhat more leisurely life, but for Gabriel, retirement simply freed him for additional research and professional activity.

Ideas and their dissemination are what motivates and excites this uncommon man. I remember remarking, several years ago, that his publication record—during retirement—far exceeded that of most of his less energetic junior colleagues such as myself. He can be said to have had two professional lives: his preretirement life and an active postretirement life that shows no sign of diminishing.

What characterizes Gabriel, and is reflected in his writing here, is a frank and open, sometimes even blunt, analysis of events and interpretation of individuals' behaviors and motives. Yet such interpretations are usually balanced with humor and often affection. Gabriel laughs a lot, and conversations with him are always punctuated with the wit of himself and of his wife, Bunny. His approach to recollection and reporting provides the reader with insight into the depth and complexity of the personalities and beliefs of those who played a part in Gabriel Lasker's life.

There are several interesting themes embedded in these recollections. First is the notion of how the successful pursuit of a life and career is a complex mix of several elements. These elements include luck (serendipity, good fortune, opportunity); a nurturing and supportive home environment, with value placed on knowledge and intellectual pursuits; and, always, the need for initiative to be taken by the individual. Gabriel was fortunate to come from a family of science, both social and natural, and his honesty and "moral leadership" almost certainly arise from this background and reflect the guiding principles of scientific inquiry, which are truth and validation.

A second theme displays his dedication to anthropology as an intellectual arena. Anthropology is truly a biobehavioral science, and Gabriel's approach to biobehavioral inquiry is probably related to some of his early family experiences. Moreover, for a biological anthropologist married to a cultural anthropologist, there can be only one of two outcomes: divorce or an increasing sense of the importance of biobehavioral and biocultural relationships. Gabriel and Bunny chose the latter outcome. A dedication to anthropology as a profession can be displayed in a number of ways; Gabriel chose several. When he could not teach anthropology students because of his appointment in anatomy, he took visiting professor posts when opportunities arose, and he dedicated several summers to the Viking Fund Summer Seminars in Physical Anthropology and other intensive short courses for graduate students and junior PhDs. Other contributions that he made to education in anthropology were co-editorship of volumes on teaching anthropology, published by the University of California Press and as monographs of the American Anthropological Association; several basic textbooks on biological anthropology (I used them all); and avuncular guidance that he gave to junior anthropologists who were publishing, with trepidation, their first articles in the journal *Human Biology* (I was one of those, too).

A third theme is the development of biological anthropology during the more than half a century of Gabriel Lasker's involvement with the profession. This also incorporates the pervading subtheme of "race," a concept that has been a part of anthropology since its nineteenth-century origins and is still a topic of debate and discussion.

When Gabriel Lasker began his graduate studies in biological anthropology at Harvard University in 1937, the prevailing view of human variation was that our species was made up of several unvarying races or "types" and that any deviation from these types resulted from racial mixing. These views persisted in anthropology despite Franz Boas's pioneering study during the first decade of the twentieth century which demonstrated that racial "types" did change in their shape, size, and skeletal dimensions when exposed to different environments. Views of racial typology also persisted in spite of the growing body of literature that demonstrated the processes of selection, adaptation, and evolution in other species, processes that we know now have contributed to the worldwide variation that we see in human populations today. An awareness that human races, as fixed entities, do not exist was a concept that developed slowly after World War II. Gabriel Lasker and several other biological anthropologists recognized early on the fallacy of fixed, typological races, and they conducted their research work accordingly. Perhaps because his dissertation research followed the migration model of Boas, human variation and plasticity were seen by him in a different light. The idea of racial typologies has been discarded largely by a younger generation of biological anthropologists, although the transition has been a long one. Modern approaches to human biobehavioral variation include studies of human functional morphology, physiology, biochemistry, growth, health, and genetics, often within environmental and evolutionary frameworks. This latter area of genetics research is one modern approach to understanding human variation that Gabriel has pursued for many years.

We owe a debt of gratitude to Gabriel Lasker for documenting the significant events of his life from which others can read and learn. His colleagues owe him a further debt for all of the ways he has contributed to the development and strengthening of biological anthropology as a science and a profession, and for the assistance that he has provided in helping the younger members of the profession to develop their scientific careers. All biological anthropologists and those students preparing for a career in biological anthropology would profit by reading this account by someone whose life in our profession has been among the most distinguished.

Michael A. Little
Binghamton, New York

Preface

When I was entering the field of physical anthropology, Earnest A. Hooton was writing entertaining books such as *Up from the Ape* (1931 and 1946) which explored the subject for generations of students. There was little in the literature then about the people involved in the science, since virtually everyone knew everyone else personally, at least in the United States. That cannot be said now. In this memoir, I try to convey the way the subject was developing by writing about the people I encountered, their ideas, and my reactions, then and now.

I speak out critically, but I hope it will be understood that I learned much from most of the same individuals I criticize and that I respect them and am grateful to them. With hindsight, I can now find fault with views that were once generally agreed upon, including some of mine. All of us have strengths and weaknesses. For instance, in my own research, some samples were too small or not sufficiently representative for definitive results. Likewise, I think I can recognize errors even in the work of those I admire most.

For example, I have something to say about my principal teachers of anthropology: Earnest A. Hooton and Carleton S. Coon, physical anthropologists at Harvard. They were always encouraging and sympathetic to students, but the research of both was flawed by an erroneous notion of the importance of race and overemphasis on the role of genetic determination of human morphology and behavior.

Detail from a portrait of Gabriel Lasker by Glenn Michaels, 1994. Michaels is well known for his mosaiclike assemblages such as a mural at Gordon Scott Hall of the medical school of Wayne State University.

Eliot Chapple, while he was at Harvard, developed a research methodology for studying the duration of each individual's speech activity in interactions between two or more individuals. His idea of studying aspects of speech interaction independently from the content still deserves further development and use even if the perfect consistency he found in behavior of individuals fails to hold up. I thrived on his Socratic method of teaching, which seemed difficult for some of the other students to appreciate.

Clyde Kluckhohn, who later was professor of anthropology in the Department of Social Relations at Harvard, gave a course I took on the physical anthropology of American Indians. It was nothing more than undigested bibliography and must have been an unwelcome task for him. However, he also tutored me in social anthropology in an incomparably effective way and with an obvious interest in trying to help me master material that I was encountering for the first time. When he became interested in psychological anthropology, Kluckhohn put himself back in the role of student to participate in Abraham Kardiner's seminar on the subject at Columbia University.

I admire Hooton as a teacher and supporter; Coon for his wide knowledge, openness, and friendship; Chapple for brilliant original thinking; and Kluckhohn for his inquisitiveness and scholarship.

Biological anthropologists may enjoy sharing my recollections of anthropologists they have known or for other personal reasons. Other readers, including some interested in liberal education, social history, or pacifism, will find something about my experiences with those issues in these pages. My time in China and my anthropological journey will be, I hope, of interest to others.

A number of people have read and criticized earlier versions of this work: members of my family, my colleagues Drs. Mauricio Lande and Jerald A. Mitchell, and others of my friends. Readers and critics included Professor Derek F. Roberts, Dr. Ralph Garruto, Professor Michael A. Little, Professor Michael H. Crawford, Professor William S. Laughlin, Dr. C. G. N. Mascie-Taylor, Professor Barry Bogin, Dr. Douglas Crews, Professor Leslie Sue Lieberman, and two anonymous critics. Wendy Warren Keebler was a competent copy editor.

Dr. Pamela Raspe did more than suggest; she put the manuscript on her computer and introduced into it not a few changes for the better. I am grateful to all these readers and have made revisions in an attempt to take account of their suggestions.

Some works by others that are mentioned are given in the bibliography. Those by myself are included in the appendix. Most of the
photographs in this book are my own or my wife's snapshots. Others
are acknowledged in the captions. Some of the photographs and their
legends attempt to tell their own little stories.

Gabriel W. Lasker

1

Family Background and Early Years

I was born in 1912 in New Earswick, a model village, created from scratch by the owners of the Rowntree Chocolate factory to show that their workers could have good, affordable housing. It is a mile or perhaps two outside the walls of the old city of York, England. The family of my mother, Margaret Naomi Ward Lasker (1884–1976), was poor. I believe my grandfather Thomas Lambeth Ward, a wool merchant in the wool-weaving city of Bradford, drank away his money. His wife, Jenny, was of Jewish origins and was born in Hamburg, Germany. My sister has said that my father's family, also Jewish merchants in Hamburg, disapproved of my father's marriage because they considered my maternal grandmother's family nouveau riche.

There was a history of educating women in the family. My mother's great-granduncle was a schoolmaster, and his two daughters, Mary and Naomi Bewley, attended his school, Mr. Bewley's Academy in Leeds. We still possess Mary's school copybook, in beautiful goose-quill calligraphy, written in 1831 when the sisters were ten and twelve years old. Twenty-eight years before Darwin published *The Origin of Species* in 1859, one passage addresses the problem of geological and biological origins as a question for rational inquiry:

> Research. If to trace the origin of particular nations is to mark and
> to account for the rise and progress of empire, the revolution

of states, the discovery of new worlds,—be an interesting and useful exercise of the human mind; how amusing, interesting and instructive must it be, to trace human nature up to its source,—to observe how the heavens and earth took their beginning, and by what means this globe was at first peopled, and continues to be filled with men.

My great-great-granduncle evidently considered the passage suitable to include with moral adages for his daughter Mary to copy.

My mother was tutored in Latin by a minister and received a King's Fellowship to go away to university, but she was forbidden by her father to leave home to take it up. Instead, she enrolled at the University of Leeds and commuted daily by bicycle from Bradford, about ten miles away. My mother obviously enjoyed her college years, and she treasured her photographs of outings with fellow students. Of course, most university students at that time were young men, and I believe my mother was fond of one or more of them. She was obviously an enthusiastic, active, and happy young woman. In 1906, she was the first woman, or one of the first, to receive a bachelor's degree in chemistry from the University of Leeds. She qualified as a teacher and subsequently taught at the Heckmondwyke Grammar School. She told me about demonstrating chemistry from a high podium wearing her academic robe, but I cannot imagine that she presented an austere figure. She always made friends very easily with everyone, whatever their age or station.

Several years ago, Marie Lawrence, a biological anthropologist and fellow of Lucy Cavendish College, a college for mature women at the University of Cambridge, was interested to learn about my mother and secured the record of her employment at the Heckmondwyke school. It shows that when she married in 1909, she was fired from her job. In England at that time, any female teacher would automatically lose her job if she married. Mother was a suffragist and, with others, refused to be counted in the English census of 1910 since women could not vote.

My father, Bruno Lasker (1881–1965), was born in Hamburg. He and his three siblings all left Germany. His two brothers migrated to the Argentine, where they engaged in international trade in hides. His sister married a Frenchman and converted to Roman Catholicism. Despite being Jewish by descent, she and her son survived the Nazi occupation of France during World War II.

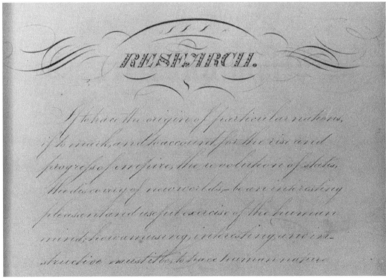

Facsimile from the copybook of Gabriel Lasker's great-grandaunt, written in 1831.

Margaret Lasker in about 1930. Research was not part of her job description at the hospital, so she did part of her research in this kitchen "laboratory," where she had a separate refrigerator for samples and reagents.

Bust of Bruno Lasker, Gabriel's father, in Hamburg in 1899, when he was nineteen, by Felix Leinweber.

My father did not go to university but was sent to work in the business of an associate of his father's in England. He lived in Manchester in a social settlement, an early form of social welfare agency. He never talked about those years—1900 to 1909—but it seems that he was involved with social reformers in Liberal Party politics. His sense of social responsibility extended to every aspect of his life. He was involved with the early years of the settlement movement, living at various times in settlement houses, where volunteers like himself worked to alleviate the problems of the poor, among whom they had settled.

My father hated the business and eventually quit and moved to York, where he became private secretary to B. Seebohm Rowntree, the Quaker philanthropist, sociologist, and progressive employer who owned the Rowntree Chocolate Company. In this capacity, my father conducted social research, and their study of the city of York, among the very first social surveys, was published as *Unemployment: A Social Study* by Rowntree and Lasker in 1911.

In August 1914, when I was two, the German army attacked Belgium. We were on vacation at a seaside resort in Holland, and as it was not yet clear that Holland would remain neutral, we all returned to England. There my father was considered an enemy alien, so his Quaker friends arranged for him to go to the United States rather than be interned. He did not remit enough money to provide for her needs and those of her two children, and for the next two years my mother had a very hard time raising two small children alone but managed with the help of neighbors and friends in New Earswick.

After his arrival in the United States, my father embarked on a lifelong career as a social scientist and editor with various organizations. His first job in America was on the New York City Mayor's Committee on Labor. During this time, he lived in another settlement house, the Henry Street Settlement on the Lower East Side. Thereafter, he held editorships on the two social work magazines, the *Survey* and the *Survey Graphic*. Then, under the auspices of a project called "The Inquiry," originally "The Inquiry on the Christian Way of Life," he wrote a book on the race attitudes of children and completed a study on Jewish experiences in America.

One of the sponsors of the Inquiry was Edward C. Carter. He was a Hawaiian and, like other intellectuals from the islands, was much concerned with political, economic, and social conditions in countries of the Pacific Rim.

5

With other supporters and scholars, Carter formed the Institute of Pacific Relations (IPR), and the group took my father along from the Inquiry to be a member of the International Secretariat of the IPR. There were national councils in the United States, United Kingdom, Soviet Union, France, Holland, Canada, China, Japan, Australia, New Zealand, and elsewhere. My father became expert at organizing international conferences and writing up the proceedings. He also wrote a book on Philippine immigration to the United States at about this time.

Eventually, the American Council of the IPR came under attack by Senator Joseph McCarthy for alleged communist connections, and the funding dried up. Whatever my father was, he was not a communist. One of his relatives, Edward Lasker, had been a member of the socialist opposition to Bismarck in Germany, and my father came from a liberal Reformed Jewish tradition. He had little regard for doctrinaire individuals who followed any leaders, political or religious.

Throughout the years of World War II and after the demise of the IPR, my father was the secretary of the Southeast Asia Institute, whose members, like those of the IPR, were mostly academic economists, political scientists, and, especially, anthropologists. His office was in the Department of Anthropology of the American Museum of Natural History, just a floor below that of Margaret Mead. He continued to edit, manage, and write, and after he left the IPR, he authored another book concerning migration, *Asia on the Move* (1943), and one on *The Peoples of Southeast Asia* (1944). These works were more concerned with the populations undergoing urbanization than with the remaining isolates that were then the focus of virtually all anthropological studies.

There were other books and many articles in the more than twenty years that my father was with the IPR and the Southeast Asia Institute. These included a book on how to hold discussions, numerous periodical articles, and the editing of a great many books by others. His work involved several periods of residence in what was then the Dutch East Indies and in China. His last post was as a member of the United Nations Committee on Slavery directly under Secretary General Trigvie Lie. In that position, Dad wrote *Human Bondage in Southeast Asia* (1950). He later wrote manuscripts for a children's book on the second week of creation, a novel about a marriage between a Japanese woman and an American man, and a work on the art of prediction, none of which has been published. He recorded his memoirs in the first important oral history project, which was at Columbia University. The historians responsible for it did not preserve the wire recording, but the transcript is on file in the Columbia University library.

My earliest memories have changed over the years. At first, they were vivid representations of sights and sounds, like the performances of actors in a play. They are now more like a script with much of the action represented by words. The first thing I recall firsthand, not remembered and recounted by other members of the family, is fleeing from Holland to England after the outbreak of war in 1914. I also remember my father leaving us when he went to the United States to avoid internment in England. And I remember a zeppelin raid and a time when we watched a seemingly endless column of soldiers bound for France marching four abreast out of the York Minster Cathedral. When we had arrived back at New Earswick several miles away, there was the same column of soldiers marching up the Huntington Road to their barracks. I never saw the end of the column either at the cathedral or on the road, and it seemed to go on forever. Events connected with the war must have had a considerable impact on me to have been remembered from such an early age. The pacifist attitude of my father and his liberal friends also pervaded my early years and influenced my later thoughts.

From my first four years in England, I remember one playmate, perhaps because there were photographs of her. The Rowntrees believed in an integrated factory operation and owned a farm for the production of milk for their milk chocolate. The farmer, Carl Sorensen, and his wife, Bee, were my mother's closest friends. They and their daughter, Ann, lived at the Garth (*garth* is a Scandinavian word for "farm," which has continued in use in northern England since the period of Viking occupation). The farmhouse was later converted into a home for the elderly, and Bee, who outlived both her husband and her daughter, returned to live there again.

A few years ago, at a meeting of the Society of Applied Anthropologists at York, a tour was organized of two model villages, one of which was New Earswick. I spoke to one resident, a Mrs. Rowntree, who was the sister-in-law of Ann, the only playmate I remembered. That kind of continuity in village life over seventy years or more must be very rare in the United States, but perhaps it is not unusual in England.

The only other non-family member I remember from England was Jimmy Mallon—Uncle Jimmy, as we called him. He was the warder of Toynbee Hall, the original settlement house founded by the Reverend Barnett in London. Many of my father's friends were involved in settlement-house work. Uncle Jimmy was famous for his Irish sense of humor. My father described one occasion when he was being honored by King George VI. The queen, apparently accustomed to being amused by Uncle Jimmy, who turned to the royal family for sponsorship of the settlement house, broke out laughing when she saw this short impish man in his court costume of pantaloons.

My mother, my sister Helen, and I sailed to join my father in America in the summer of 1916, when I was four. When we landed in New York, there was an epidemic of polio, and to avoid exposure, we were immediately driven up along the Hudson River to Nyack. I remember the girders supporting the elevated train tracks that ran up New York's West Side. There were cases of polio at Nyack, too, so late in the summer, we moved to a farm in Brewster, New York. Lillian D. Wald—the founder of the visiting nurses movement in the United States and the philanthropist behind the Henry Street Settlement where my father had lived—owned the farm. Miss Wald, by courtesy title my Aunt Lillian, had five adopted children who were my first American friends.

My parents soon found a house for rent in Nepperhan Heights, a part of Yonkers that was a bedroom suburb of New York City. They later bought the house and lived there for forty-one years.

That part of Westchester County had once been farmland, and there was still a farm half a mile from our house that sold unpasteur- ized milk dipped from twenty-gallon cans into bottles that the cus- tomers brought with them. Our neighborhood was in the "country" but was becoming built-up. A small brook at the back ran through an empty lot to a culvert under our road and down to a pond where my sister, other children, and I collected tadpoles (we called them polliwogs) which we kept so we could watch them sprout legs.

Some of the neighbors were "old Americans" with at least three generations born in the United States, but they also included an Italian nurseryman with his wife and five children, an Irish Catholic family, and a family with a Japanese father and European-American mother. The handyman who tended our furnace was an Italian immigrant, and the woman who came once a week to do laundry and cleaning had come from Poland. The nearest Jewish family, that of Morris

Cohen, a professor of philosophy at City College, lived a half mile away. I knew all these people, but my first awareness of ethnicity and race came slowly.

One day, I joined some neighborhood boys in drawing cartoons of the kaiser with his upturned mustache and helmet with a spike on top, and I was scolded at home for saying "Kill the kaiser." Something about race that I picked up on the street and said at the age of six is said to have appeared as one of the anonymous examples in my father's book *Race Attitudes in Children* (1929), but I do not know what it was, and I did not know any African Americans and did not become sensitive to issues of race until I went away to college.

By 1917, my mother had enrolled in a master's degree program at Columbia University. Mother finished her degree and took a job at Post Graduate Hospital. She then worked as a biochemist at Montefiore Hospital in the Bronx until she and my father retired.

Besides performing routine blood and urine analyses, Mother developed a test to differentiate kinds of sugars and conducted research on patients with conditions in which sugars are excreted. Some of the rarely found sugars result from hereditary conditions, so she also traced other members of the families and drew up their pedigrees. Patients loved to talk with her about their family histories. The research was not viewed as part of her job, however, and some of the chemistry was done at home in our kitchen, where there was an extra refrigerator for reagents and specimens.

My sister and I started at the local public school in Yonkers. I remember my shock on the first day to find out that most of the other children in my class could not read and that only one other student could count properly. My mother had taught me to read *The Little Red Hen*. After only a few days, we were transferred to a private school, the Leete School on East Sixty-first Street in New York City. For the first year there, my mother took us on her way to the university, and she taught science in the school in lieu of paying our tuition. A year or so later, my sister and I began to commute alone. The school changed its name to the Washington School, but, along with many other schools I have attended—the Raymond Riordon School, the Experimental College at the University of Wisconsin, and the College of Chinese Studies in Peking—the Washington School no longer exists.

My mother's science classes were fun. The youngest students built a siphon out of glassware and rubber tubing arranged across the stage of the auditorium and demonstrated it to the rest of the school.

Another group blew bulbs in glass tubing and made thermometers by filling them with mercury; letting children handle mercury would now be taboo, of course. There were all sorts of arts and crafts. Most of the students were girls, and at folk dances I would be mobbed by girls looking for a male partner. I understand that one of the wealthy parents wanted a coeducational experience for his daughter and that my gender was one reason my sister and I were given scholarships even after my mother ceased teaching there.

My sister and I were each given a dime every day for the two trolley rides between Grand Central Station and the school, but we almost always walked and spent the money on candy instead. As we walked up or down Madison or Fifth Avenue, each of us could "buy" one thing in each shop window. My favorites were clocks in glass cases with "perpetual motion" mechanisms activated by marbles running down a tortuous ramp to an endless belt that lifted them up to the start of the ramp again.

I did well at school, but, unlike my sister, I caused great trouble for my parents. I was naughty and unruly, no doubt. In England, it was common to send young boys to boarding school, and, as my mother was working, it was convenient for my parents to follow that course. In 1924, when I was twelve, they shipped me off for my last year of grade school and the three years it would take me to complete high school to the Raymond Riordan School in the country, six miles from the nearest village, Highland, in Ulster County in the foothills of the Catskill Mountains.

In the boarding school, the classes were so small, rarely ten in any one, that several classes went on in the same room. We had classes in the morning and study hall in the evening, and after lunch every day, each of us received a work assignment. In the fall, we cut wood on the three-thousand-acre grounds for winter heating; in the winter, we cut and stored ice from the lake for use in the summer; and in the spring, there was plenty of building and rebuilding and other outdoor tasks. One of my assignments involved reforestation, and thirty-five years later, I happened to see some of the white pines I had helped to plant around the school, and they were huge. There was also John Burroughs Memorial Forest some miles to the north and west, where, on a south-facing slope, we planted five thousand or more white pines and white spruces in what must have been abandoned farmland. We sharpened sticks, impaled the wormy apples on the points, and, using the sticks like an Australian spear thrower, hurled the apples a long way. I wonder if the grove of evergreen trees and the John Burroughs marker plaque still exist. The school eventually closed down, and the buildings were sold to the State of New York. They were turned into a reform school, and my alma mater is now a correctional institution.

I was the youngest and smallest boy of the seventeen in my graduating class, and probably the most intellectual, so I was made the school librarian. I had already learned to bind books among the many industrial arts I learned in elementary school. In the library, I repaired and rebound many books, but I spent most of my time reading. Besides the required readings for my classes, I read several of the novels of Sir Walter Scott and all of the comedies and some other plays of Shakespeare.

I did not spend the summers at home, either, but from the age of ten, I spent two months each year in summer camp. In my last year of school, I went on vacation to Europe with my mother and sister.

Life as a teenager was not always placid. Once, when I was about fifteen, my father sent me to serve as gardener for a friend of his in an affluent suburb of Pittsburgh for the weeks before school reopened. My mother was in England for the summer, and my father was also away. I slept alone in a large musty attic, and one night I woke in a fright and thought I could not breathe. I was sent to an ear, nose, and throat specialist who treated me for sinusitis.

My stay in Pennsylvania, however, was not dominated by my anxiety. I learned a game that was as much fun as Spin the Bottle. Four of us lay on our backs in the grass in a sort of swastika shape, each one with his head on the next one's belly, a boy and a girl and a boy and a girl. When one started to laugh, the whole circle would erupt in laughter. When your head started bouncing, it was impossible not to laugh.

In 1928, at the age of sixteen, I was sent to the Experimental College at the University of Wisconsin, a two-year program in general education. The radical ideas of the school's founder, Alexander Meiklejohn, are described in his book *The Experimental College* (1932). The students all lived together, as in an Oxford University college after which it was in some ways patterned, and we all studied fifth-century B.C. Athens for one year and the roots of modern American society for another. Then students were expected to transfer into a degree program and select a major. I had no trouble being away from home, despite the fact that I knew few people in Madison. The president of the university, Glen Frank, knew my father and once addressed me by name on campus. A professor of education called Kellogg who also knew my father invited me for dinner once. Another guest was anthropologist Charlotte Gower. She was a close friend of anthropologist Ralph Linton and was also said to have been a friend of Radcliffe Brown. Later she went to China, and after Pearl Harbor, she was interned by the Japanese for the duration of World War II. After her release, she married a sea captain and had nothing further to do with anthropology. However, her notes on her early work in Sicily survived, and a book based on them was published after her death.

I had been at a boys' school and boys' summer camps and had scant experience in getting to know girls. That became one of my major interests in college, an interest that kept me from doing much studying.

Up to that time, I had no sense of being Jewish, as there was no religious observance of any kind at home. The only holidays we celebrated were secular or Christian. We made a big thing of Christmas—a tree with candles and a star of Bethlehem on top, decorations, cards, and many gifts. We ate pancakes on Shrove Tuesday and usually a ham at Easter, when, like the neighbors, we often wore new clothes, but we did not go to church.

One day, I met a freshman coed in the library and chatted with her. I later took her to dances and saw her often. Soon her parents asked to meet me, but when I arrived, she was not there. They made it quite clear to me that they considered it inappropriate for their daughter to go out with a Jew and that she was upset and not able to study. This was quite a surprise for me. Most of the girls I knew and dated in college were not Jewish, but that experience probably made me conscious of which ones were Jewish and why some of the others were not interested in me.

My sister says her first realization that she was being taken to be Jewish was when, after three summers of summer camp, she was not invited back for another.

After the two years at the Experimental College, I entered the University of Michigan as a student of architecture. Back at Wisconsin, I had spent a day with Frank Lloyd Wright at his home in Spring Green, and I ended up with a very idealistic attitude about that profession. At the university, I soon learned that architecture is more business than art, so I transferred to the College of Liberal Arts, where I took a number of courses in sociology, economics, philosophy, and a variety of other subjects, few of which I found of much interest at the time.

My undergraduate training included no course work in anthropology. At the University of Wisconsin, I had attended one public lecture by Ralph Linton, but all I remember from it is that in Madagascar he had required an extra bearer for his sedan chair because he was so heavy. In later years, after I had read and admired his book *The Study of Man*, I liked to talk with Linton at meetings of the American Anthropological Association. He was always interested in the status of physical anthropology and what I had to say about it.

At the University of Michigan, I lived in a small apartment with a roommate. Although he belonged to a fraternity, the Roman Catholic one, we ate most of our meals in restaurants. I did the minimum to get by academically and eventually barely graduated with a bachelor's degree and without a major.

2

Unemployed and Off to China

When I graduated from the University of Michigan in February 1934, I was unemployed except for volunteer work in several social service agencies. The country was in the midst of the Great Depression, but both my parents were employed, and we did not suffer personally. My first work was at Sloan House, a former YMCA in the West Fifties in New York City. It was a residence for young white-collar unemployed transient men who were a federal responsibility because they could not claim residence in any state and therefore could not be sent back home. I stayed in the residence with them, helped with minor tasks, but was given limited management responsibilities. My window in the house looked out on the tracks of the Sixth Avenue elevated train, and trains roared by every few minutes all night long.

One resident I remember was an artist who either couldn't draw or didn't want to; he needed lots of paint to daub on his canvases, and I bought him some. I tried but failed to see the point of his art.

I thought that the relief efforts were making a positive difference, but there were disillusioning episodes, too, such as when a client who was given a position of trust in the office eventually absconded with everything he could find of value.

Next, I worked as a volunteer for the so-called Poor Office of the township of Eastchester, New York, where I investigated potential clients for the Federal Emergency Relief Administration (FERA) and for the Civilian Conservation Corps (CCC). The township had two villages. The first, Bronxville, was affluent, and none of our clients lived there. The other village, Tuckahoe, was home to the families of those who had built the houses, roads, and aqueduct and, when their patrons had more money, had served as day servants in Bronxville.

At the Poor Office, one of my coworkers was a "Negro," the first one I had come to know and care about. I had him to my home for dinner, but he never invited me to his place in Harlem; I presume that was because of conditions there.

Of course, desperate poverty was not limited to African Americans. Poverty reached into families of all kinds, including many that had been reasonably well off. We certified families for relief with a budget of $2.10 per week for a single man, $3.25 for a couple, $5.15 for a family of five, and so on. Under FERA rules, only the shortfall of wages relative to this slim budget was paid out in cash. After the Works Project Administration (WPA) was established, a skilled workman such as a steam shovel operator was given only enough work to cover this same budget. That might amount to a few hours a week. If we learned of any income from an outside source, the recipient would get only enough work to cover the deficit in his budget.

Many people often went hungry. Some young men were certified for the CCC; they lived on the job, received ample army-type rations, and built roads, trails, log cabins, and other structures in the national parks and forests. Some of their work is still in use today.

One young man boasted that he had once made more money in two minutes than anyone else had ever made in a month; he was an unemployed jockey. Such sudden riches are no guarantee of security, of course; the ex-jockey was in as deep financial trouble as most of the rest of the unemployed.

More important in relation to my future career, during the latter part of the year and a half between my graduation and the fall of 1935, I assisted my mother in her research on the genetic analysis of an inborn error of metabolism, essential xyloketosuria (excretion of a pentose sugar in urine), which she and a clinician, Morris Enklewitz, were investigating.

In order to help with the genetic analysis, I visited the Cold Spring Harbor genetics laboratory. Charles B. Davenport and his associates are now remembered for their leadership of the elitist

American eugenics movement, but at the time it seemed that their collection of data on relatives was advancing knowledge of human genetics, and it was there that I learned how to plot a pedigree. I also taught myself genetics by studying at medical libraries. Dr. Madge Thurlow Macklin's review article "The Role of Heredity in Disease" in the journal *Medicine* in 1935 was an important source for me. It describes in clear terms how, beginning with the pedigrees, one can distinguish the mode of inheritance. Xyloketosuria, I discovered, met the conditions for a Mendelian autosomal recessive. Macklin herself was very kind and helpful. My mother, Morris Enklewitz, and I published our article, my first, in the journal *Human Biology* while it was still under the editorship of its founder, Raymond Pearl. I could not have imagined that someday I would edit that same journal myself. My mother later collected information on cases of essential fructosuria, an even rarer condition, and I helped her with a genetic analysis. It is also a Mendelian recessive and is so rare that almost all the cases occur in individuals known to be inbred.

Since I didn't have a job, I had lots of free time. While my grandmother in England was alive, my mother used to visit her in the summers. Sheldon Jacobson, while he was a premedical student, sometimes substituted for her in the hospital laboratory. He later became a lifelong friend of Mother's and mine.

In 1932 or 1933, when he was a resident pathologist, he'd been able to buy a yacht that someone who had lost everything was forced to sacrifice. It was a forty-nine-foot gaff-rigged ketch and cost less than the new sails that he bought for it. I greatly enjoyed many coastal cruises up as far as eastern Maine and down the New Jersey coast. Sheldon loved the sea. During the war, he was in the U.S. Navy Medical Corps, but he applied repeatedly for transfer to the line. His request was always refused, but he did serve at sea and was eventually promoted to captain in the Naval Reserve.

My father was often away for long periods in the Far East, and at one time, after my sister and I had left home, my mother went to work for a professor of biochemistry at Yale. I never really thought about these times as separations, but my daughter, who must have heard it from my sister, believed that my mother once left my father for a year. In retrospect, I suppose my mother felt deserted with her two small children in 1914, and again at times later.

In 1935, my father was at Nankai University in Tientsin, China. He wrote suggesting that I learn Chinese or Japanese so that I could always find a job. At that time, my mother was at the International Congress of Physiology in Moscow, the only international congress held in the Soviet Union during the whole of the Stalin epoch. On her return home, she gave me the funds necessary for the trip, and I wrote informing my father that I was coming to China to learn Chinese. There was no airmail in those days, and I set out without waiting for a possible reply from him that might have said, "Don't come."

I crossed the country by bus and arrived in Seattle several days before I was due to sail. The first night there, I stayed in a hotel, but I figured that with about fifty fraternities at the University of Washington, I could phone around and persuade someone to take me in. I had not belonged to a fraternity at college, but one of my first phone calls resulted in an invitation. I stayed at a fraternity house that was in the midst of rushing freshmen, and I helped entertain the rushees (and myself). The sororities were also rushing freshmen, and I went around to dances and surprised one of the boys by taking him around to introduce him to some coeds. The university students showed a lot of interest in a person of more or less their own age who was setting out for China in the hope of finding something to do. Several of them, both men and women, came to see me off. I bought a bottle of applejack, and we had a party on board the small Japanese liner before I sailed.

In Japan, I disembarked in Yokohama. The customs agents were so concerned about the cigarette allowance that they even stamped the cigarettes in my pocket cigarette case. Then, after I landed and took out a cigarette to smoke, another customs agent accosted me and examined all my cigarettes again.

One of my father's associates in the Japanese Council of the Institute of Pacific Relations met me. He took me to Tokyo, but without seeing that my luggage had been unloaded. We went back the next day and found it, still safe, on the dock. A couple of days later, this friend freed himself of his duty to my father by sending me on to China. After three days, the little ship on which he had booked my passage had crossed the Inland Sea of Japan and the Yellow Sea and had anchored on the bar beyond view of land. The Yellow Sea really is the color of the earth, and I was soon to learn that in the North China Plain during a windstorm, the whole sky and everything else is that same color.

Unlike the serious Japanese, the money changers and other Chinese who came aboard from the lighter that was to take us to the harbor at Taku were laughing and joking. I remember that they seemed to be playing with captive birds or possibly were trying to capture small birds that had come looking for food on the ship.

I joined my father in Tientsin, where the IPR had assigned him to edit manuscripts in English by Chinese members of the Economic and Social Institute at the university. Tientsin is a city of canals; my father arranged for a rowboat, and I became a sort of gondolier for him in this Chinese Venice. All we could see from the streets were the blank walls of houses, but on the canal side there were no walls, and from the boat we could see the activities within the compounds. After three or four days, he sent me off to the College of Chinese Studies in Peking. My father stayed in China several months more, but he was busy, and so was I, and we did not get together again before he returned to the United States.

In 1935, the foreign community in Peking contained an extraordinary group of people. There were virtually no businessmen; their activities were in Shanghai and other commercial cities. There were, however, missionaries of many denominations, and I met them at the language school, which was a first stop for many of them, as it was for me. I did not have very much in common with most of them, although by then the churches were usually sending only individuals with some education as well as a "call."

In 1899, the foreign legation quarter in Peking had been besieged during the Boxer Rebellion, and after the siege was lifted by an international army, the area remained under foreign control. By 1935, the embassies had been removed to the new capital at Nanking, a day's ride away by train, but the large legation buildings in Peking were still staffed and guarded by foreign troops, including a small detachment of U.S. Marines. I had a friend from college in the American legation and met him and other consular officers there, as well as members of the British Foreign Service, during my occasional visits to the area.

That leaves the other large group of foreigners, the intellectuals, and it was among them that I found the majority of my associates throughout nearly two years in Peking. Almost all the people I came to know well had already written, or would subsequently write, books, many of them about China. Those few who did not were teaching at the Peking Union Medical College (PUMC) which had been established by the Rockefeller Foundation. There were also a few artists and experts on aspects of Chinese art among my acquaintances.

I eventually got to know well the Chinese I lived with and some Chinese students and other young people, but the Chinese take friendship very seriously, and I did not have casual relationships with them of the kind I had known at the university.

The language school taught using the direct method. Some of the teachers were Manchus whose families had been associated with the imperial court; they spoke the Chinese equivalent of the King's English. The teachers were very effective. Bertrand Russell had been there sometime before I arrived and had described one of them as "great." Most of the students at the language school were missionaries, but there were other foreigners, to me generally more interesting, studying Chinese there. Among them were the Marxist historian Karl August Wittfogel and his Russian-born wife, Olga Lang, who has also written a book about China; Henry MacAleavy, a recent graduate from Cambridge; John de Francis, an American who was a serious student of China and the Chinese; Otto Klineberg, a social psychologist, and his wife; also James Bertram, a New Zealander fresh down from New College, Oxford, where he had been a Rhodes scholar. The Klinebergs—he was on temporary leave from Columbia University—remained at the language school, but all of the others sooner or later moved on to private residences of one kind or another or left for other parts of China.

The Wittfogels established their own menage. One episode manifests the Chinese concept of "face." Like many foreigners, the Wittfogels boarded with their cook, giving him so much per week to cover both the food and his pay. On the first day, he asked them both how they liked their potatoes, but he only served them once the way Olga preferred. It happened because she had offended him in some way, and the next time they had company, he punished them by providing inadequate food. The cook would not serve the potatoes the way she had said she liked until Olga had apologized to him.

Henry MacAleavy was the son of an Irish mother who worked in a mill in Manchester. He showed promise in school, so, with the financial aid of an aunt, he went to the University of Manchester and studied Latin. He excelled, and someone suggested that he should be at Cambridge where he could receive further instruction in Latin. Once there, he studied Chinese instead, and with the help of his teacher went to China, where he also studied Japanese. During the war, the Japanese allowed him to return to Britain with the diplomats on the Swedish liner *Gripsholm*, but, because of his knowledge of languages, the British government sent him back as a language officer to Chunking, which, throughout the war, remained under Chinese control.

John de Francis ventured through Inner Mongolia and across the Gobi Desert to Kansu and returned with opium smugglers on a raft on the Yellow River. He had a Chinese cook with him but nothing to eat but flour, so the cook made noodles and, for a change of diet, cut them in different shapes on different days. Once a local headman gave them a sheep. In later years, de Francis taught Chinese at Yale and published a number of textbooks on the Chinese language.

When not on his adventures, de Francis lived in the private house of Mrs. Ruth Yang, a Christian who had learned excellent English from missionaries. Another American who lived in Mrs. Yang's house for a while was the journalist Haldore Hanson. After about a year at the language school, I also moved into Mrs. Yang's house and secured a tutor for my study of Chinese.

When he left Peking for further adventures elsewhere in China—described in his book *Human Endeavor: The Story of the China War*—Hanson turned over to me his job teaching English at the YMCA night school. The college-age girls who were students there were much more apt than the boys. Merchants who wanted their children to learn English sent their brightest sons to university, but the most they would do for bright daughters was allow them to go to night school.

One day, Mrs. Yang introduced me to a delegation of students from Chao T'ung University, the government university of the railway administration that trained executives. The students had come to her for aid in finding a teacher of spoken English. The students took me to their English professor, who talked with me only in Chinese, and from then on, I taught English at that university twice a week for as long as I stayed in Peking. The students brought me my pay, and that first formal meeting with the English professor was my only contact with the faculty of the university.

My students, first at the YMCA night school and then at the university of the railway administration, were like many I later encountered at Wayne State University in Detroit. That is, they saw an education purely as a route to a career and financial success and were learning English solely to enable them to do business with foreigners. At Chao T'ung University, they were aiming to become station masters and rise in the bureaucracy of the railway system.

These students did not seem to be much interested in current events, and although it would have interested me, the students did not wish to discuss politics. However, at other universities in Peking, such as Peking National University (Pei Ta), Yenching (the American college with a Harvard connection), and Tsing Hua (where I also knew some faculty members), the students were in ferment. James Bertram helped some Chinese students produce a magazine in English called *Democracy* which carried attacks on the authoritarian central government policy. Ironically, some of the very same students were probably instrumental in establishing the communist state that, half a century later, would violently suppress other students clamoring for democracy in Tienanmen Square. In 1937, the object of the students' most bitter denunciation was the Japanese encroachment and the Chinese government's attempts at accommodation. At the time, I was sympathetic with the students, and I remained so about democratic socialism, but I never supported Soviet militarism and became completely disillusioned with communism after the Russian attack on Finland in 1939.

In December 1936, when one of the warlords (Chang Hsueh-liang) took Generalissimo Chiang Kai-shek hostage, Bertram attempted to reach Sian, where Chiang was being held, as he recounts in his book *First Act in China: The Story of the Sian Mutiny*. By the time Bertram got to Sian, however, the roles had reversed, and the generalissimo was holding General Chang in Nanking. The student demonstrations gradually led to a situation in which the regional warlords and the Chinese central government said "No further" to the Japanese. The next Japanese provocation was the spark that led to the conquest of most of China by the Japanese army and their holding it for the duration of World War II.

I managed a social life of sorts. The phone service worked pretty well, but we still continued the practice of calling in person and handing a calling card to the servant at the gate. Some of my father's friends in Peking were kind to me. Owen Lattimore, an expert on Mongolia, and his wife, Eleanor, had me to dinner more than once. The Lattimores had made several trips through inner Asia, and both wrote books about it. Owen Lattimore looked at China from a Mongolian point of view. Like many students of Chinese affairs at the time, he apparently was not convinced that there was much of a future for the country under the corrupt government of the Kuomintang. As there was no plausible democratic alternative, most of the intellectuals I knew in Peking were interested in the communists. Lattimore, however, was not a communist, but later, while he was on the faculty of Johns Hopkins University, he would be denounced by Senator Joseph McCarthy. Although supported by many at the university, he would leave the United States and finish his academic life at the University of Leeds in England.

The houses of the foreigners I visited in Peking were compounds surrounded by high walls that were usually topped with broken glass in lieu of barbed wire. They were laid out like miniatures of the old imperial residence, the Forbidden City, with the main hall at the north and the entry at the south, flanked by rooms for the gatekeeper and other servants. Other rooms were on the east and west, and all faced inward. The outer walls had no windows. There was a great deal of activity in the streets—foot traffic and food stalls—but the residences were cut off from the hubbub, except for the cries of peddlers.

Peking was a walled city at that time, or rather two walled cities, a Chinese one to the south, where much of the commercial activity such as jade cutting and silk embroidery took place, and, separated by a high wall, a Manchu one with the imperial Forbidden City and the foreign legations to the north.

On one occasion, in the company of a few young American and Chinese friends, I went outside the walls for a picnic. It was winter, and the terminal part of the Grand Canal that once had brought rice to the imperial court over a thousand miles from East-Central China, was frozen. We hired two iceboats, flatbed sleds pulled by men, and went to a cemetery, just about the only unused open land in that part of the North China Plain, to eat our American-style frankfurters. The tomb of a princess was an ideal picnic site. However, two peace preservation officers, armed with staves, like the watch in a Shakespeare play, came by. They thought we were in great danger; grave robbery was a capital offense, and if there were grave robbers about, they would be desperate. So our guards sent for a squad of six more officers armed with rifles. Our picnic was scant for so large a party, but we shared our hot dogs as far as they went. Furthermore, we had to hire another iceboat, since our guardians obviously had too much "face" to walk. When we got back to the city wall, we were glad to have our protectors. The huge, heavy wooden gates had been shut for the night, and our guards had to shout to the soldiers on the wall to open them and let us back into the city.

The Princess Tomb outside the walls of Peking. The Manchu princess was said to have been buried alive here on the death of her husband. This is where Lasker and his companions had to share their picnic with a company of riflemen who came to protect them.

Ida Pruitt was the first social worker at Peking Union Medical College (PUMC), the medical school sponsored by the Rockefeller Foundation. We became good friends, and I called her by the Chinese name for aunt, which translates as "the older sister of my father." She was the daughter of missionaries, was fluent in Chinese, and was at the center of a circle of intellectuals in Peking. She translated and published *Daughter of Han,* the oral history of one of the last attendants of the dowager empress, the power behind the throne during the last years of the Ch'ing Dynasty. I was there when the old lady, whose story the book tells, came to Ida Pruitt's house to display proudly the elaborate robes in which she would be buried. Funerals and weddings were virtually the only occasions when Chinese families showed their status by public displays. Families would put themselves into debt and hire many people to form processions for these rites.

Ida Pruitt in Peking in 1936. Ida, the daughter of missionaries to China, was a social worker at Peking Union Medical College. She held a popular open house each Thursday evening at the home she shared with two adopted daughters, P'u Kwei-ching and Tania Manooiloff.

I went to Ida Pruitt's weekly open house almost every Thursday, where I met interesting visitors, such as anthropologist and psychologist Kimpton Stewart. If Ida Pruitt organized an outing, as she once did for a picnic in the western hills at a monastery for the surviving eunuchs of the old imperial court, I was always invited.

Ida Pruitt introduced me to several faculty members at PUMC. One was a dietitian who had been at Montefiore Hospital in New York where my mother worked. When we were on summer holiday on the coast, she and I went to walk on a little-visited segment of the Great Wall, and she slipped under the barbed wire into Japanese-controlled territory as if to defy them. Another was a doctor at PUMC who talked me into playing a tiny part in a charity performance of a play, *Men in White*. Eventually, Ida Pruitt was my link with PUMC, where I had my first opportunity to do work that related to my future study of biological anthropology.

The Wittfogels also took me along when they went to interesting places or to see interesting people. Some were Chinese scholars such as Hu Shih, the person who introduced use of the spoken language

Part of a funeral procession in Peking for the mother of a general. The band with Western-type instruments played "Auld Lang Syne" and an American college drinking song (the University of Maine "Stein Song"). They played the same tunes at weddings. The catafalque carried by thirty-two or sixty-four men was too big to go up the alley to the house, so a second, smaller catafalque (left) was used for that.

(pai hua) into literature. It is the language of the people, and authors who wrote in it were regularly accused of being communists, but Hu Shih himself was later made ambassador to the United States by the Chiang government.

I met most of the foreign scholars who spent any time in Peking during my two years there. Norbert Wiener, the founder of cybernetics and one of the fathers of the computer age, would have conversations with Jim Bertram and me over beer at the coal hill or the Pei Hai.

The coal hill was an artificial hill that was supposed to be filled with coal for fuel in case of a siege; actually, it was probably just the earth dredged up to make the artificial lakes. The Pei Hai, or North Lake, was in a park. In winter, I used to skate there, but there is no rain in winter, and much dust from loess (loamy soil allegedly blown from as far away as Mongolia but probably mostly local) covered the ice. They had to flood the top of the ice daily to cover the dust and provide a surface for skating.

A better place to skate was at the YMCA in a temporary structure made of grass mats that protected the ice from the dust. I would go alone, since none of my friends was interested in exercise. I would

The Great Wall of China at a place near the coast not usually frequented by foreign tourists and not well preserved. It marked the boundary with Manchukuo, the puppet country set up by the Japanese in Manchuria before they invaded other parts of China. Lasker's companion slipped under the barbed wire just long enough for him to take this photograph.

take with me, and study as I skated, a stack of small square word cards with a Chinese character printed on one side and the pronunciation, definition, and phrases on the back.

Spoken Chinese consists mostly of "phrases," which are the equivalent of words in English. The single words of written Chinese are often too ambiguous to be understood when spoken. Of course, if there were young women skating, I would look up from my cards, but I never made friends or met friends at the skating rink.

Wiener, the boy-genius son of the professor of Slavic languages at Harvard, had learned celestial navigation as a child. He explained feedback to Bertram and me by analogy with a ship's automatic pilot controlled by a gyroscopic compass. If it is set to correct the course as soon as there is any deviance, the ship will vibrate. Instead, it must allow the ship to yaw and fall off its heading before feedback from the compass to the rudder pulls it back. He wrote two autobiographies, and it seems clear that his relationship with his father left an enduring mark on him. For one thing, Wiener competed with his father by

Norbert Wiener, right, and Lasker having a beer and discussing feedback by analogy with a ship's automatic pilot. Wiener was very proud that although he was a theoretical mathematician, he and a Chinese student had sold a patent for five thousand dollars. Their patent turned out to be important in the development of the first computers.

devouring languages. In later years, when I saw him at MIT, one of his friends was the U.S. Marine officer in charge of the ROTC unit. The basis of the friendship was that the colonel had been the language officer at the American embassy in Peking, and the two of them could speak Chinese together. Wiener also practiced his Chinese on me. On one later occasion, Wiener spoke in German to my father, who afterward asked me, "What does that man think I am, his language teacher?"

3

First Exposure to Anthropology

T he Rockefeller Foundation established and continued to support Peking Union Medical College with Davidson Black, a Canadian, as head of the anatomy department. In 1920, the foundation arranged a visit by Ales Hrdlicka to the department, and that stimulated interest in human paleontology. Black had described the Choukoutien fossils as a new hominid species, *Sinanthropus pekinensis*. By the time I arrived in Peking in 1935, Black had died of a heart attack while in the United States, and the college had installed two anatomists to replace him: Franz Weidenreich, to write the monographs about the fossil hominids from Choukoutien, and Paul H. Stevenson, to teach the medical students.

Stevenson had been a student of T. Wingate Todd at Western Reserve University in Cleveland, Ohio, and had collaborated in studies of the relationship between the age of individuals and certain traits of their bones. Those studies were based on the famous Todd collection of skeletons from dissecting-room populations. These were individuals of known sex, age, "race" (white or "Negro"), and cause of death, whose details were recorded, often together with photographs, hair samples, and other personal data. Stevenson was the scientist at PUMC whom I came to know best, and he helped me the most. He guided my study and later sent letters of recommendation for me when the time came to leave China. During the war, Stevenson, an

MD, stayed in the part of China that was not occupied by the Japanese and headed an antimalaria project, but I lost track of him after that.

I also met Franz Weidenreich at the anatomy department at PUMC. He had taught anatomy at the University of Strasburg until, at the end of World War I, France took the city from Germany and fired German members of the faculty. Weidenreich then became a professor at the University of Heidelberg, where he did pioneering work in hematology, but his interests later shifted to human paleontology. As a Jew, he found himself again without a job when the Nazis came into power in Germany, but he escaped the worst consequences when the Rockefeller Foundation created a position for him at PUMC to study the human fossils that had been excavated at Choukoutien near Peking. Weidenreich showed me the "Peking Man" *Sinanthropus* fossils, but I did not know enough to make useful observations or to remember any details. That is especially unfortunate, since the original specimens disappeared after Pearl Harbor, when the American Marine contingent, which was carrying them, was attempting to flee the former embassy. Fortunately, Weidenreich has described them in great detail. He took pains to demonstrate to me what he saw in the fossils and how he interpreted them. He was a magnificent teacher, ready to explain his views to anyone who was interested, and it is a tragedy that after he came to the United States, he took up a purely research appointment at the American Museum of Natural History and was never asked to teach at Columbia University. In the United States, he had good opportunities for research at the museum but no chance to reach students. Harry L. Shapiro, the curator of anthropology at the museum, taught at Columbia, but he was not a regular member of the faculty.

In 1943 and 1944, my wife, Bernice Kaplan ("Bunny," as she is called), was working as an assistant in the anthropology department at the American Museum of Natural History. She was also serving there after hours as a manuscript typist for Weidenreich. During this period, G. H. R. Von Koenigswald, who had another set of *Homo erectus* and *Gigantopithecus* fossils in Java, was being interned in Java by the Japanese. He had hidden his precious fossils, and when he was at last free at the end of the war, he sent the *Gigantopithecus* teeth to Weidenreich in New York for examination. Bunny says that when they arrived, Weidenreich, in great excitement, went down the hall to Shapiro's office to say the fossils had come, but Shapiro was "too busy" to go back down the hall to look at them.

I saw Weidenreich often in later years. He was puzzled that I could be teaching anatomy to medical students without having a medical degree. On the other hand, the hematologists at the medical school were amazed to learn Weidenreich, whom they knew from his early publications in their field, was a prominent figure in paleoanthropology.

While I was in China, my father, concerned about the standard of living of the Chinese, edited a three-volume work, *Land Utilization in China* by the agricultural economist J. Loesing Buck (first husband of novelist Pearl Buck). My father asked me to look into the question of metabolism in the Chinese, because, he reasoned, a lower basal metabolic rate might imply a lower individual calorie requirement. Stevenson gave me a desk in the anatomy department and access to the excellent medical library at PUMC, and I began to read everything I could find concerning the applied physiology of the Chinese. Some studies of basal metabolism of the Chinese showed higher average levels in emigrants to the United States than prevailed in China. The same was true of blood pressure. Under conditions of limited food intake, many ways to lower the output of energy have evolved, some of them automatic and not just the result of the psychological lassitude that comes with hunger.

At about that time, my father also asked me to write a review for the *Nankai Quarterly* of Otto Klineberg's book *Race Differences*. Klineberg had applied the Boas model for studying environmental effects on human biological variables by comparing groups of genetically comparable migrants and nonmigrants. That was the original source of the research plan for many later studies, including my eventual research on the Chinese and on Mexicans. The idea is simply that if two samples of individuals are very similar genetically but differ in the environments to which they have been exposed, biological differences between the two samples can reasonably be ascribed to the environmental differences. What Klineberg found was that the IQs of "Negroes" in Harlem were higher than those of others in the South. Furthermore, he found that school grades of those who later went to the North were no higher than grades of those who stayed in the South, so he concluded that the difference in the IQ scores should be ascribed to some aspects of the different environments and was not an innate difference.

While I was still in China, I wrote a paper on the growth of Chinese children, and it appeared four years later, in 1941, during the war with Japan, in the anthropological journal *Anthropologica Sinica* of the Academia Sinica. The study introduced me to some of the literature on human growth. The studies I reviewed did not offer convincing evidence of the importance of nurture relative to nature in height and weight growth of Chinese, however, because the South Chinese children who were outgrown by those of North China were not merely displaced northerners. To assess the role of diets requires studies of genetically similar samples of people growing up under different conditions.

In my second year in China, I was earning a bare subsistence by teaching English, first at the YMCA night school and then at Chao T'ung University. I still received funds from my parents to pay for my Chinese tutor, with whom I was translating short stories. My more experienced friends pointed out that for a real career based on knowledge of the Chinese language, one would also need to be an expert about some subject matter. Furthermore, although I had moved into a private Chinese home and was learning the language faster than the missionaries I had met at the language college, the scholars I knew were more apt than I. Norbert Wiener had a large vocabulary (although I thought his accent worse than mine); John de Francis would one day be a professor of Chinese language at Yale; Henry MacAleavy was on his way to becoming the outstanding authority on Chinese law at the London School of Oriental and African Studies; and Karl August Wittfogel was submerged in documents of the Liao and other dynasties. All were learning written Chinese while I was struggling with the written form of the vernacular. Most Chinese literature other than fiction is written in a more difficult sort of shorthand style. My developing interest in anthropology, a subject I had never studied and in which I therefore had no mediocre university grade to discourage me, suggested itself as a career area.

Chinese society was puritanical, and I had few social contacts with young women. I knew the daughter of a missionary who liked to dance, and on a couple of occasions I put on my tuxedo, and we went to nurse one drink all evening and dance at the Grand Hotel. I must have been a sight coming and going on my bicycle alongside the young lady in the rickshaw. I was also friends with Ida Pruitt's adopted daughters and a few other young women, but my social life was not like that during my years at university or in New York.

After nearly two years in China, I was ready to return to the United States. Stevenson and Klineberg made it clear that for a career as an anthropologist, I would need a PhD, and they wrote letters of recommendation.

Bert and Ethel Aginsky, recent doctoral students under Franz Boas at Columbia University, were in China for a brief period. I don't think they did any real research there, because they were on their honeymoon. When Bert learned that I planned to study anthropology, he also offered to write a letter of recommendation for me. It was favorable, but the Aginskys apparently considered me to be outside their social class, because when I came to talk to them about my application, they were giving a party, and Bert talked with me in an anteroom without inviting me to join his party.

Bernard Gallen had a somewhat different reaction to the Aginskys when he first returned from fieldwork and Bert offered to help him with his thesis. Gallen was invited to dinner at the Aginskys' Park Avenue apartment, and when he "came as he was," he found the other guests and his hosts dressed up, with the men wearing dinner jackets and black ties. After dinner, Bert deserted his other guests and took Gallen into another room for a long and helpful conference about how to produce a thesis.

In later years, the Aginskys had a very expensive town house in New York (just across the street from the Wenner-Gren Foundation). One of their topics of research was the lateral cultural behavior of the international yachting set, of which, one presumes, they considered themselves a part.

For many years, the Aginskys conducted a summer field school among the Pomo Indians. One story is that the Aginskys would drive around in their station wagon and pick up Pomo hitchhikers, who would ride in the front seat while students were instructed to ride in the back and take notes as the Aginskys interviewed the riders. Another story is that the Aginskys stopped the station wagon every so often to make the students change seats because they "didn't want cliques to develop."

When my father had sailed home from Shanghai, he had counted his numerous pieces of luggage, as travelers who sometimes had dozens used to do. However, someone had given him a good-bye present, and his old Corona portable typewriter was left behind on the dock. Eventually, one of his associates from the Institute of Pacific Relations sent it to me in Peking. That machine and two-finger typing stood me in good stead for many years. There was no airmail service across the Pacific until much later, so I wrote applications only to

Harvard and in duplicate with carbon copies. I sent one copy via the Trans-Siberian Railway and Europe, the other with Chinese stamps and a U.S. airmail stamp via sea from Shanghai to San Francisco and then by air to their destination.

Perhaps my eagerness as demonstrated by the duplicate application letters plus the contents of the letters of recommendation, which apparently were glowing, did the trick. Despite mediocre undergraduate grades, I was admitted by E. A. Hooton into the graduate program in physical anthropology at Harvard. I did not qualify for a grant because of my prior C average and would have to rely for a year on monthly checks from my ever tolerant and hardworking mother.

I think that Hooton was so enthusiastic about his subject, and the faculty in anthropology at Harvard was so helpful to young people interested in their subject, that they took on most applicants. Bunny, in her usual perceptive manner, points out that when the country was only beginning to come out of the financial depression, there were few applicants for graduate training in anthropology, and even elite departments were inclined to accept almost any student they could get.

4

The Long Trip Home for Graduate Study

*I*n the summer of 1937, I started a long, slow trip home to my parents' house in New York State. I knew very little of any kind of biology or anthropology, but I did know about the swelling resentment toward Japanese military adventures in China among Chinese students and intellectuals and their distrust of the Chiang Kai-shek central government's will to resist. On my way home, I stopped in several Chinese cities to visit anatomists and social scientists, stayed in Japan for a month and called on opinion makers, and then traveled across America to visit departments of anthropology. Besides carrying news from one place to another, I had information of my own from Peking and other places in China through my contacts throughout the country. For instance, I had spent an evening listening to Edgar Snow tell about the things he later published in *Red Star over China*. He was the only American journalist to have visited the communist enclave and army holed up at Yenan in western China.

After leaving Peking, I stopped in Tsingtao to talk with the anatomist at the medical college there and at Nanking University to meet an American sociologist working on rural development in the cotton-weaving industry. In Soochow, I just visited the sights. An old lady there tried to sell me a fan, a young girl tried to sell me some flowers, and another child tried to sell me some candy. None of those things cost more than a few pennies, and I tried to joke a bit and perhaps buy something, but they spoke the local dialect, and none of them could understand my Mandarin. A young woman, perhaps in her twenties, there with three men of similar age, came over to translate for me, very much to my surprise. In the north of China at that time, a young woman would never have spoken to a stranger like that. It turned out that they were Chinese tourists from Shanghai, where they were employed by the railway administration. When they learned that I was a teacher at the railway university, they invited me to visit them when I got to Shanghai.

In 1937, the commercial center of Shanghai was still under control of foreign governments. The French and the Japanese had their own concessions. The Americans had never seized extraterritorial concessions in China, and the Germans, Austrians, and Russians had lost theirs after World War I. I stayed in the YMCA in the French concession but had to find acquaintances in the international concession where the Sikh policemen spoke English. I did not speak Shanghai dialect, and I did not know the English names of the addresses given to me by the young people I had met in Soochow and other acquaintances. For directions, I had to hunt for educated people, whom I identified by their long blue gowns. People who dressed that way almost always knew the national (North Chinese) dialect. When I did find the young men and the woman, they had prepared to entertain me. One of them came from Kweichow Province, and he insisted on my eating some delicacies he had received from home, which included dried beetles; one stripped off the wings and got a tiny but intense taste of something like anchovies.

Presumably to preserve the "face" of long-nosed, hairy foreigners, the United States Steamship Line would not sell a third-class ticket home from China to a white U.S. citizen. However, the Canadian Pacific Steamship Line did sell me one at their lowest third-class fare from Shanghai to Kobe, Japan. It called for Oriental food, which would have suited me fine, but the stewards on board the ship did not think it appropriate for a clean-shaven American youth to eat with the Chinese seamen who were returning to their ship, and they insisted on having me dine on European food with some White Russians (who had paid five dollars more for their meals). I did not enjoy the food and could not converse with the Russians; I would have preferred to eat with the seamen. They spent the voyage playing mah-jongg, moving the tiles so rapidly that I could not see what was going on, let alone dare to participate.

The food on the Canadian ship was the first of its kind I had
eaten for nearly two years. In China, I had avoided ice cream and
raw food. On the street in front of the house in Peking, a peddler had
sometimes sold sugared fruits skewered on slivers of bamboo. I used
to buy and eat them until Mrs. Yang stopped me from breaking the
bamboo slivers, "because we get a new fruit kabob free for every ten
bamboo slivers we return." I was worried that the slivers would not
be properly washed between uses, and I did not eat those candied
fruits thereafter.

In Nagasaki, the ship, the *Empress of Asia,* took on coal. A continuous line of women, each with a full sack of coal, climbed up
from the barge and then descended with empty bags. After being
accustomed to the smiling but generally dirty working-class Chinese,
I was surprised that the women who came to carry the sacks of soft
coal up from the lighters wore spotless blue and white clothes. Of
course, after the first sack of coal, they were covered in soot, but they
obviously cleaned up thoroughly every day after work.

From Nagasaki, the ship put into the mouth of the Sea of Japan.
It was on the south shore of the strait, at Shimonoseki, that the ship
stopped for a day. I took the ferry across to the small city of Moji
on the north shore and had my first experience at being taken to be
deaf. Most Japanese could understand written Chinese, of course, but
the spoken language is completely different. I could write and read
some Chinese characters and carried a Chinese-English dictionary
arranged by pronunciation, so if I knew the oral Chinese, I could
find the printed characters. By writing on the palm of my hand, if I
knew the Chinese written character, or pointing to the character in
the dictionary, I could make myself understood. For instance, it was
raining, and I was able to bargain for and buy one of those fabulous
large Japanese umbrellas with bamboo ribs and working parts and
a yellow oiled-paper cover. The person selling it assumed from my
behavior that I was deaf and dumb and answered by poking my
shoulder to get my attention and tracing the answering characters
with his right forefinger on the open left palm without uttering a
sound. I ended up spending a month in Japan as a deaf-mute without
learning any spoken Japanese.

From Kobe, I went to Kyoto, where Walter Hochstetter was installed at the Railway Hotel. Walter, who had also lived in Mrs.
Yang's house in Peking, was a collector of Sung Dynasty porcelain, an
occupation in which he was single-mindedly absorbed and at which

he subsequently earned his livelihood. I did not want to spend as much as he was paying for a room, and the hotel clerk kindly referred me to a Japanese inn. Fortunately, it was one that had beds rather than mats on the floor.

There were only a few guests at the inn, and the next morning I discovered that the other guests were women, probably being kept there by men who were not their husbands. The women came into the bathroom while I was shaving and tried to talk to me, but of course I did not understand. Using a cake of soap, I wrote a few words in Chinese on the mirror to indicate that I was an American student. Responding in the same way with characters written in soap, one of them indicated that she wanted me to meet her man. They later entertained me at a Japanese movie and took me to the railway station to see me off for a day's sightseeing in Nara, where there are some beautiful ancient temples. The inn was evidently not a bordello, because the other guests all left in the mornings and were away all day.

The innkeeper's daughter was studying English in school, and she was called in by her parents to translate. The family was very hospitable and insisted on my eating with them on one or two occasions.

I saw the sights of Kyoto as a tourist and went on to Tokyo, where I met Gilbert Bowles, the father of anthropologist Gordon Bowles. The elder Bowleses were Quaker missionaries and knew a great deal about Japan.

On July 7, 1937, conflict broke out between China and Japan with a skirmish at Marco Polo Bridge. Although we did not know it at the time, that started the war. I bought and tried to read a Japanese newspaper, but it had too many Japanese characters among the Chinese ones I knew. I was staying at the same hotel as Jim Bertram, the New Zealander with whom I had become a close friend in Peking. The two of us went to visit Ushida, the secretary of the liberal prime minister. Ushida said, and apparently believed, that, like many other incidents incited by the Japanese army in China, this one would be negotiated and passed over. A day or two later, Bertram and I went to see Oxford-educated Prince Saionji, the grandson of the chief adviser to the emperor. The prince had the same opinion as the prime minister's secretary. They did not expect that the Chinese would feel forced to resist.

The communists in the hinterland, the warlords already pushed out of their provinces by the Japanese, and the radicalized students in the cities forced Chiang Kai-shek's hand. Indeed, as the war intensified, Chiang's Kuomintang government apparently tried to position its army so that the armies of the provincial warlords would be chewed up first. The communists had the same idea vis-à-vis Chiang's army, and since they previously had been relegated to the most marginal area, Yenan, in Shenhsi Province, the communists managed to preserve enough resources to defeat Chiang after the war with Japan.

Following a month's stay in Japan, I sailed on a Japanese liner, the *Chichibu Maru*, to San Francisco. A group of about fifty Japanese students on their way to a conference in California were fellow passengers in third class. I got to know some of them, especially because their chaperones traveled in first class. Several came to me with the texts of the talks they had prepared and sought my help with their English. Their papers had been vetted in advance by foreign office functionaries, but I managed to put a few of my own more radical antiwar ideas into their mouths. Two of the students were from Japanese colonies, Korea and Formosa (Taiwan), and knew Chinese. They both sought me out and spoke to me very openly in Chinese about their anti-imperialist attitudes.

The ship stopped in Honolulu for a day, and I spent it with Romanzo Adams, a sociologist at the University of Hawaii. He had just written a book on interracial marriage in Hawaii. Those who think that whenever diverse peoples meet they tend to intermarry will find strong support from the example of Hawaii as told by Adams and in later studies by Newton Morton, among others. The integration of the different immigrant groups into Hawaiian society was probably one of the reasons Japanese Americans there were fortunate enough not to be interned as mainland Japanese Americans were during World War II. Adams drove me up to Diamond Head, where it was, as usual, raining, and down to Waikiki Beach, where it was, as usual, sunny. All the time, he was giving me an account of the social structure of the islands, the occupations and status of the various immigrant groups, and where and how they lived and were adapting to the Hawaiian geography and economy. After about nine hours, I was getting nervous because it was almost time to sail. Before taking me to the ship, however, Adams insisted on one more stop to buy me a huge glass of pineapple juice, memorable because I had had nothing of the kind for the previous two years.

After docking in San Francisco, I continued my trip home overland through the Southwest and Midwest and eventually on to New

York. Everywhere I exchanged talk about China and the war there for knowledge about the discipline of anthropology and its organizations. At that time in the United States, there were no more than a handful of individuals employed full-time in the discipline of physical anthropology. The majority of these were professional anatomists, many of whom considered physical anthropology as an ancillary occupation. Except in the case of Harvard, which offered a program leading to a PhD, expertise in physical anthropology was to be found primarily in university anatomy departments or in museums. I set off across the country from San Francisco, intending to visit as many of these institutions as possible and also to talk with as many anthropologists as I could find.

In Berkeley, there were two distinguished professors of anthropology. Alfred Kroeber was out of town when I arrived, but I went to see Robert Lowie. Both Kroeber and Lowie were students of Boas and therefore trained in all kinds of anthropology. Then I visited Felix Keesing at Stanford. Keesing was a New Zealander who had trained outside the American anthropological tradition of integration of all four fields of the subject: social anthropology, linguistics, archaeology, and physical anthropology. Neither Lowie nor Keesing had much to say about physical anthropology. The University of California program covered all those aspects, but Keesing's department at Stanford never did.

I saw Keesing again much later, in 1961, the evening before he died. He had just been to see his doctor for a checkup and believed that he was in fine shape. The next day, he played tennis with his wife, Dorothy. She urged him to play just one more set, during which he collapsed and died of a heart attack. She never recovered from her subsequent depression and shortly afterward committed suicide.

I next took the bus to Los Angeles. I cannot now remember whether I met Ralph Beals there, but I do remember that everyone was very cordial and tried to be helpful. One thing I later appreciated about Beals was his generous help to Norman Humphrey when he was ill with kidney disease and drinking too much. Humphrey had done fieldwork in Mexico on a project that never would have been finished but for the fact that Beals did virtually all the data analysis and saw that it was published under Humphrey's name. The project concerned professionals in Mexico who had received advanced training in the United States but found on their return that those who had stayed behind had built their network of connections and controlled practice to the exclusion of those who had gone away and believed themselves better qualified.

In New Mexico, I visited the department at the University of New Mexico in Albuquerque as well as the Institutions of Anthropology then still housed in the old Spanish government buildings in Santa Fe. The sheer quantity of archaeological material in the Southwest was what most impressed me.

Another anthropology department I visited on that trip was at the University of Chicago, where Fay Cooper Cole received me. By that time, the Department of Anthropology was separate from the Department of Sociology. Bunny, who was a graduate student and completed her PhD at Chicago, says that the separation happened after Leslie White took his degree there. One of the sociologists, she thinks it was Robert E. Park, challenged White during his oral exam and nearly reduced him to tears. White had written critical reviews of the work of some of the sociologists at the University of Chicago and, although still a student, had apparently identified himself as being in their department. The faculty was furious and is said to have taken revenge on White at his examination. Cole would not stand for having his students treated in that way and soon after organized both the separation into two departments and the elimination of the PhD oral qualifying examination. Cole was a well-rounded anthropologist with an old-fashioned interest in all four fields. His student White was purely a cultural anthropologist, but he had respect for physical anthropology, as I later inferred from his high opinion of the work of his colleague James N. Spuhler, whom I also admired. From Chicago, Cole sent me on to Cleveland to see Wilton M. Krogman, who had a position on the Chicago faculty but was spending the summer at Western Reserve University.

I converted part of my Greyhound bus ticket and traveled from Detroit to Cleveland by the D&C steamship line. There I met Krogman, but T. Wingate Todd was away, so I did not then see his famous skeletal collection. Krogman was very person-oriented and never said an unkind word about anyone. He wrote dozens of book reviews and always found something favorable to say. I am glad that there are some colleagues one can always count on for a favorable reaction and a kind word. He encouraged many students, and they were all loyally appreciative. He was a great organizer of facts, and for a long time all of what otherwise would have been white spaces in the *American*

Journal of Physical Anthropology were filled with fascinating snippets from Krogman's collection of out-of-the-way or ancient works.

After Cleveland, I finally went on to my parents' home in Yonkers, a suburb of New York City. At the American Museum of Natural History, I had a talk with Harry L. Shapiro, who had already published a preliminary account (1929) of his study with William Lessa of Chinese migrants in Hawaii. Later, when I would talk with Shapiro about my proposed thesis on Chinese immigrants, his lack of great enthusiasm was presumably because he had in his possession, but had not yet published, the results of Lessa's fieldwork. Shapiro never did publish more than the preliminary report. Lessa had been a graduate student at the time but was not permitted to use the data he had collected on the Chinese for a thesis. In fact, he left for the University of Chicago to complete his degree. His eventual thesis was on data from the major government postwar research program in Micronesia.

Frederick S. Hulse had collected all the data in Japan and Hawaii for a study with Shapiro of Japanese migrants. Some aspects were apparently similar to those of the study by Lessa. Hulse was still a student, but he also did not get a thesis out of the project and instead wrote his dissertation on Puerto Ricans. However, the results of the Japanese study were published in *Migration and Environment* by Shapiro "with the assistance of F. S. Hulse." Geoffrey A. Harrison always cites the work as "by Shapiro and Hulse." I thought that was the best way to give Hulse due credit. I have spoken to him about it, but he indicated that he did not wish to be cited in that way. It may have been modesty, but I think it probable that Boas was the source of the research plan; Hulse, hired by Shapiro, did the fieldwork; I don't know who did the statistics; and Shapiro wrote the report by himself. Perhaps the reason Hulse would not have wanted me to indicate that he was a joint author is some disagreement Hulse had about the conclusion Shapiro reached. He wrote that the first-generation migrants were "selected," that is, were physically distinct. Hulse once indicated that some of the Japanese migrants to Hawaii went there at an early age, and he may have suspected that the differences in physique they showed from those who never left Japan (the sedentes) were the result of growing up in the new Hawaiian environment. Analogy with my later study in Mexico suggests such an explanation. Whether or not Hulse thought so, at least some of the differences between the sedentes and the migrants may have resulted from the

Hawaiian environment rather than from the selective migration as stated by Shapiro in the book.

Shapiro wrote well, but Bunny says that he struggled over the task and constantly revised. Whatever the reasons, much of his research was published only after a long delay, or not at all. William Pollitzer says that much unpublished data still exists at the American Museum of Natural History.

Unlike the experiences of Lessa and Hulse, Robert Meier says that Shapiro helped him with his dissertation on data collected by measuring inhabitants of Easter Island. When he consulted Shapiro, who had made anthropometric measurements there thirty years previously, in some instances of the very same individuals, Shapiro dug out his original data and made the material available for Meier to use. Shapiro also helped the graduate students who in about 1949 were pioneering the field of anthropological genetics in a program at Columbia University organized by geneticist Theodosius Dobzhansky.

The advice I received from these visits clarified for me that I had made the correct choice in applying to Harvard, since my interests lay in physiological and genetic aspects of physical anthropology. There was more or less universal agreement among those I talked to on that point. This view was also shared by Florence Hawley and the other archaeologists I met and by cultural anthropologists such as Lowie and Keesing.

It is more surprising that some physical anthropologists gave the same advice. Krogman advised me to study under Hooton at Harvard rather than with himself at Chicago. Shapiro gave the same advice, but in his case it was not too surprising, as he had studied with Hooton himself. He also never really trained physical anthropologists at Columbia; his chief job was at the American Museum of Natural History. Marcus Goldstein had completed his PhD in physical anthropology at Columbia University but did so under Franz Boas. Goldstein's first fieldwork was with Shapiro among French Canadians, but I have never seen any publication of it except for some anecdotes in Goldstein's recent memoirs.

5

Cambridge, Massachusetts

*I*n the fall of 1937, I arrived in Cambridge, Massachusetts, and found a place to live in the 1820s house of Mrs. Grace Botinelli on Cambridge Street. After a year, I moved up a ladderlike flight of stairs into an even less costly garret. The only spot where one could stand erect was in a dormer. The good thing about the room was that the rent was only a dollar and a half per week. In time, Mrs. Botinelli, her husband, her two adult sons, and her other roomers became my friends. For cooking, I had access to a single gas burner in the hallway, and Mrs. Botinelli let me keep food in her refrigerator. For a year, I shared meals with a law student who kept track of our shares of expenses down to the half-cent.

Others on the periphery of the university were even poorer than the students. I had one friend who bought nothing to eat that cost more than five cents a pound. He earned ten dollars a week by singing in the choir in the Old South Church in Boston, and on that he supported himself as well as a brother who lived in New York City. To supplement his diet of potatoes and cabbage, he sometimes treated himself to codfish that cost six cents a pound on the pier. The rest of us sometimes shared what we had with him.

Hooton's door was always open to students. He would put aside whatever he was doing to listen to them. When I went to talk with him about my program, he told me about a new university policy

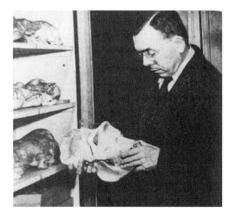

Earnest Albert Hooton with a gorilla skull. In the decades before World War II, Hooton and the Department of Anthropology at Harvard that he chaired trained far more professional physical anthropologists than any other university. In the subsequent years, Hooton's former students dominated the field. (From *Human Biology* Vol. 26, no. 3, 1954, following page 180.)

that would allow one to plan an individual degree between two departments, such as physiology and anthropology. The drawback was that one would have to satisfy the requirements of both departments, which would take more time. I therefore decided to become a straight anthropology student.

I have no formal training in biology, nor did I ever study physiology. I did work at the biology laboratories on two occasions, however. The first time was to look at details of social behavior in pairs of caged mice, a study suggested by Eliot Chapple. He had been studying the timing and duration of activity in humans engaged in social interactions. The idea of analyzing such objectively observed details had a great deal of appeal to me. I did not achieve worthwhile results with the mice, however. My other stint at the laboratory, which I describe below, came the following summer.

The main course I took that first year was Hooton's full-year Anthropology 2, Physical Anthropology. Hooton read tables of data from Martin's *Lehrbuch der Anthropologie* which he translated into English and annotated by digressing at length to interpret the findings, sometimes discussing technique, sometimes defining the implications, and occasionally presenting other findings. His general point of view was that the details of form reflected in the measurements were essentially inherited as an aspect of general morphological combinations that defined racial types. To accommodate evolutionary change in such a scheme, it had to be assumed that such changes were caused by migrations from elsewhere.

Hooton had a keen sense of humor. His speech was interrupted with pauses for effect punctuated with an exhaled "heh." Since these often followed a joke, one automatically laughed out loud or at least smiled inwardly whenever Hooton exhaled his "heh" with a rising tone.

In addition to the lectures, there was laboratory work, which consisted of assignments in measuring and observing selected bone specimens Hooton had previously examined. Hooton graded the papers himself, but the person in charge of the bone lab was Kay Young, a fellow graduate student. Some of the students (Harvard then admitted only males) had a crush on her; at least, her amiable presence made it agreeable to spend a lot of time there.

On her own initiative, Kay would set up a "skull of the month." These were chosen in an effort to fool us; they were not typical of the population from which they came. Our task was to guess their provenance. Quite often, one or more of us would place the specimen very accurately, probably based on knowledge of the particular series in the Peabody Museum collections. However, other students would invariably guess the wrong continent for these unidentified specimens. For instance, one skull was of a Chinese from Szechuan. I had been looking at some of the Szechuan skulls in the collection and guessed correctly, but most of the other students thought it was of an American Indian, and some placed it in West Asia and even Africa. This voluntary student activity was very educational. It greatly enhanced my skepticism about racial typology; I was impressed with the difficulty of correctly placing an individual in the right part of the world solely on the basis of features of the skull. On average, there are clear differences, but individuals vary greatly.

The bone lab was on the fourth floor of the museum. One privilege of being a graduate student was getting a key to the elevator. I lost mine, and, rather than admit it, I climbed the stairs for the rest of my stay in Cambridge except when someone else opened the elevator door.

During the second semester, the lab work involved individual projects of one's own invention, and I wrote a paper based on measurements of palates and teeth. One result of that project was that Carleton Coon asked me to give the sessions on teeth in his course for three Radcliffe College students. Radcliffe and Harvard courses were separate, although all were taught in the Peabody Museum.

Coon sat in while I talked, and that was the first experience I had in teaching anthropology.

One requirement of Hooton's course was a periodic quiz requiring the identification of bone specimens passed from one student to another at the sound of a signal that rang every minute. Those of my fellow students who had done fieldwork in archaeology were much better than I at identifying scraps of bone. With my poor past performance at university, I was very apprehensive about passing that course, but the students all helped one another prepare, and I got through.

Hooton's reputation at Harvard was largely based on his popular undergraduate course, Anthropology A, in which he aped the apes and told limericks. The flavor of it is preserved in his book *Up from the Ape*. This course was tremendously influential in the teaching of anthropology. Bunny attended the physical anthropology lectures of Harry Shapiro at Columbia University and then in 1947 served as instructor and managed eleven discussion sections including that of William Howells at the University of Wisconsin. Somewhat later, she taught during the summer session at the University of Michigan, where Mischa Titiev taught the course. She reports that these three courses were virtually identical, all by former students at Harvard, and apparently all based on notes taken in Hooton's popular class. No doubt, some of Hooton's ideas also have crept into my textbook writing, but I missed the pleasure of taking his most entertaining course and cannot be accused of ever reusing material from notes taken during those lectures.

Teaching from another's lecture notes may have been common at Harvard. After Roland B. Dixon's death, his courses were taught by others using his notes or notes taken in his lectures. Stanley M. Garn remembers that when Carl Coon left to join the Office of Secret Service (OSS) during World War II, Lauriston Ward taught the course on Africa from the very note cards that Coon had used.

That certainly was not true of Eliot Chapple. In my first semester, I took his course on social relations. Although he did use a great deal of material from the Yankee City (Newburyport) project of Lloyd Warner, Chapple spent most of the time charting who interacted with whom and for what durations they talked. These interactions were plotted and statistically analyzed without reference to the subject being discussed. Chapple taught by the Socratic method which had been used by the instructors at the Experimental College at the University of Wisconsin and which I had discovered by reading translations of Plato's dialogues. Some of Chapple's other students were accustomed to lectures and note taking and found it difficult to distinguish what was important through so much give-and-take discussion. One of my friends in the course was Lin Yueh-hwa, a Chinese student who later finished his foreign study under Raymond Firth in England and then for years (with an interruption during the Cultural Revolution) worked in the Institute of Minorities of the Academia Sinica in Peking. Chapple's method was in sharp contrast to the typical Chinese method of learning by word-for-word memorization.

The final examination in Chapple's course consisted of two questions. One, for 5 percent, was a factual question covering material in the course. The other, for 95 percent, was a long section from the laws of Massachusetts concerning organization of schools followed by a single word: "Analyze." I wrote that everything requiring a law involved interpersonal interactions that did not normally occur and therefore required a formal reversal. For example, spelling out regulations regarding the ability of a schoolteacher to put something before the school board implied that it was normally the principal who would do so on behalf of the teacher; a law was required for situations when the normal interactions failed to work. I worried whether I had passed; my fellow students had apparently all carefully plotted the interactions described in the laws and had not considered the laws as rare sanctions in a system where other interpersonal behavior was the norm. It was the first grade I received as a graduate student, and it was an A+. I was never again allowed to worry out loud about grades to the law student and others at Mrs. Botinelli's lodging house. I also never again got an A+; most members of the faculty did not give them. I have always thought of Chapple as perhaps the most intellectual of my teachers, but I am probably prejudiced.

During this time at Harvard, there was a group of faculty members who lacked permanent tenure: Coon, Chapple, Conrad Arensberg, and Clyde Kluckhohn. Of all of them, only Kluckhohn was reappointed in the end. Chapple and Coon coauthored a very original introductory textbook, *Principles of Anthropology* (1942). It examines human society from the point of view of human behavior. Arensberg was also involved in developing the approach, and Kluckhohn cited Chapple's ideas in his own teaching.

I had to take courses in archaeology to prepare for my "general" oral exam covering all four fields. Lauriston Ward taught the two

Stanley M. Garn, one of the last of Hooton's students, has probably published more research, mostly about human growth, than any other living biological anthropologist.

archaeology courses I took. One was on the Far East, and I wrote my term paper on the Chinese Neolithic; the other was on the Near East, and I wrote about the site of Uruk. I received B's in both and was told that A's were reserved for students majoring in archaeology. However, William S. Laughlin, who was also a student of physical anthropology but who had experience in archaeology in Alaska, did earn an A in a course that Ward taught.

While I was at Harvard, I did not have much to do with undergraduates, but I met Stan Garn on the steps of the Peabody Museum in September 1939, when he was just starting his anthropological studies. At one time, I cautioned him not to get involved with "anomaly anatomy," advice I could better have heeded myself. From the start, I thought Garn would succeed. I cited his undergraduate thesis in the *Yearbook of Physical Anthropology*. When I edited *Human Biology*, I used one of his papers as an example of the style for references, so it appeared on the inside back cover of every issue. As Garn moved from the Forsythe Dental Infirmary to the Fels Research Center to the University of Michigan, I have kept his telephone numbers handy. A call to him is an easy way to find an answer for many questions and will almost certainly be accompanied by other interesting facts and entertaining anecdotes. So many biological anthropologists now have narrow specialized careers, but those such as Garn who have broader interests are often the ones who connect insights from different fields to create new knowledge.

Although I took only four courses at a time and they lasted a semester or even a year, not a quarter, there were quite a few. I took Hooton's course on the ethnology and archaeology of Europe, in which he used the Latin classics as well as modern sources, and I occasionally sat in on the parallel course on the New World taught by Coon, who studded his lectures with the firsthand accounts of ethnologists. I also took Kluckhohn's course on the physical anthropology of the American Indian, but I learned more talking in the bone lab with fellow students who had worked in the Southwest. Of course, I read a few obligatory works, such as Hooton's Pecos Pueblo monograph. It is the best example of Hooton's method of sorting the skeletons from a single population into a number of morphological types that represented to him evidence of distinct sources of origin. Because of Hooton's broad knowledge, keen observations, and persuasive presentation, it took years for most of his former students to realize that the various characteristics of the types actually have different causes, including independent inheritance. At the time, some of the supposed relationships were already ruled out by accumulating genetic evidence. Hooton later admitted to that. He did not see that the method itself was flawed, but he did shift his main interest to an enthusiasm for the somatotyping system of constitutional types of William H. Sheldon.

I took Coon's course on primitive arts and industries. It covered things like the different methods of making and decorating pottery and identifying them from archaeological shards. I had gone to a progressive school, so by the age of twelve I had made pottery by coil, by slab, and by slip-in molds. We had made and had decorated pottery in every conceivable way. We also constructed looms and tried every textile method from knitting to Persian rugs. There seemed to be little in so-called primitive arts and industries that I had not tried to do as a child. I believe that I passed that course in graduate school on the basis of what I had learned in the fifth grade.

Kluckhohn did something for me that probably stemmed from his experience as a Rhodes scholar at Oxford; he met me in the smoking room every second week for an Oxford-style tutorial. The works he gave me to read (unlike the bibliographies of his course that I had previously taken) were the classic works of modern anthropology, such as Bronislaw Malinowski's *Argonauts of the Western Pacific*. At our sessions, after I had my say, Clyde would explain what he thought. That is virtually all the cultural anthropology I was ever taught, undergraduate or graduate, but it was the best it could be.

In 1942, I was living among fellow pacifists in a Quaker-managed Civilian Public Service camp for alternative service to military conscription. I wrote a piece about anthropology for our mimeographed magazine and sent copies to a number of friends including Clyde Kluckhohn. After his *Mirror for Man* appeared, I read a review of it in the *New York Times* that complained about the sweeping generalizations and held up as an example of what was wrong with the book a ringing phrase claiming that anthropology might contribute to peace. I laughed because the phrase was taken verbatim, and without ascription, from my mimeographed article.

The various courses had final exams, of course, but the tests that caused the most apprehension were the orals. There were three: a general exam covering all of anthropology, a special exam covering physical anthropology, and the defense of the thesis. About a dozen faculty members, along with visitors, sat in on each set. Leslie Spier sat in as a visitor on one of my exams. I do not remember what he asked, but I would have an experience with him later. In 1954, I published an article in the *Southwest Journal of Anthropology* which Spier edited. My article used several examples drawn from populations of small size and low admixture rates to demonstrate the opportunity for random genetic drift. Spier's response to the submission was to contribute an additional example, the Havasupi, in carefully counted detail, to enhance the article.

I always thought I could do well in speaking, and I did pass my general exam the first time I took it, although many fellow students, including some who would become distinguished anthropologists, had to try more than once. Coon helped me once. I never was good at cramming for exams, either starting too early, which normally proved counterproductive, or cramming too near the date, when it was already too late. The day before one exam, I had audited Coon's lecture in his course on American Indian culture. At the exam, he asked me a question straight out of that lecture.

Perhaps it was at the same exam that he handed me a tooth and asked what I made of it. The tooth was of a similar color to some material I had seen in the archaeology laboratory that had been excavated from the High Cave in Algeria. The notion did flicker across my mind that Coon thought he had found a Neanderthal tooth there, but I did not take advantage of the opening. I said that it was probably a human tooth, and I told the story about *Hesperopithecus*, a pig's tooth that had been reported to be a primate fossil. Then I opined that the tooth he was showing me was a molar and hemmed and hawed about upper or lower, left or right, and first, second, or third molar. I missed the chance to suggest that it seemed taurodont and large, perhaps suggesting Neanderthal. One should never get stuck in a narrow frame of reference; I should not have considered the question to be purely morphological, because I missed my opportunity to wow them.

When I took my special oral exam in physical anthropology, R. Ruggles Gates, an English geneticist, was visiting. I had prepared by reading all of his papers on genetics of corn but was given no opportunity to display that knowledge. Gates's anthropological genetics were dreadfully racist. At one point, he argued for considering races as species, and he contributed to the disgustingly racist journal *Mankind Quarterly*. I was already agnostic about any claims for inherent superiority in intelligence or other characteristics of one "race" over another. Hooton and, especially, Coon did not share my extreme skepticism, but I must say that neither of them ever impeded my progress as a student or my subsequent career because of our differences of opinion. I may have been relatively persuasive with fellow students. One of them, Sherwood Washburn, has reported (in *Human Biology*, 1982) that I influenced him to more liberal views. Of course, it may have been the other way around. Most of my fellow students have been free of any hint of racial prejudice in their published discussions of human variability, and some, such as Jim Spuhler, have published well-reasoned criticisms of studies purporting to show some sort of racial superiority.

Whatever their personal views and my disagreements with some of them, I doubt that a greater group of teachers of anthropology has ever been assembled. Hooton, Coon, Chapple, Kluckhohn, and the others with whom I had less contact all had a knack for encouraging learning. Nevertheless, an even greater influence may have been the other students.

6

Hooton's Students

While I was at Harvard, I met many of Hooton's previous students. Gordon Bowles had received his PhD in 1935. His fellow students included Carl Seltzer, who finished two years later, and, I believe, C. Wesley Dupertuis, who did not finally finish until 1940. Their careers were apparently handicapped by the Great Depression of the 1930s.

Bowles wrote a very interesting monograph comparing the physiques of Harvard students with those of their fathers when they had been students at Harvard. On average, the sons were larger than their fathers had been at comparable ages. Bowles found similar differences between mothers and daughters at elite women's colleges, too. He stopped working in anthropology for a while during and immediately after the war but returned to a faculty position at Syracuse, where his patient manner and his experiences in the Far East must have contributed considerably to his teaching. For many years, Bowles continued to work on expanding his thesis on the people of the China-Tibet borderland into a book on the peoples of Asia. It was published by Oxford University Press in 1977 and contains a great deal of information. However, the frame of reference is that of the time when he started to collect the data, when races were defined in terms of morphology and assumed to have a biological distinctiveness, which now, thanks to such studies as Bowles's own on the Harvard students, can no longer be sustained.

Carl Seltzer struck me as bright and knowledgeable. He retained a connection with the anthropology department at Harvard while he carried on a family shoe business. His early work was in the Hooton mold, but his further contributions to anthropology concerned obesity. Leslie Sue Lieberman, professor of anthropology at the University of Florida, told me that she met him in 1965, and she reminded me that his study of subjects in a camp for overweight girls was among the first in nutritional anthropology.

Dupertuis was sent by Hooton to Ireland to measure ten thousand subjects throughout the island. Later, at the College of Physicians and Surgeons at Columbia University, he specialized in studies of constitutional type in relation to disease. In 1944, I was working on a very rare syndrome, a hereditary disruption of normal development called cleidocranial dysostosis. Dupertuis told me that he had photographed a case in New York for his vast file on constitutional types. It turned out to be the same patient I was studying in North Carolina. I consider the constitutional approach essentially sterile, since it lumps together features of human physique that have various causes rather than trying to separate them by more analytical methods. Nevertheless, studies sometimes have value quite aside from the hypotheses that motivated them, and I saw potential value in William Sheldon's collection of somatotype photographs. I was very disturbed recently when, in a display of yellow journalism by the *New York Times Sunday Magazine,* the nude photographs were sensationalized, and the Smithsonian Institution, which was supposed to preserve them, allowed them to be removed and destroyed because some of them were of college students who later became famous. I hope Dupertuis's pictures of patients, with their permanent value to medicine, will not meet a similar fate.

William W. Howells and Frederick S. Hulse received doctoral degrees from Hooton at Harvard in 1934. Howells achieved his in near record time. His *Mankind So Far* (1944) was a very successful book. Howells writes very well, in clear and concise English prose. Some think that advances in science are limited to technical achievements conveyed in scholarly reports to a few other equally specialized investigators, but I believe that the authorship of successful serious books for a wider circle of well-informed readers deserves acclaim. Indeed, it is what makes most scientific reputations. Howells also retrained himself in new techniques (multivariate analysis), and his successful academic career was uninterrupted. He went on to a job at the University of Wisconsin in Madison but apparently had his eye on the professorship at Harvard from the first. He kept a foot in the door back east until 1954, when he finally got the professorship there. For instance, he kept his dentist in Boston and never sought one in Madison. In fact, during about twelve years in Madison, he never acquired a house but lived in a rented squash court. All that while, he had two sets of household furnishings in storage. William Laughlin, the physical anthropologist who succeeded Howells at Wisconsin, says that he and his wife received much of the furniture Howells had used in Madison. At Harvard, Howells continued his surveys of world distributions of aspects of human skull form using the multivariate methods that he was among the first to apply in biological anthropology.

For the 1947–48 school year, Bunny was instructor of anthropology at Wisconsin and conducted sections of Howells's Introduction to Anthropology course. Four of the students in one of Bunny's sections eventually achieved doctoral degrees, three in anthropology and one in animal behavior, but none of them did graduate study under Howells. He had the reputation of working in his office with the door closed, and it was not easy for students to get to know him the way they did his mentor at Harvard, E. A. Hooton. In fact, the two individuals I know who received PhDs in physical anthropology at the University of Wisconsin during the Howells epoch both had anatomist Walter Sullivan, and not Howells, as their thesis adviser.

One of these was Earle Reynolds, who went from Wisconsin to the Fels Research Institute in Yellow Springs, Ohio. There he pioneered research on the distribution of subcutaneous fat in childhood and adolescence. After Reynolds left Fels, Stanley Garn and, much later, Alex Roche and their associates carried on the important longitudinal growth study. Reynolds went from there to join the Atomic Bomb Casualty Commission in Japan to study victims of the attacks on Hiroshima and Nagasaki. He became an anti-nuclear weapons activist and, in a protest against the development of atomic weapons, sailed his little yacht into a U.S. nuclear test site and into a restricted military zone in the Soviet Union at Vladivostok.

Hulse was another of the early Hooton students. He received an appointment in the anthropology department at the University of Washington. Hulse is best known for his study of a Swiss Alpine population. In his paper "Exogamy and Heterosis," published in French but translated into English in the *Yearbook of Physical Anthropology*, he found that the offspring of parents from the same village tended to be smaller than those with parents from two different places, and he ascribed the difference to hybrid vigor in the latter, the factor that makes for larger size in corn from hybrid seed. There are genetic as well as environmental influences on variation in human size, but some other studies show no special growth "vigor" in outbred humans, and it will take further research on a large scale to determine the circumstances and extent of the phenomenon.

When a new head of the department, James Watson, who had been trained at the University of Chicago, came to the University of Washington in about 1959, he brought other social anthropologists from Chicago with him. Watson was happy enough to see many of the old crew leave, including Hulse. At about this time, Hulse received a letter with an offer of a post at the University of Arizona, and when he showed it to Watson, he was advised to take the job. When I visited the University of Washington soon after and talked about it with Frederick P. Thieme, who had recently become provost, he expressed his disappointment that his position had not permitted him to play any role in the anthropology department's affairs and, specifically, to do something about retaining Hulse. (Thieme also once said that he would have liked to recruit me but that he could do little to further physical anthropology from the provost's office.) Hulse published a few papers during his eight years or so at the University of Washington, but when he moved to the University of Arizona, his research took off, and he also wrote *The Human Species,* published in 1963.

Hulse had an easy way with other people. Toward the end of his life, after his wife, Leonie, had been killed in an auto accident, he visited us in England for two weeks and pitched in to help me edit a book. The Thiemes also visited us in England. One of the advantages of being at the University of Cambridge for part of each year is that many interesting people who never pass through Detroit would come looking for us in England.

Many of the graduate students of anthropology who were at Harvard when I was there already had experience of fieldwork, and I learned a lot from them. Hooton used to read to us the letters he received from Joseph Birdsell, who was in the field with Aborigines in the Australian outback. When Birdsell returned to Harvard, he gave a seminar for Hooton's class. He had originally studied engineering and came to anthropology with a very different background from most of us. Stan Garn tells me that Birdsell's wife, Esther, was Dupertuis's niece. Garn seems particularly interested in such details of kinship because his own wife and that of another Harvard anthropologist, C. Loring Brace, are sisters. As students, we were not all so literally interrelated, but we were very close.

J. Lawrence Angel was a great help to me; he learned more easily than most of us and had a great deal to teach about the archaeology and physical anthropology of Greece. Alice M. Brues was at Radcliffe, and, because women were not admitted to the Harvard courses, she had to sit in the open door rather than in the lecture room to audit Hooton's course at Harvard and get credit for it at Radcliffe. Brues is the daughter of a biologist and had a background in the subject, including genetics, about which many of the students and even the faculty were more or less ignorant. Later, she took over Kay Young's post as mistress of the bone lab. I think that whatever these two Radcliffe students were deprived of in not being admitted to Harvard classes was probably more than compensated for by being central to the student-to-student learning situations in the lab.

Charles E. Snow was a conspicuous fixture; after presentations of papers at meetings of physical anthropologists, he made his presence heard by clapping much louder than any others did or could. I was told that he arrived at Harvard in plus-four knickers with loud "barber pole" stockings. According to one story, early in his stay he called Professor Alfred Tozzer by a nickname only the family used, and Tozzer rushed up the flight of stairs to Hooton's office shouting, "He called me Fuffy, he called me Fuffy!" Laughlin held a Thaw Scholarship in 1946, and Tozzer punned that they "could not give it to Snow; it would have made slush."

Paul Gebhard was considered an archaeologist but was studying physical anthropology. His subsequent career has been in Alfred Kinsey's sex study institute at the University of Indiana. One of Hooton's many projects involved measuring people's back sides to provide data for seat design. Garn reminds me that Hooton referred Gebhard for the job and that "Paul Gebhard measured bottoms for the Sleepy Hollow chair in South Station which gave him a proper foundation for heading the Kinsey Institute."

Jim Spuhler came from New Mexico and was at Harvard during part of my time there, but I got to know him better later when he was at the University of Michigan. In fact, having met several future anthropologists while we were students together made it possible to know them much better later. In 1953, a year after I became editor of *Human Biology*, the journal needed a new source of support.

James N. Spuhler, the first PhD in physical anthropology who was also professionally trained in human genetics. He maintained an up-to-date genetic perspective in anthropology and a broad understanding of the cultural environment in human population and behavioral genetics. (From *Human Biology*, Vol. 66, no. 4, 1944, p. 555.)

Spuhler arranged for us to receive it from Lee R. Dice's Institute of Human Biology at the University of Michigan. In the end, I found an alternative source of support and did not take Dice up on his offer, but I was always appreciative of it.

When we were still all at Harvard, my best friend among the anthropology students was Marshall T. ("Bud") Newman. He was the one who understood genetics, with which I had already had some experience, but he also had been in New Mexico doing real anthropology and knew many of the things I was trying to learn. He and his first wife, the daughter of the director of the Harvard Museum of Comparative Zoology, Thomas Barbour, were very kind to me socially, too. I was welcome at their apartment, and on the day of my oral general exam, I went to their place to prepare. In fact, I must have been excessively nervous and seeking comfort, because they had to call me out of the toilet to get me to the Peabody Museum on time. One of the examiners was Tozzer. I had seen him in the library (since named after him) almost every day, but I did not take his general cultural anthropology course that most of the students took. I understand that after my examination he told Hooton, "There is a young man I never saw before in my life, and I do believe he has memorized my syllabus."

In all, I spent three years in Cambridge, Massachusetts. Other courses I took included auditing Allen's course on mammals (I recall that there are mammalian species with females larger than males—weasels, I believe) and Romer's on vertebrate paleontology which left me astonished at the great numbers and variety of extinct species known from fossils. I also enrolled in a course that Hooton had scheduled on the primates, but he turned all the lecturing over to Sherry Washburn, who had just returned from the Asia Primate Expedition. That field trip had been organized and presumably paid for by Harold Coolidge, of the Boston branch of the family whose poor cousin from Northampton had been president of the United States. The other members of the expedition were Adolph Schultz, the leading primate anatomist of the time, and Charles Ray Carpenter, the first researcher to succeed in studying the behavior of individually identified primates in the wild.

The following summer, Washburn offered me a job helping him to prepare the bones of macaques and langers that had been shot in what was then Siam. I have visions of Schultz and Washburn with hunters trying to collect the very gibbons and monkeys that Carpenter was trying to observe. When Michael Little learned that I had daydreamed of such a notion, he said that when he was a student at Penn State University, Carpenter gave a seminar in which he indicated his distress about just that matter.

The carcasses of the monkeys had been defleshed roughly in the field, and the remaining tissue had dried and mummified on the bones. We tried several methods to remove it without damage to the bones. Dermestes beetles, raised for that purpose, simply died of starvation rather than eat the remaining tissue. In the end, Washburn acquired some activated sludge from the city sewage department. We heated our laboratory to about ninety degrees Fahrenheit and put the skeletons in large canning pots with the sludge and water. The work was done in the biological laboratories, and we had an exhaust fan, but that did not prevent complaints about the stench from elsewhere in the building. Even a Fourth of July weekend at the beach in the blazing sun did not completely free me from the smell, but I became inured to it. Washburn was then courting his future wife, Henrietta Pease, daughter of the professor of classics and president of Amherst College, and I wondered how she felt about the smell.

Washburn wanted more help with our work, and I brought along Lin Yueh-hwa, who, like myself, could well have done with a little extra income. Lin worked bravely for one or two days and then gave up. The stink was too much for him, or perhaps for his future wife, who was then a student at Wellesley. They later returned to China, and she died during the very hard times of the Cultural Revolution. He was eventually reestablished at the Institute of Ethnic Minorities in Peking, and a son came to the United States to study anthropology as his father had done.

In my second year at Cambridge, Hooton secured a fellowship for me, five hundred dollars, that I learned many years later was from a fund that was really supposed to be for archaeologists. Hooton did everything he could to promote an interest in studying physical anthropology. The following year, he got me a job working for Vilh-jalmur Stefansson, the Arctic explorer. Stefansson had demonstrated that one could live on animal food alone, first in six winters in the Far North and then in a yearlong experiment in New York. In grati-tude, the American Meat Institute had provided him with funds for research for a book on diet that he wanted to write. Stefansson hired two of Margaret Mead's graduate students at Columbia University to

Bunny Kaplan with Lin Yueh-hwa in Detroit on his first visit to the United States since he had been a graduate student of anthropology at Harvard.

work under her supervision to make a cross-cultural study of foods eaten. I was to review the literature on diets of nonhuman primates. On this and my other projects, I haunted all the biological libraries of Cambridge and Boston—about a dozen—and I brought back to my room books and journals in many languages. On one such occasion, I had with me a work in Norwegian, and a fellow student asked me if I could read it. The scientific terms are much the same in every language, but the connecting words give the trouble. "Oh, yes," I said, "but I don't know whether it says it is so or it isn't so."

Stefansson lived in Greenwich Village in New York City. It must have been like a real village at that time, because he once saw my sister, who also lived in the Village, on the street, and although she did not know who he was, he gave her a letter to give to me. I sometimes met Stefansson, Margaret Mead, and the others at Romany Marie's, a restaurant in the Village. My sister often ate at that restaurant, and perhaps someone had pointed her out to him at some time.

I once had lunch in Cambridge with Stefansson and Hooton at the Harvard Faculty Club. Hooton ordered an omelette and explained to Stefansson that usually he ate meat but he had been ill. Stefansson eyed him with suspicion and replied, "When I'm too sick to eat meat, I'm too sick to eat."

7

The Anatomy Department at Harvard

*H*uman anatomy was one of the requirements in Hooton's program. I met it by taking the course that Edward Edwards (the first person to use spectrophotometry to study skin color) taught for dental students. The others who dissected with me were Larry Angel, Jo Birdsell, and a Greek physician called Coucouvitis whose chief concern was learning the English nomenclature. On the first day, I spent some time dissecting cutaneous nerves, and Coucouvitis came with scissors or scalpel and cut them in a second, saying each time, "Of no importance." Angel was by far the most apt of we three anthropologists. Birdsell was more than adequate, and I squeezed through with the minimum acceptable grade for a graduate student, B−. It was all very new for me; I had taken no previous comparative anatomy or other relevant biology course work.

I knew about Walter Cannon, who wrote *Bodily Changes in Fear, Hunger, Pain and Rage,* because of my earlier interest in physiology. My first contact with the medical school was through Cannon's student, neurophysiologist Birdsie Renshaw. I once helped Renshaw operate on a rhesus macaque. It was my first exposure to animal surgery, and I was impressed by the skill and anatomical knowledge required. Renshaw died at a very young age, but a distinguished Australian neuroanatomist once told me that he had made a major contribution during his short professional life.

In Cambridge, the former home of Walter Cannon had become an international house. How the International Club obtained it, I do not know, but it was not subsidized by John D. Rockefeller Jr. as those at Columbia and the University of Chicago had been. It was a co-op residence. I had many friends in the club who lived at the house, and I spent considerable time there. The members ranged from the son of Hitler's friend Putzi Hanfstengl to refugee Italian antifascists. The mix had its effect more in practical jokes than in arguments. For instance, a student, unknown to most members, was dressed up in formal attire, brought to the club, and introduced as the Portuguese ambassador. A supporter of the fascist regime in Portugal fawned over the fake ambassador to the amusement of those antifascists who had concocted the stunt.

The club once held a masquerade ball, and I went as the Man in the Iron Mask, with my head encased entirely in a mask and the rest of me covered with a raincoat and gloves. It was hot in that costume, and one of my friends, who had come without dressing up, wanted to get into my get-up while I cooled off. He then looked for the girl I had brought and started to dance with her. When I stepped up to cut in, she nearly fainted from shock because she thought she had been dancing with me the whole time.

Because of the club and the rooming house, friendships were not limited to one's own department, and conversations ranged over many topics, intellectual and otherwise. That kind of enriching social life now seems rare among graduate students with the present stress on the limited objectives of many university graduate programs. These days, there is much discussion about interdisciplinary research, but opportunities may be lacking to establish lifelong friendships such as I have had with William Leue, a graduate student of philosophy, and his friend from St. Louis, Jack Pickering, who later made his career in publishing and helped me greatly as editor of my first book. Even short-lived acquaintanceships with students in other disciplines, such as mine with Birdsie Renshaw, can allow one to participate in various branches of science, rather than merely to read about them.

I cannot remember how I met Harold Coolidge, but we were both active in Chinese war relief organizations. I served as stage manager for a charity performance Coolidge and his wife had organized, in which actress Anna May Wong and dancer Ruth St. Dennis performed. I remember that Anna May Wong, famous for her performance with Douglas Fairbanks Sr. in the movie *The Thief of Baghdad*, took it for granted that I would light a match for her every time she smoked a cigarette.

Later, Coolidge, who knew about my research on the primate diet project and my interest at that time in teeth, asked whether I could put together a bibliography on primate teeth for Dr. Warren Sisson, a pediatrician at the Forsythe Dental Infirmary. When I had finished the bibliography and was about to pass it on to Coolidge, I remembered a story Washburn had told me about the expedition to Siam. Coolidge had malaria, and the first day he felt well enough to work, he was very busy in his tent. They found him removing the labels Washburn and Schultz had put on the specimens and substituting ones preprinted with "Collected by Harold Coolidge." This story prompted me to phone Sisson at the dental clinic, ostensibly to ask exactly what he wanted, but in fact to make clear that I had done the work. The phone call resulted in an invitation from Sisson to lunch at the posh Harvard Club in Boston. Sisson's kindness and interest in a student he had not even met surprised me. At lunch, he asked what career I intended to follow. I replied that I was so busy trying to get my degree that I had not given it much thought. He suggested that I try to get a job in the School of Dental Medicine at Harvard, a new program leading to both medical and dental degrees. Sisson sent me to see Dr. Percy Howe, a grand old man in dental research, at the Forsythe Clinic. He was the first person to examine experimental vitamin C deficiency in monkeys. He was happy to talk about his research and give me his reprints but said that as he was retired, no one consulted him about the program in dental medicine. There was, he said, a committee managing the program, and he suggested that I see George Wislocki, the head of the anatomy department at the medical school, who chaired that committee.

When I reported this to Hooton, he said, "You didn't do very well in anatomy, did you, Lasker? He may not be very interested in you." In retrospect, I think Sisson may have gone before me to Wislocki. It is less likely that Hooton could have influenced Wislocki, because, according to Garn, Wislocki disliked scholars who, like Hooton, were always talking with the press and appearing in the newspapers.

It is also possible that Coolidge had put in a good word for me. He paid for the Asia Primate Expedition, and he helped Laughlin and others financially with a 1948 expedition to the Aleutians. Laughlin built a distinguished research career by continuing fieldwork there.

William S. Laughlin (right), with R. S. Vasilievsky (left) and academician V. E. Larichev (center), a friend of Hrdlicka's. They are discussing excavated stone tools at Anangula Island in the Aleutians in 1974. Laughlin is the leading authority on the physical anthropology of the Aleuts. He always enjoyed the outdoors and was evidently happy when working in Alaska. (Photo courtesy of Professor Laughlin.)

Although none of the tasks Coolidge ever asked me to do involved money, he did give me opportunities. In any case, when I went for an interview, Wislocki said that although there was no suitable job in dental medicine, I could come into his department as a predoctoral fellow.

I accepted with glee, moved to Brookline, and taught gross anatomy to medical students for a year. Alan Grafflin, later head of the anatomy department at Johns Hopkins, and Edward Bennett, later head of anatomy at Washington University in St. Louis, were involved as instructors in the course. Don Faucett, later head of the department at Harvard, was another predoctoral fellow. They were very kind to me as I struggled to keep ahead of the students. The one lecture I was asked to give to the freshman medical students at Harvard concerned my own research interest at that time, dental anthropology. In fifty years at Wayne State University, I was never asked to lecture on my own research work to the freshman medical students. It seems that at Harvard intellectual curiosity was valued in itself, whereas at Wayne they were only concerned with training the physicians in their trade.

While I was in the anatomy department at Harvard, Wislocki read the papers I was working on and showed me how to construct a scientific paper. He read virtually everything that came out of his department. After the five hundred dollars per year in fellowships I had received for the previous two years (plus continued subventions from home for tuition and some other needs), the nine hundred dollars from the anatomy department made me completely self-sufficient for the first time. In fact, I was offered a 33-percent raise for the next year, but the war and the draft would intervene.

My thesis project was a migration study of Chinese in America using the Boas model, in which the offspring of migrants born and brought up in a new environment are compared with migrants of the same stock who grew up before they moved. It was purely anthropometric and anthroposcopic, that is, anthropological measurements and observations of physical traits. I had not obtained the training in physiology that had been my original intent, and I did not extend my research to those characteristics. Hooton also wanted me to examine regional racial variability in China, so I measured any Chinese men I could—students, laundrymen, restaurant workers. Women were not included because they were greatly outnumbered by men in the Chinese immigrant community. Even for men, I exhausted the easy possibilities in Boston and Cambridge and added subjects from elsewhere in the eastern United States. In New York's Chinatown, my contacts were through the family of Robert Chin (later professor of psychology at Boston University). He and I used to go to Chinatown in the company of his friend Herbert Hyman, also later a distinguished social psychologist. It was not easy to persuade some subjects to submit to measurements, but others made jokes about it. One of them called to a passing out-of-state tour group to come in and see him being measured for his coffin.

When I was in New York, I consulted Boas, and he did a power analysis and estimated that under some assumptions he made, I would be unable to measure enough subjects to demonstrate a change in cephalic index in the offspring of the migrants. That prediction eventually turned out to be so, but there were statistically significant differences in stature. Despite flaws in design (a difference in mean

Bronze bust of Franz Boas by Roberto Bertoia of Cornell University. It was commissioned by the Human Biology Association as a prize for achievement by a human biologist and awarded to Gabriel Lasker in 1996.

age of the two subsamples) and execution (small numbers), the thesis work added to my education. Seeking advice outside my own university seemed perfectly natural to me, and I think Hooton encouraged his students to do so. Perhaps such exchange of information used to be easier. Another Harvard student, Paul Gebhard, went to work with Hrdlicka at the Smithsonian Institution. One of Boas's former students, Marcus Goldstein, worked on Eskimo teeth in Hrdlicka's department, and Goldstein, for his part, once permitted me to publish an analysis of data he had collected.

Also in New York, I often would drop in at the anthropology department at Columbia University. Gene Weltfish always found time for a talk. Others have said that she was a radical feminist and disliked men, but apparently that did not include me, perhaps because I was of a different age group and was eager to learn from her about aspects of anthropology, such as her ethnographic studies of American Indians, that I had largely missed at Harvard. I saw and talked with the other faculty members occasionally, but I do not recall learning anything else substantive except for the interview with Boas. I did sit in on one of the Kardiner seminars on psychological anthropology that strongly influenced many cultural anthropologists, including Kluckhohn. At Columbia, the psychology department was housed in the same building as anthropology, and I called on Chin and Hyman whenever I came home to my parents' house in Yonkers.

After I entered graduate school, I started attending meetings of professional societies. These included meetings of the American Association of Physical Anthropologists (AAPA) and the first meeting of the Society for Applied Anthropology. I always met many friends at society meetings and never hesitated to get into conversations, even when I had scant prior information on a subject. Being caught out always rolled off me, and I tried to learn and remember and not make the same mistake again. I still enjoy discussion and interjecting opinions and try to learn from the responses.

After one visit to Otto Klineberg in the psychology department at Columbia University, he took me home with him to Scarsdale for dinner. As we arrived, his wife confessed that she had bought a subscription to a magazine. Young people were being recruited to sell subscriptions door-to-door under the pretext of earning a scholarship to college. Actually, they were just working for a small commission. Mrs. Klineberg had obviously been overly sympathetic many times, because Otto reacted with resignation: "Oh, not again." She replied brightly, "We never sent anyone to Cornell before."

A serious hurdle for me, as for many other graduate students, was the requirement for the PhD of a reading knowledge of German and French. Hooton examined me in German, and Coon examined me in French. I failed both the first times I tried. Such German as I had learned at university and French at school had never sunk in, and my review was inadequate. Since I had learned quite a bit of Chinese, however, I imagined that I could manage with other languages, too.

When I retook the German test, Hooton gave me a section of Martin's *Lehrbuch* to translate. His lectures consisted of his translations of that ponderous work (with inserted commentary), so I knew what it said even before I tried to read it and passed.

Coon had a hearty sense of humor that some would have described as coarse. On my first try at passing in French, he asked me to translate, among other things, a French-language newspaper clipping about a strike of prostitutes in Beirut. I think he was trying to be helpful and had made the assumption that any young man studying French on his own would have been reading French pornography. After I failed, my father hired a tutor for me, a student who had just returned to the United States after a long stay in France. I spent the ten days of my Easter vacation at home in Yonkers, drilling sixteen hours a day on those little prepositions and adverbs that gave me so much trouble. The second time I took the French exam, the text was one on physical anthropology, and I managed to pass.

The spring of 1942, my last Easter vacation before being drafted, was also given over to sixteen-hour-a-day work. Coon asked me for a report on physical anthropology in wartime Germany. I did not know of the existence of the Office of Strategic Services (OSS), but that must have been the source of the request. Garn called the OSS "Oh So Secret" and has said that Coon was involved "before it became full of Yalies." The war in Europe was two years old, but German journals were still reaching the United States via Spain. Reading German was slow and tedious for me. Some of the publications were sheer Nazi propaganda, but others, such as the *Zeitschrift für Morphologie und Anthropologie,* reported empirical studies, sometimes decorated with the hope that they would benefit racial hygiene. The only copy of my report was apparently given a security classification, and I was subsequently unable to find out where it went or even if it existed. In my rush to meet the deadline, I did not keep a copy.

8

Conscientious Objection

I had held pacifist views at least since high school. My sympathy for the Chinese and Spanish antifascists did not lead me to believe that military victories would be an adequate solution. As for Germany, I probably did not know of the worst excesses of anti-Semitism, or it would have been even harder to decide to become a conscientious objector. I had no connection with Jewish organizations of any kind, and few of my friends were Jewish, so I had no pressure from that source. But I had been reading some German journals, and I was associated with Chinese people, whose country had been subject to aggression for nearly five years by the spring of 1942. It was not easy, but I had declared myself a conscientious objector, and I stuck to it when my number came up in the draft. Others who taught anatomy had their draft call-ups deferred, at least for a while. Alan Grafflin was later drafted and had an experience at Darwin, Australia, that seemed to leave him bitter after the war. I think George Wislocki felt he could not ask for a draft postponement for a conscientious objector because of the common lack of sympathy for COs among the public at large. Later, he may have felt guilty about it; after the war, he went out of his way to praise me to others and to see that I was well placed in a suitable job.

In the spring of 1942, Selective Service called me up for the draft, but I had registered as a conscientious objector and had made up my mind to resist war. My brother-in-law, a Unitarian minister, wrote to the draft board about what I had said to him concerning my pacifism and about my father's avoidance of service in Germany during the previous world war, and I was granted CO status without any argument, although I later met men who had had a very difficult time with the same draft board. My family supported my decision, as did several Quaker friends, so the only real problem I had was with my own doubts.

Selective Service assigned me to a camp in the White Mountains near Plymouth, New Hampshire. The camp was managed by the Friends (Quaker) Service Committee, and the work was for the U.S. Forest Service. In the winter, my foot was injured by a falling rock in a gravel pit. I spun out my recovery for a couple of weeks in order to work on my dissertation. While we worked in the woods, Frederick Riggs, the son of a former Presbyterian missionary to China and now a political scientist, and I conducted a class in Chinese to prepare some of the others for relief and rehabilitation work in China after the war, and some of them actually did that. The work at the Forest Service camp involved evaluating growing timber, clearing out blown-down trees, building a fire tower, and improving forest roads and trails.

The other conscientious objectors I met were a mixed lot. Those who belonged to two of the traditional peace churches, the Brethren and the Mennonites, had no doubt about what they should be doing. They generally came from rural communities and fell into the routine of outdoor work in the Civilian Public Service camp. The Quakers also generally showed little visible emotion about their position, but most of them were well educated and given to intellectual explanation of their pacifism. I was comfortable with that. There were others, however, for whom it was a constant struggle. Some belonged to churches, like the Roman Catholic, which condone "just" wars, but groups like the Franciscans and the Catholic Workers Movement and individual clergymen of all denominations offered support to the COs. The decision was particularly hard on those who had brothers or other close relatives in the military constantly exposed to death. For such individuals, the moral struggle surfaced all the time. Their difficulty affected me, especially when, as sometimes happened, one of them would leave camp to join the army or, more often, to report to the authorities and be sentenced to prison rather than cooperate with the government in wartime even in a civilian capacity.

In the spring, I volunteered to become a research supervisor and a subject in an experiment with insecticides to kill body lice which we grew and fed. We lived in an isolated camp, but during the day we worked in the forest, and I had the additional task of counting lice. We were never told what the insecticides were, but one was probably DDT, which was first put to actual use during a typhus epidemic in Naples in 1945.

The next year, I was transferred to a unit in eastern California. After a week there, I volunteered to serve as a lookout in a fire tower on top of a mountain near Carson City, Nevada. They told me to take supplies for a couple of days and that they would be up the next day with whatever else I needed. Unfortunately, there was a forest fire the following day, and no one came with more food and water for nine days. Long before they brought more supplies, I had to ration water only for drinking, and by the end, the only food I had was several kinds of dried beans. When others talk about monotonous diets, I shut them up with this story.

Between scanning the horizon for fires every few minutes, I did thousands of calculations with pencil and paper on the data I had collected for my dissertation. When I first went up to the tower, I thought that I would work on the thesis all day every day, but as time wore on, alone without social stimulation, I found myself wasting time reading and rereading the same few magazines. I also spent a lot of time just watching buzzards soaring back and forth beneath me and a small herd of horses that grazed nearby. Someone would bring me food and water once a week. The only other visitors I had all summer were a couple of prospectors and a man and woman who camped on the mountain one night.

For the last two years of the war, I was transferred to Duke University as an attendant in the hospital psychiatry department. Because of the opportunity for meaningful work unconnected with the war effort, the unit, sponsored by the Methodist Church, was probably the most sought-after in the Civilian Public Service system. Dr. Richard Lyman, the head of the psychiatry department, believed in making maximum use of the men in the unit by giving them opportunities for further training. For instance, we all participated in his ward rounds. In my time off, Dr. Markee, the head of Duke's anatomy department, gave me an opportunity to conduct research on the blood supply to the brain. Nothing came of that, but I did do some genetic research on the family of a patient on the ward, which was published, and I collected data on teeth and on twins that I eventually published. One of my papers of that period attempted (with the aid of a fellow conscientious objector who was a mathematician) to formulate some inferences about symmetry into estimates of genetic penetrance. Charles Windsor, the editor of *Human Biology*, accepted the article and appended some further formulations of his own. The editor's addendum was nearly as long as my paper and was illustrated with several text figures. In all the years that I later edited the same journal, there were times when I thought I could have had much more to say about somebody else's study. However, I never added an editorial appendix.

During the war years, many of the articles appearing in the *Proceedings of the National Academy of Sciences (PNAS)* were unaccompanied by author abstracts. The editor of *Biological Abstracts* asked me to review all of the articles on biological subjects appearing in *PNAS* each month, to edit any author's abstracts or summaries, and to provide abstracts for those that had none. It was an extraordinary learning experience for a person still without a PhD. I had to read papers in every field—bacteriology, immunology, genetics, botany, embryology, and so on. Even if I did not fully know the meaning of some biochemical or other term, I had to understand the relationships among the terms well enough to reduce the papers to a few essential sentences. As far as my training was concerned, the exercise, which lasted several years, was a great success. Although I never received thanks from the authors, I also never received any complaints.

Dealing with the mental patients as an attendant had its difficulties. One afternoon, I took a group of female patients for a walk in the Duke gardens. The locked mental ward is in the main hospital, which occupies a central position on the campus. The adjacent gardens, with their attractive plantings of azaleas, are open to the public. I did not wear my white coat on such occasions, so as not to attract attention. That afternoon, one of the patients took it into her head to take off all her clothes then and there. One of the other patients was a blind woman who was being treated for depression. Fortunately, I had established rapport with her by letting her teach me to read braille, and I managed to place her as close to, and myself as far away from, the naked lady as possible. Finally, I found someone to send back to the ward for a female nurse. None was available, but eventually another male attendant came, and we were able to coax the woman back into some clothes for the return trip to the ward.

Normal shifts in the hospital were eight hours per day, five days a week, plus time for reports on patients before and after. The night shift was the least desirable. I volunteered to work every night of the week, from one A.M. until eight A.M., about the same as a normal work week. After work, I slept until lunch and had afternoons and evenings free. I even managed some social life. The other attendant on that special night shift was Charles Ray ("Chuck") Elliott, who was always full of enthusiasm for learning and doing. After the war, he married one of the nurses, and, like many of the other conscientious objectors from the Duke unit who later finished doctorates in medicine and related fields, he completed his PhD in psychology, going on to teach speech therapy at Northwestern University. Another Duke CO became the medical artist at Duke Medical School, and yet another became the business manager of Duke Hospital.

I do not recall anyone going into anthropology because of experience as a conscientious objector. Bill Laughlin, who was a conscientious objector, was already studying anthropology when he was drafted. He served in Civilian Public Service as a smoke jumper with the Forest Service. In his view, that was the most sought-after and perhaps the most meaningful assignment available. As COs were not paid, on days off he sometimes parachuted at county fairs to earn a little pocket money. Years later, when I was with him at a conference at Burg Wartenstein, Austria, he was the only anthropologist there who was completely at home scampering about the Alps. He seems to have enjoyed the rough life of work in the national forests and fieldwork in inhospitable environments.

While I was assigned to the Duke hospital, I made friends among the psychologists at the university, including Sygmund Koch, who used to lecture lying prone on his desk with a cigarette in his mouth, and pathologist Dr. Black-Schaffer. At the nearby University of North Carolina at Chapel Hill, anthropologist John Gillen and his wife also befriended me, and I had a chance to discuss my work on my thesis with them.

In Durham, I called on Carolyn Day Bond, who had received a master's degree from Hooton with a thesis titled "A Study of Some Negro-White Families in the United States" (republished in 1970). In her monograph, many members of the pedigrees are not illustrated because they were passing for white. From the unpublished photographs that Bond showed me, I could see how they might do so. Housing was still completely segregated in North Carolina, so when I went to visit the Bonds at their home in the African-American section of the city, the bus drivers would ask me if I had forgotten to get off.

The opportunity for social interaction at Duke made a big change from being alone in the fire tower. I had friends among the nurses and female students, but I must admit that dealing with mental patients was a strain. That, along with the free evenings, was why I preferred the night shift, when most of the patients were asleep. Under the regulations for COs in the Civilian Public Service, we received no pay (just two and a half dollars per month for toothpaste and shaving cream), but in the period before Christmas, Chuck Elliott arranged a part-time job for himself and then for me in Mr. Marlow's bookstore. I enjoyed getting young children interested in books that they then would persuade their mothers to buy. Chuck always had so many schemes. He collected postage stamps and was so enthusiastic that he got me involved in a first-day cover business on one occasion and in Christmas cards on another. I never made (or lost) much money at these businesses, but I learned about entrepreneurship and wound up with many unsold stamped envelopes and Christmas cards.

I wrote to Hooton to ask about the formal requirements for the dissertation. He replied that two copies were required and that they should be typed. With aid and advice from others, I finished my thesis, submitted it, and appeared in Cambridge in 1945 to defend it. Hooton's comment was: "Biggest God damn thesis I ever saw. Really two theses: the one I wanted you to write and the one you wanted to write yourself." The thesis was three and a half inches thick, but Wislocki taught me how to reduce the main points to two short articles; they finally appeared in the *American Journal of Physical Anthropology* in 1945 and 1946.

Hooton's house in Cambridge was always open to the students for tea at five o'clock. Garn has since told me that some of the students were regulars. I had gone only rarely, but being back in Cambridge, and with nothing to do while staying at a hotel awaiting the exam the next day, I went. Hooton himself was not there. Carl Seltzer, who, having received a PhD in the program, had retained a position in the department, was there and, to my surprise, apparently thought I had come to Hooton's house for reassurance, because he took me aside to say that the exam was routine and everyone passed. Perhaps he was the one who needed to show the senior examiners how much he knew, because the next day, he was the only one who asked what might be considered a hard question. In those days, I was always ready with answers, especially in oral discourse, but I couldn't get a word in edgewise as Hooton and Coon jumped in to reply themselves to Seltzer's question.

After the war, I looked for permanent employment. At that time, physical anthropology and anatomy were very closely associated. The American Association of Physical Anthropologists had been founded at a meeting of the American Association of Anatomists and usually held its own meetings at the same places and times. Many anatomists were leaders in the field of physical anthropology, such as Franz Weidenreich, Adolph Schultz, Mildred Trotter, and William L. Straus Jr., of an older generation, but also some who were my age or younger. For instance, Phillip Tobias, who was chair of the anatomy department at Witwatersrand University, has a medical degree (and a DSc) and has published in other branches of anatomy as well as voluminously about paleoanthropology and about the human biology of contemporary peoples of southern Africa. John Clegg's anthropology deals with contemporary human biology, and he was Regius Professor of Anatomy at Aberdeen, Scotland, one of only two British chairs of anatomy that are appointed by the queen.

Before World War II, newly appointed faculty in departments of anatomy were, for the most part, young MDs, who often considered this as a temporary step in their careers. But during the war, virtually all young MDs were practicing medicine or surgery and afterward were intent on staying in practice. Besides, as reported in *The Teaching of Anatomy and Anthropology in Medical Education* (1956), from about 1913 on, medical educators wanted to staff departments of anatomy with scientists rather than practitioners. Several of my friends and former fellow students of anthropology got jobs in anatomy during that period: Ashley Montagu and Earl Count at New York Medical College, Sherry Washburn at the College of Physicians and Surgeons, Larry Angel at Jefferson Medical School, Alice Brues at the University of Oklahoma, and George Erikson at Harvard. Of these, only Erikson stayed with anatomy until retirement. Many others, including James Gavan, Daris Swindler, and Matt Cartmill, have taught anatomy.

In the spring of 1946, I went to Detroit for an interview at Wayne State University. F. Gaynor Evans, who had been trained in vertebrate paleontology by William King Gregory at the American Museum of Natural History and had then taught human anatomy at the University of New Hampshire and the University of Maryland, was on the faculty. Apparently, he had met me at a meeting of the American

A lively discussion at the annual meeting of the American Association of Physical Anthropologists in 1997. From left to right, Phillip Tobias, the honored guest of the association, who invited the others to meet with him in South Africa, which he helped free of apartheid; Roberto Frisancho, Professor of Anthropology, University of Michigan, whose distinguished professional career started when he was a local assistant to Paul Baker in Peru; William Pollitzer, Professor of Anatomy at the University of North Carolina, one of the group of anthropologists trained by Theodosius Dobzhansky at Columbia University; and Michael Little, Paul Baker's first doctoral student and coauthor with Baker of many of the works that shaped the study of human adaptation.

Association of Physical Anthropologists, where he had heard me give papers. Gordon H. Scott, the department head, interviewed me, and at the end of the interview, he offered me a job as instructor. I was on my way to Cleveland to a meeting of the AAPA held jointly with the American Association of Anatomists, and I had some other interviews planned, but I replied that I would let him know promptly. He said that he would hold the position open for my reply since he hoped to get me and keep me.

On the train to Cleveland, it occurred to me that if Scott was holding the job open for me, he would not be able to offer it to someone else at the anatomy meeting; that is, he really was keen to get me, and I should have said yes then and there. Before I had reached Cleveland, I had made up my mind to go to Wayne. I accepted and joined the anatomy department at Wayne State University in September 1946.

9

The First Years in Detroit

My wife and most of my friends are anthropologists, and this account is predominantly about biological anthropologists. However, the academic enterprise can best be understood by comparison with other occupations. My best friend from college, whom I introduced to his future wife, was Charles Hugh ("Sandy") Stevenson, a man who made his living primarily in real estate. When I came to Detroit, he found me an apartment in one of his buildings close to the campus, and we got together at least once a month until he and his wife, Mary, eventually retired to Florida. Sandy was a very intelligent person; for instance, he invented a game based on the history of railway mergers, and he usually won, even though Bunny and Mary and I would make a concerted effort to beat him. He was an amateur actor, an expert at bridge, and curious about everything. I always thought it was a pity that he was not an academic. It seems to me that even the least accomplished of my university colleagues have been able to chip away at some little corner of the previously unknown. For me, that activity is infinitely rewarding, and I find it hard to imagine that the rewards from winning at cards or making lots of money could substitute for it.

Another friend who was not an academic was an executive of an automobile company, and we soon learned that we were "his professors," about whom he could talk to his associates. Likewise, he was "our auto executive," and we would carry stories from that world back to the university. Why, for instance, after investing so heavily, did Detroit not build a small car to compete with the Volkswagen Beetle? Short-term profits are all-important in business. Initially, it would have cost as much to build a car that was inferior to the Volkswagen but would have to compete for sales at the same price. If the industry had been able to plan farther into the future, the problems of the 1972 oil crunch would have been mitigated and the important small-car segment of the market might not have been ceded, first to European and then to Japanese manufacturers.

When I met other automobile executives at my friend's house, they sometimes sounded envious of the lesser pressures of academic life. Most of my colleagues would not agree, and some of them envy the greater financial rewards some businesspeople receive. In the medical faculty, some of the practitioners envy the researchers, and vice versa. However, I am not among those who think that academics are underappreciated.

Since moving to Detroit, I have been employed as an anatomist but have also been continuously involved as a physical anthropologist with organizations and journals of the discipline and consequently have been in correspondence with most of the biological anthropologists active in research. During the decade following World War II, I served from 1946 to 1951 as secretary-treasurer of the American Association of Physical Anthropologists (AAPA) and from 1952 to 1957 as secretary of the anthropological section of the American Association for the Advancement of Science (AAAS). Sherry Washburn was my predecessor as secretary-treasurer of the AAPA. He liked to run the association his way. For instance, the nominating committee customarily presented a single slate for office, and election was a mere formality. In 1950, Franz Weidenreich was on the slate for president, but Washburn, aware that he could not manipulate Weidenreich, said that such a president would be a mere figurehead and that we needed what would now be called a more proactive candidate. The slate that was presented to the members contained the name of Krogman rather than Weidenreich, and Krogman was elected without dissent. In fact, Krogman, who was too blind to read easily, let the secretary run the society, including its annual business meetings. I assume my own election as secretary-treasurer was also because Washburn knew I admired him and would be likely to see most issues his way. In 1952, with Krogman still president, I was expected to conduct the annual business meeting of the members. I had no prior knowledge or experience, but I managed by doing things the way I had observed during the previous five years. However, the next year, T. Dale Stewart was the elected president, and I naively overstepped my authority by starting to run the meeting the way I had for Krogman. Stewart promptly put me in my place, and we got on well together thereafter.

When the anthropological section, Section H, of the AAAS needed a secretary, they turned to me. The conditions of the office included being a fellow, and I was not even an ordinary member. As soon as I sent in my dues, they elected me fellow and secretary simultaneously. Through those experiences and subsequent service in other offices of these and other professional societies, I remained in touch with many of the members.

An office I once held in the AAAS was as a member of the nominating committee. No anthropologist had been president for some years, and I suggested Margaret Mead, who was a member of the executive board and was well known to all kinds of scientists. The other members of the committee decided that at age sixty, Mead was too old, and she was passed over. Ten years later, Bunny began to collect the fifty signatures necessary to add Mead's name to the slate for president. When the ballot appeared, that nominating committee had put Mead's name on it rather than letting it appear by petition. Mead was so much better known than the scientist who opposed her that she was easily elected, even though it was ten years after she had been labeled too old. Those like Mead who make themselves known outside the profession can represent the interests of the group so much better than a cloistered scholar.

At Wayne, I always received what encouragement and assistance the department chairman, Gordon Scott, and his chosen successor, Ernest Gardner, could give for my research. Their administrative style of throwing away their aces inspired loyalty. After I had been in Detroit two years (far short of enough time for paid leave), I received a grant from the Viking Fund (later the Wenner-Gren Foundation) to work in Mexico for five months, but with no provision for my salary. Scott reasoned that if I had been in Detroit, I would have been doing research in the spring and summer (gross anatomy was taught only in the fall and winter terms), and in Mexico I would also be doing research, so I should continue to draw my salary and just go. We needed a vehicle for the work in Mexico, but in order to reuse the money for the research, we would have to be able to sell it when we returned. Scott shopped for a station wagon for us and put his own name on the title for joint ownership of the car so no one would think I had diverted the money. We eventually sold the car for two-thirds of what it had cost and reused that part of the grant.

It was some years later that I received a really substantial raise, just before I was to be gone for a year on a sabbatical leave in Peru. It would have been easy for Gardner to wait until I returned to give me the raise, but I greatly appreciated receiving it before I went. Considerate behavior by administrators probably more than pays for itself in faculty morale and productivity and perhaps also financially.

During my first year at Wayne, Scott liked to come into my office, which was next to his, to chat. I recall one such occasion before the first Christmas, when the secretary, Judy Love, came in to ask whether she could take time off to shop at Hudson's, the nearby department store. When he had given his permission and she had gone, he turned to me and said, "If you want to set up restrictions, the time an employee comes to ask for permission is far too late to say no."

Bill Straus was a visitor to our department for about a year in 1949. He spent a lot of time in my office talking. He had a very critical mind and found good reasons to reject virtually every interpretation others had about the hominid fossil material. He was one of those who showed that the bent leg bones of the best-known Neanderthal skeleton, the one from La Chapelle aux Saints, were caused by rickets and were not a normal feature of prehistoric people. However, he could be overcritical. For instance, in an article, "The Riddle of Man's Ancestry," he tried to show similarities between humans and monkeys that are not shared by the great apes and was left with the now disproved hypothesis that the most recent common ancestor of humans with other primates was very ancient and at an Old World monkey level. By the same tortured type of logic, he dispensed with Raymond Dart's conclusion that *Australopithecus* was a hominid. I liked talking with Straus because he knew so much and argued so well, but I could not always agree, and I argued with him about some of his theories.

Another associate during my first years at Wayne was John D. Green, a neuroanatomist who was one of the first, along with his colleague at Oxford, Geoffrey W. Harris, to study the portal system of the pituitary gland. Green had studied medicine at Cambridge and had been exempt from military service during World War II because he suffered from Pott's disease, which left him dwarfed and stooped. He had been in W. E. Le Gros Clark's department at Oxford University teaching anatomy during the war. At Wayne, he taught histology and continued his comparative anatomy of the pituitary portal system, which was eventually published in a long, classic article in the *American Journal of Anatomy* (1951). The work involved perfusing the venous system of live animals, and he needed a live fish for his experiments. I had noticed that in Detroit's Eastern Market area, there was a Jewish fish store that sold live carp, and the two of us walked over to buy one. The merchant insisted on donating a fish "for the sake of science." Green selected the one he wanted, but the fishmonger would have none of it; we must take the biggest one, a greater beneficence on his part. That carp's pituitary is now immortalized in Green's monograph, and the merchant's good deed is recorded here.

Early in my stay at Wayne, I went to visit the Department of Sociology and Anthropology, which was housed in a former residence. In fact, at that time, Wayne had more buildings than any other university—252, I believe. There were three buildings of the College of Medicine and a main campus consisting of a former high school (Old Main, now completely rebuilt on the inside) and numerous former private dwellings.

All the members of the sociology and anthropology faculty had been trained in sociology, but Norman Humphrey considered himself an anthropologist and had conducted studies in Mexico by the participant-observer method. He appointed himself my protector against what he, not I, perceived as slights by the chairman, Alfred McClung Lee.

Sometime later, when I was the secretary of Section H of the American Association for the Advancement of Science, I noticed that few anthropologists had been appointed as fellows, and I nominated for fellowship those individuals on the membership list whom I knew to be professional anthropologists. When Lee learned that Humphrey was on my list but that he was not, he let me know that he thought he should have been, because he had once worked for the anthropology museum in Santa Fe. His only association with anthropology in any formal sense turned out to be that he had helped the museum as a consultant on public relations and fund-raising over a period of a few weeks.

Another member of the faculty in the joint department was H. Warren Dunham. He had been a PhD student of sociologist R. E. L. Farris at Chicago, who may have been one of those who had given Leslie White so much trouble there. Dunham's thesis concerned the social epidemiology of schizophrenia, and it was later published as a book by Farris and Dunham. The conclusion reached in the book contributed greatly to Dunham's reputation. He continued his interest in psychiatry and did research in the psychiatry department. Some twenty-five years later, Dunham published a second book on the same subject, which contradicted the thesis of the first. His reputation was further enhanced, of course. We surmised that Dunham had been forced to express Farris's opinions in the thesis and then had waited all those years until Farris died to have his own say. For a graduate student, the relationship with the thesis adviser is often more difficult than conducting the scholarly research.

Several physical anthropologists visited the Department of Anatomy at Wayne State University over the years. When I first met Ronald Singer, he was a bright young South African anatomist with experience at the University of Cape Town in both studies of human fossils and research into genetic and other biological variables among his country's contemporary populations. He visited Detroit on a Rotary Club fellowship and flattered us by pretending that he already knew all about Wayne State University but was unfamiliar with the University of Michigan. Another South African visitor was Phillip Tobias of the anatomy department at Witwatersrand University. The anatomists at South African medical schools have made contributions to physical anthropology out of all proportion to their small numbers. Dart and Tobias made major discoveries, but the influence of anthropology on anatomy there was general, and Ronald Singer, Herta de Villiers, Maciej Henneberg, and George Nurse are among those who continued to contribute.

When he was first appointed to the faculty at the University of Michigan, Marshall Newman was another visitor. His father, who had conducted the first classic study of identical twins reared apart, and his first father-in-law were both academics. They apparently did not take him very seriously, and I think that made it difficult for him professionally. Furthermore, at the Smithsonian Institution, he had been a subordinate of Dale Stewart, and he claimed that the position gave him limited opportunity to pursue his own research interests. When he quit and joined the faculty of anthropology at the University of Michigan, he needed access to Weidenreich's monograph on the skull of *Sinanthropus pekinensis* published by the Geological Survey of China. It is a rare volume and was not in the University of Michigan library. He asked if I could help him find a copy. I told him that the last time I had needed to make reference to it, I had waited until I could examine the copy at the American Museum of Natural History in New York. Later I would discover that I had a copy that had been given to me by Weidenreich, in its box with the pages still uncut. Bill Laughlin recently reminded me that after I had told him this story, he asked Weidenreich about the monograph and also received a copy. Weidenreich was always generous with young anthropologists and ready to spend time with them. Newman was also always helpful to others. I regret that I was not more helpful to him, not simply in lending him a book but more importantly by encouraging him to follow up an important study of his. He, along with Derek F. Roberts, initiated studies on the interrelationships of climate, nutrition, and human physique.

10

Teaching Anthropology

*A*t Wayne State University, my only significant teaching responsibilities were in human gross anatomy in the medical school. However, I took several leaves of absence to teach anthropology: at the University of Chicago in 1953, at the University of Wisconsin in Madison in 1954–55, and at Northwestern University in the summer of 1955. I also spent a year at the University of California, Berkeley, in 1960–61 on a project on the teaching of anthropology and, on three occasions, commuted to East Lansing once a week for a term to moonlight teaching seminars at Michigan State University.

In 1953, Bunny was busy on the faculty at Wayne in Detroit and writing her dissertation for the University of Chicago. By then, Krogman had left Chicago, and they had hired Washburn, who had been in the Department of Anatomy at the College of Physicians and Surgeons in New York. Washburn's interests were in primatology and the kinds of experimental anatomy related to problems of human evolution that he had been pursuing in New York. So, ostensibly to have someone to teach contemporary human variation, Washburn invited me to lecture for an academic quarter. I think his real or main motive may have been to allow Bunny to interact with Robert Redfield, her adviser, and with other members of her thesis committee whom she had not consulted before she submitted. They, as might have been expected, had responded with criticisms. Eventually, she complained to Redfield that she was receiving contradictory advice and asked what she should do. He responded that she should please herself. She replied that she had tried that already, whereupon Redfield and the others acceded and set a date for the defense. For candidates for the PhD, the proper balance between acceptance of the positions of mentors and a show of independence of thought is often difficult to achieve.

As a visitor, I had an easy relationship with the graduate students at Chicago, and there was a lot of intellectual ferment among them. Most of those in my seminar course were cultural anthropologists, but it was then generally expected that all graduates should be familiar with both social and biological aspects of anthropology. I had brought along a photometer that measured reflected light, and the students examined the skin color of a wide range of people. We learned that some of the foreign students from the Near East and South Asia had darker skin color than some of the African Americans who were designated at that time as "Negroes."

Washburn inherited a number of Krogman's physical anthropology students who had not yet finished their degrees. In fact, although Krogman later granted many PhDs to students at the University of Pennsylvania, some of his students at the University of Chicago had not been pushed to finish. Georg Neumann and Richard Snodgrasse each took more than twenty years to complete their degrees. In the short time that I was at Chicago, Washburn hurried them and several others through the final stage. James A. Gavan defended his thesis on the growth of chimpanzees. I helped examine him and eventually secured a manuscript based on that work for publication in *Human Biology*. Melvyn Baer had been working with two dentists on experiments with rats. By injecting a dye that marked the growing bone, Baer could determine the progress of bone formation in the skulls and jaws of the animals. He did not finish at that time but accepted a position at the University of Detroit School of Dentistry and was able to consult with me often. He applied his ideas on bone growth to the human skull and published the findings in *Human Biology*. Clark Howell, who had entered the department only after Washburn had arrived, wrote a dissertation based on the kind of studies Washburn was then doing on stress lines in bones, and he defended his thesis that term, too. He had already been publishing regularly.

Another person we got to know in Chicago in 1953 was Albert A. Dahlberg. He was a practicing dentist—in fact, he took care of some minor problem with my teeth—but he also spent much time and effort in dental anthropology, and he established a laboratory at the University of Chicago for the anthropological study of teeth. In later years, his lab became a refuge for graduate students who could always count on a sympathetic hearing from Dahlberg. Anthropology owes much to this man who, in an adjunct capacity at the university, was a major contributor to the study of human dental variation. The development of standards for observing the morphology of human teeth, largely thanks to Dahlberg, has permitted others to apply these methods to anthropological problems. One of Dahlberg's former students, Christy Turner, is a leader in the field and, in turn, has trained other dental anthropologists.

In 1954, Howells left his position as professor of anthropology at the University of Wisconsin at Madison to become professor at Harvard. Laughlin was appointed to succeed him but was not free to take up the post for another year. I was eager enough to fill in at Wisconsin for the 1954–55 academic year, although the main task assigned me was very different from the one I had enjoyed at Chicago. I again held seminars with cultural anthropology graduate students, but the department at Wisconsin was a joint one with sociology, and I also lectured to a freshman class in a course called Anthropology-Sociology 1. I managed somehow despite the fact that my graduate assistant was a sociology student who knew even less of anthropology than I did of sociology. He had no realization of his limitations and pontificated before his sections. Again, as at the University of Chicago, some of the students remained friends later and tended to keep me aware of developments in those sociocultural areas with which they were involved.

The Department of Anthropology at Northwestern University at that time was very much the child of its chairman, Melville Herskovits, and its graduate students were devoted to his interests in Africa and in African elements surviving in peoples of African origin in the Americas. However, Herskovits had been a student of Boas and had himself been interested in biological aspects of the subject, at least to the extent that these intersected with social constructs of race. Since there was no physical anthropologist on the regular faculty, he had arranged for Spuhler to spend one summer in his department, and I was invited for the summer term of 1955. Again, we were closely associated with graduate students and others who were cultural anthropologists.

One story about Herskovits concerned his relationship with Ralph Linton. It is well known that Linton did not get on with Boas's former students. Ernestine Friedl has recently recorded in print that Linton and Ruth Benedict were barely on speaking terms. One rumor had it that Benedict used Pueblo magic and Linton used Madagascar magic on each other when both were candidates to succeed Boas as head of the Department of Anthropology at Columbia University. The story about Herskovits, who no doubt also wanted the Columbia post, was that when Linton returned from fieldwork, he gave Herskovits a present of a fine Madagascar textile. Herskovits, who valued culture with a capital C as well as a small one (he wrote and published poetry and loved classical music) draped the cloth on his grand piano. As the story goes, someone else who knew Malagasy material culture was visiting Herskovits and exclaimed in surprise, "What a beautiful Madagascan shroud."

In 1955, the American Association of Medical Colleges organized a conference on "The Teaching of Anatomy and Anthropology." The appropriate balance on the organizing committee seemed to them to be four anatomists to one anthropologist. I was the one anthropologist, and I placed on the panel several biological anthropologists working in medical schools on such subjects as human evolution and child growth. I also included one of the first American medical anthropologists, Ben Paul, who gave an influential talk on his role at the Harvard School of Public Health before an audience that included deans of medical colleges. In my own university, I was given an adjunct appointment in the psychiatry department and gave a seminar on culture and personality to a group of residents and one lecture to medical students in the Introduction to Clinical Medicine course. I told them about a study by Thomas McCorkle of how chiropractic fits into the culture of those who turn to it for medical help. The patients of chiropractors get local help through a "laying on of hands," and they get back to work promptly. This was described as in keeping with the ethos of the Iowa farm communities McCorkle studied. The medical students were incredulous, but the psychiatry residents were fascinated. It was years before anthropologists were employed at Wayne State University in clinical departments with research projects on such subjects as alcoholism.

I later taught a seminar course at Michigan State University on three occasions by commuting one afternoon a week. Instead of covering the subject matter of biological anthropology, each week the students presented a paper on some currently controversial matter such as the number of species of *Australopithecus* or the validity of the molecular clock. This served to keep me up to date as an anthropologist while my regular job was in anatomy.

In 1960, David Mandelbaum at the University of California, Berkeley, had secured National Science Foundation funds for a major study of the teaching of anthropology. The grant was to conduct a series of about ten conferences and to gather information in other ways for a two-volume work on the topic. Washburn was teaching at the University of California by then, and, again at his suggestion, I was invited to take leave from anatomy and deal with anthropology for a year. There was considerable tension among faculty members in such a large department, and I soon learned how Mandelbaum dealt with it. Bunny and I were invited to parties at the homes of many on the faculty, and the Mandelbaums would always attend, stay a few minutes, and leave early. By being the first to leave, Mandelbaum avoided hearing and participating in most of the backbiting. In organizing the project, Mandelbaum found a role with some benefit, such as travel money to a conference, for each of the tenured members of the department, and the roles seemed to me to be strictly graded according to formal status, the more important tasks being assigned to the more senior members. The only one left out was an old professor who drank too much.

Some graduate students at Berkeley were caught up in the professorial rivalries, but they had a resource. Theodore D. McCown, who had helped describe important human fossils from Mount Carmel in what is now Israel, was always available to them and was himself uninvolved in the unpleasantness and ready with detached and supportive advice. His was a role in some ways similar to that of Dahlberg at the University of Chicago.

11

The New Physical Anthropology and the Old

Between the two world wars, Paul Fejos, a Hungarian with a medical degree, came to America and began to make movies in Hollywood. Axel Wenner-Gren was a very successful Swedish industrialist who held the profitable patents on the Servel gas refrigerator and the Electrolux vacuum cleaner. He was never involved in the Swedish match monopoly and thus preserved his fortune during the collapse that ruined many other wealthy Swedes. Fejos and Wenner-Gren apparently got on well together, and when Wenner-Gren organized an anthropological expedition to Peru, Fejos also went along and made a pioneering anthropological movie.

During World War II, Wenner-Gren was persona non grata in the United States because his Swedish companies (Sweden remained neutral) were doing business with Germany. In fact, there was a scandal in Great Britain because the former prince of Wales and king of England, the duke of Windsor, had accepted hospitality on Wenner-Gren's yacht. Probably to maintain some control over his American assets and prevent their possible confiscation, Wenner-Gren created a charitable trust, the Viking Fund. It supported such institutions as the Red Cross and British War Relief. Fejos, however, was able to persuade Wenner-Gren and the trustees that the fund should be devoted to supporting anthropology, and this was accomplished immediately after the war, with Fejos as director. Eventually, the new purpose was indicated by a change of the name to the Wenner-Gren Foundation for Anthropological Research.

Anthropologists in New York soon learned of this source of financial support. Some were wary of accepting such funds because of rumors about Wenner-Gren's dealings with the Nazis, but Ralph Linton, then recently appointed chairman of the anthropology department at Columbia, helped Fejos find useful projects. One of those who was distrustful was Ruth Benedict, but ironically, when she died, it was the foundation that organized an elaborate memorial to her and published the proceedings.

Whatever Wenner-Gren's relationships with Nazis may have been, and despite his close ties with the managing board and with Fejos, the director of the Viking Fund, there was never any display of anti-Semitism in the dispensing of the funds. By far the largest expenditures on projects were those in support of schemes of Sol Tax, professor of anthropology at the University of Chicago, who had an interest in internationalizing anthropology and empowering native peoples. One of those expensive schemes was the commissioning of an opera by Gian Carlo Menotti for an international anthropological congress, the first opera commissioned for an event since Verdi composed *Aida* for the opening of the Suez Canal. The opera, *Tamu-tamu*, has an anthropological theme: the relationship between people of different cultures when two families are thrust together. It was considered a commentary on the Vietnam War and on intercultural relations. The libretto, by the composer, is in English and Indonesian. The opera was quite risqué by the standards of the time, because one of the cultural traits it deals with is the women baring their breasts.

Another of Sol Tax's ambitious schemes supported by the Wenner-Gren Foundation established the journal *Current Anthropology*, with a system of soliciting dozens of reviews of each manuscript and publishing the comments of the reviewers as well as the work itself. Besides the additional costs of such a mode of publication, the journal was made available to scholars throughout the world either gratis or at rates that required a subsidy, and the foundation must still meet an annual deficit for this very significant means of interchange of information in the world anthropological community.

Financial considerations now seem to drive the directions of research in anthropology in American universities, but that is part of a tendency in science in general that has accompanied the increased role of support from federal agencies. In this environment, the alternative of the smaller Wenner-Gren beneficence has had a decidedly positive effect, since it has often been made available with a minimum of red tape and at critical times in ways where even modest funds are of maximum benefit. For instance, they granted me six thousand dollars early in my career (1948) to collect data in Mexico which I have since used to illustrate many hypotheses, and they granted me ten thousand dollars at the time of my retirement (1982) which I used to begin a series of studies of the structure of English populations from surnames.

For whatever the studies may be worth, the latter grant started a line of research that has since been emulated by others. Many graduate students of anthropology have had support from Wenner-Gren that would not have been available from any other source.

After World War II, Washburn, then on the faculty in the anatomy department at the College of Physicians and Surgeons in New York and secretary of the American Association of Physical Anthropologists, saw an opportunity to revolutionize physical anthropology with the help of the Viking Fund. To him, the old racial ideas were of virtually no use in dealing with historic and prehistoric problems. He was particularly critical of typologies, by which individuals with a set of characteristics in common, such as hair color, head form, and nose shape, are considered to be related to one another even if they are members of different breeding populations. Furthermore, these ideas had been completely discredited through use and abuse by the Nazis.

It is now clear that such groupings have little, if any, genetic justification. Now, once again, more than fifty years after Washburn turned the discipline away from typological analysis, some overspecialized molecular geneticists are unaware of the evidence that there can be no consensus about the numbers and nature of "races." Thus, the myth of race persists even among some savants, although the genetic evidence itself shows that some DNA configurations, called haplotypes, occur in various populations, while other haplotypes that are geographically restricted to one area generally occur in a minority of the people there.

Washburn had his own agenda concerning the concept of evolution in physical anthropology and strong ideas about how to promote the subject. In 1946, he was one of the central figures in the reorganization to widen the professional membership base of the American Anthropological Association. To further his vision for the field, he organized a series of major conferences, the Viking Fund Summer

Seminars in Physical Anthropology, at the foundation's headquarters in New York. The first seminar (1946) lasted six weeks, the second one a month. Although subsequent summer seminars were shorter, the impact was phenomenal. All the recent PhDs in physical anthropology and many advanced students were there for the full period; although practically every significant figure in American physical anthropology also came, the senior anthropologists did not stay for the duration. Many from abroad also attended for at least part of one or more of these conferences, but the major impact was from Washburn and other younger members who always attended and stayed for the whole time.

Washburn sharpened his ideas about the direction of the "new physical anthropology" during the first two Wenner-Gren summer seminars in physical anthropology. The result was a true paradigm shift within the discipline. This new direction was rooted in the following assertions:

The best way to understand the human biology of shape and form is through experimental procedures—the better to understand the actual formative role of the various muscle and tendon groups. Functional anatomy was the end result of this endeavor. Methodologically, there was an imperative need to tailor all data gathering to the particular research questions being asked. Washburn railed against the routine gathering of a laundry list of measurements and observations (as on the standard Harvard anthropometric and anthroposcopic data sheets where the observer had no idea what problem any of the observations could possibly address). The earlier practice had been to collect *everything* in the hope that some of it might prove valuable at a later date. Washburn held for a more focused and economical use of scarce resources and research time.

Problem-focused research led Washburn to emphasize the need to pay greater attention to the applications of genetics to the understanding of human variability.

And this would lead ultimately to an awareness and acceptance of the basic inappropriateness of typological analysis at the *Homo sapiens* level as an analysis that was neither functionally nor genetically based. This insight led to the diminution of the concepts of race and of racial "types" as no longer useful in explaining problems with which human biologists and physical anthropologists dealt.

Following the first and second summer seminars, where the level of discussion of challenging ideas was intense, the direction of virtually all research in physical anthropology was dramatically changed. New paths of research came to dominate, as the following brief list will show.

Washburn and Irven DeVore turned their attention to the study of baboon and other primate behavior highlighting the interrelationship between biological and social factors in behavior. The whole field of nutritional anthropology expanded. Awareness of the possible contributions of human biology to epidemiology, demography, and further subspecialties moved contemporary physical anthropology miles away from the earlier emphasis on measurements of human dimensions. These shifts in research interests ultimately led to a better understanding of human variability, which in turn has further expanded as the expansion of human genetic studies with an anthropological base has grown increasingly important. Along with the growing reliance on genetic modes of analysis has come the elaboration of population genetics, followed by the "discovery" of DNA and of MTDNA, and now the exploration of the genome as a possible key to better understand human variation.

Washburn himself was pursuing functional anatomy and conducting experiments that observed the effects on the morphology of bones of surgically altering soft tissues. He ran an anatomy course for the students attending the summer seminar in his dissecting room at the university. Others, including Bud Newman and Jim Spuhler, were interested in genetics (which got them away from holistic racial types). Not everyone was influenced, of course. Jo Birdsell studied genetics, but he had collected his data in Australia before the war using a framework of racial types, and he continued to publish on the basis of the regional distributions of three types that, he argued, arrived in Australia by three waves of migration. Although the basis for Birdsell's conclusion that there were three major prehistoric migrations into Australia is insecure, the possibility of repeated migrations exists, and there probably were further migrations of Malays and those from New Guinea before the first Europeans arrived.

Larry Angel also held out and continued to talk about racial and constitutional types, but his main research focus shifted to paleodemography. The average length of life was much shorter in ancient times. Angel showed that in Greece, as elsewhere, it varied from period to period as conditions of life deteriorated or improved.

My own understanding about race developed slowly. By the time I started studying anthropology, it already seemed clear to me that the concept of racial superiority could not be established objectively. Although I had begun studying human genetics on my own in 1934, I do not think that I had assimilated the genetic reasons that racial "types" are not transmitted and hence are not a satisfactory representation of human variation, until the discussions of the issue at the annual Viking Fund Summer Seminars beginning in 1946. *Race* as a way of designating geographical populations remained in my vocabulary for another fifteen years or so, and even after I stopped talking about race, I used the adjective *racial* to designate hereditary biological traits that characterize populations that principally originated in a specific region. For instance, by 1946, I had started to file reprints about biological surveys of people under headings such as "Race, Iran," even if the author had not used the word *race* and I do not consider the Iranians to be a race. Filing-card systems have a life of their own, and mine reminds me how difficult it is to alter mental categories, even when one realizes that the concept of race is not useful, either to judge individuals or even to help with historic and prehistoric reconstructions.

The last bastion of race in science is in epidemiology. Some diseases attack different segments of the population with very different frequencies. For instance, in the United States, sickle-cell anemia is largely confined to people now designated as "African Americans." The use of that as a racial term, however, may in itself turn attention away from other approaches to the problem. Whether the gene for sickling first arose in an African, the simplest and most probable assumption, or arrived there from elsewhere is of less importance than that it thrives in areas like West Africa because it provides a degree of immunity to falciparum malaria, a major cause of premature death in that region. Thus, the gene for sickling flourishes in populations whose ancestors had to contend with endemic malaria for generations. Since the ancestors of most African Americans have been away from malarial environments for several hundred years, the gene (and the disease of sickle-cell anemia) is becoming less frequent in America than a purely racial type of analysis would predict.

There are several other hemoglobin variants and also blood group types with a somewhat similar relationship to malaria, and race is an equally inaccurate explanation of their prevalence. Prominent among anthropologists working in this area is Frank Livingstone, who had been studying with human geneticist James V. Neel, the co-discoverer of the mode of inheritance of sickle-cell anemia. Livingstone was one of the first to abandon the race concept and to explain details of the geographic distribution of hereditary traits by reference to the ecological conditions needed by malaria-carrying mosquitoes.

Besides the issue of racial types, some physical anthropologists, including Hooton, were attracted by the idea of constitutional types. However, after the demonstration of the enormous changes in the outer manifestation of so-called somatotypes of partially starved individuals, it was clear that every observable or measurable aspect of the types was subject to changes under those circumstances. There was therefore no objective way to classify any such genetic entity as a somatotype.

Stan Garn was one of the youngest participants in that first seminar in 1946, held in the first postwar summer, which had such a profound effect on the subsequent direction of physical anthropology. His chief recollection was of his amazement at being associated with the authors of all the works that were "required reading" at the university. He and Fred Thieme both took Washburn's summer course in anatomy, and he recalls how Fred began his report on the jaws. "The jaws," announced Fred, "is where the teeth live."

Garn had been working with the Polaroid company studying human hair in polarized light, and the company continued to consult him on the proposed Polaroid 77 sunglasses with a nose piece "that would fit anybody from a Chinese to an Armenian." He spent his weekends in Chinese and Armenian restaurants and looking in the American Museum of Natural History at Eskimo sunglasses. (The bone "glasses" are designed to reduce glare from the snow by limiting the amount of light passing through a single narrow slit in the bone. No lenses are involved.) Knowing of this interest of Garn's, Washburn set him to dissect the nose and its blood supply. That summer, Washburn had everyone thinking in terms of functional anatomy.

It was well known that Garn had been studying human hair, and at one session, Weidenreich, whom he held in awe, turned to him and said, "Garn, you always sit behind me in order to examine the hairs in mine ears." It was this easy mixing of academic levels from first-year graduate students to emeritus professors that made the summer seminars so successful. Washburn must also be credited with bringing together students from different universities who rarely had such opportunities to intermingle. There was also a romantic aspect to the first summer seminar, and it was then that Ted McCown began courting Libby Richards. It was McCown who invited Libby (Elizabeth) Richards to attend the seminar, and it was Libby who invited Bunny Kaplan. As Bunny and I were living at our respective homes and not in the Bard Hall dormitory where the out-of-town participants were housed, my interest in her may have passed unnoticed.

12

Editing and Publishing

Washburn decided that the Viking Fund Summer Seminars should have a publication, and he named me to edit the new *Yearbook of Physical Anthropology*. I was to report the proceedings of the seminars, summarize the state of the science, and reprint some of the year's most important papers. At that time, xerography was not available to most, there had been little exchange of reprints during the war years, and in most of the world physical anthropologists had become hopelessly out of touch with one another. As was usual in those sexist days, the two female students present, Libby Richards and Bunny Kaplan, were assigned as secretaries. They helped me write the proceedings of the first seminar, and Bunny continued to write the reports in subsequent years.

For the rest of the summer following the seminar in 1946, I worked on the *Yearbook* at the headquarters of the foundation in its useful small library. It was a comfortable place to read, and some interesting work was done there. Among the scholars who had the support of the Viking Fund for work in the library, Earl Count, who had been teaching anatomy, was there to study the history of the race concept. Count had been Kroeber's first successful PhD student at the University of California. He was fluent in most European languages, and his work had a breadth few could match. Subsequently, Count taught undergraduates at Hamilton, a small liberal arts college, for the rest of his active career.

When I was editor, the *Yearbook of Physical Anthropology* was distributed gratis to interested anthropologists. The budget, met by the foundation, was modest, about two thousand dollars per year. Most of the mailing, telephone, and other incidental expenses were not included in the budget but were covered by the anatomy department at Wayne. Some others were involved in editing the *Yearbook*, but I continued to do most of the literature search with Washburn's aid.

In 1953, however, *Human Biology* had suspended publication, and Bill Howells (after having asked Josef Brozek, who declined) asked me to reestablish it. Howells applied to the Viking Fund for a two-thousand-dollar grant, and we were off and running. I was naive and did not realize that the publishers, Johns Hopkins University Press, would request another two thousand dollars the next year and every future year. At the end of the year, when they did, I was on the editorial board of the Wayne University Press, an enthusiastic group founding a new institution. The university had until then been a city college under the Board of Education. The editorial board was keen to try to take on the journal. The members of the board of the press whom I particularly remember were the chairman, Flint Purdy, the university's chief librarian; Harold Basilius, a professor of German; Alex Brede, a professor of English who did much of the editing; and the treasurer of the press and bursar of the university, Robert Thompson, an old-time city employee. Bob Thompson suggested that I apply to a foundation for three thousand dollars, and the Wayne Press would take it over. He told me to explain that the journal, which had needed two thousand dollars the year before, would need fifteen hundred for the current year, and one thousand and then five hundred for two more years, after which the journal would be completely self-supporting. That budget, with its promise of a self-sustaining journal, must have looked good to the National Science Foundation, because they gave the press the money. Thompson cannily used it to buy the journal and the back issues from the Johns Hopkins Press, and the next time he needed a cash infusion to balance the budget and show a surplus, he sold the back issues to a commercial concern for eight thousand dollars. In fact, the press met some subsequent shortfalls by further sales of later accumulations of back issues.

I started editing *Human Biology* in 1953 by the method of trial and, especially, error. In 1957, I attended the founding meeting of what became the Council of Biology Editors, and the discussions with fellow editors at the early conferences of that group helped me learn how a scientific journal should be run. Another great help was the advice of my original board of editors of *Human Biology,* largely selected on the advice of Howells. Besides him, they were Bentley Glass, Jim Spuhler, Bill Straus, and Josef Brozek. I also exchanged information with the editors of other anthropological journals. Nevertheless, I kept my own counsel, and if there was something I wanted to publish, advisers had a hard time dissuading me.

Some scholars are very independent and have learned most of what they know from reading books. I have always found it easier to ask the many other biological anthropologists of my acquaintance for assistance. Nevertheless, I have also done a great deal of reading. As editor, I read virtually every manuscript, most of them several times, and in my letters to manuscript reviewers, I tried to ask specific questions. I consulted Alex Roche, Barry Bogin, Michael Crawford, Robert Malina, Stan Garn, and some others many times because of their knowledge in a wide range of subjects.

In 1954, when I first prepared the "Information for Contributors" for the inside back cover, I deliberately chose a reference by a young but promising author, Stan Garn, as an example of the style for references. Apparently, one of the Japanese journals copied the style and reprinted the same citation. Those uses added up to a lot of citations over many years. Garn has become one of the most published and cited authors in our field. He exemplifies the value of research in a wide range of areas as well as command of specialized methods.

Some reviewers are slow. Spuhler apparently found it hard to criticize in writing. If I eventually phoned, however, he would have studied the manuscript and would give a useful oral review.

Reviews were not the only thing Spuhler found difficult to write. When he was secretary-treasurer of the American Association of Physical Anthropologists and his term ended, he did not give a final treasurer's report, and his successor, Edward Hunt, did not receive the final accounts. Eventually, Hunt sent a friend who was a lawyer as well as an anthropologist to interview Spuhler. On his way to Ann Arbor to see Spuhler, the attorney stopped in Detroit and asked me to accompany him. I had the bad judgment to go along and had to listen to Spuhler's excuses.

Then Hunt used the excuse of not having Spuhler's report and did not set up new books with the funds that Spuhler gave him. So Hunt, in turn, did not issue a report. The executive committee held an emergency session. We set up new accounts with the funds that were transmitted and collected as dues. T. Dale Stewart was the leading voice at the meeting, so, although he previously had been the president and also the editor, we drafted him for the thankless job of secretary-treasurer. In fact, as head of the anthropology department at the Smithsonian, he delegated all the actual work of treasurer to his associate, Larry Angel. Poor Larry took it in stride with his usual good nature, and the work was done. Spuhler and Hunt turned over such funds as they thought belonged to the association, and that ended the crisis.

As an editor, I have followed the rule of trying to treat all authors equally and fairly. To do so, I have sometimes overruled the opinions of reviewers. No doubt, there were mistakes, but an editor should be more concerned about rejecting something that contains a good idea than about publishing something of limited merit. If in doubt, let the readers judge. Once someone submitted a very philosophical article about human evolution to *Human Biology*. Two biologists to whom I sent it recommended against publication, but they did not seem to me to understand it, so I sent it to several more biologists with the same result. I then sent it to two philosophers for review. Both of them wrote back with their own theories, so I published the article anyway. I would like to be able to say that the article made an important point, but in fact none of the readers of the journal seems to have had anything further to say about it.

Another incident that caused an editorial problem was a manuscript submitted by a foreigner who was a prolific researcher. Much of the English was barely intelligible. I did the best I could to construe the intent and produced a short version that simply omitted those statements that I could not understand. This reduced the length of the paper considerably. We wrote to the author explaining that all we could publish of his paper was an extended "abstract." He must have been satisfied, however, because he agreed and later proposed writing papers jointly with me. I had to explain that such editing is not authorship.

At another time, I had a misunderstanding about papers submitted by Roy Acheson, a pioneer in applications of human biology to issues of public health. While he was still on the faculty at Yale, he submitted two manuscripts about the progress of ossification during human growth. They were marked as belonging to a series with the Roman numerals I and II. One of the reviewers suggested that the two manuscripts be combined into one, and I relayed the suggestion to the author. After a short while, we received a packet from Acheson with what we assumed were the two revised manuscripts, and they were still marked as I and II. Authors deserve to have their opinions respected, so we published the two articles that way. I later learned, however, that Acheson had combined the two original manuscripts into a new number I and that the second manuscript we published had never been reviewed! Since it would certainly have passed muster, no harm was done, but I became more reluctant to allow authors to use numbers within a series. I sometimes told authors that we could not accept an article labeled with a I unless we delayed it until we could accept one marked II.

For a number of years, *Human Biology* had a coeditor. When the Society for the Study of Human Biology was established in the United Kingdom, Derek Roberts was already on the editorial board of *Human Biology*, and he explored with the publisher a role for the society in the journal. In accord with the agreement with the publisher, the society named James N. Tanner to be coeditor and three additional members for the editorial board. Tanner is the researcher on human growth whose work is most widely known both within the scientific community and among pediatricians. That reputation was based on the fact that he and his associates were major contributors to the subject and published growth standards to which other findings readily could be compared. Such an editor was obviously an asset to the journal. After a number of years, the relationship between the journal and the society broke down over financial disagreements, and the society decided to publish its own journal.

While it lasted, the arrangement for joint editors was a success. Tanner had high scientific standards, and I was never tempted to overrule any of his editorial decisions, although I think I once asked for additional work on a manuscript he had accepted. Furthermore, I recall only once when Tanner said that some member or members of the society had complained about an article I had accepted and published. It was a speculative review by Russell Newman on why humans sweat so much. It has been repeatedly cited and is apparently still of some interest long after its initial appearance.

When he was appointed to the faculty in the Department of Anthropology at Wayne, David Carlson immediately volunteered and helped with the editing of *Human Biology*. Then, when he left Wayne and Barry Bogin replaced him, Bogin served as the associate

Barry Bogin in 1997. He has demonstrated dominant evolutionary and environmental factors in human growth. He worked closely with Gabriel Lasker in editing *Human Biology* for several years.

editor for many years. We worked closely together, and I increasingly came to rely on his judgment.

Most of the biological anthropologists of my generation were trained by individuals interested chiefly in historical problems. Their work is often therefore of a speculative character. That approach has survived the changes in paradigm more in some countries and departments than in others. We had to deal with the manuscripts we received and pay attention to the opinions of reviewers, but increasingly we tried to emphasize functional studies that demonstrated biological processes general to the species rather than the specifics of history. We never formalized or limited the scope, but we tried to keep the journal abreast of the two major changes in the direction of the field: away from an earlier preoccupation with race and toward a functional integration of physiology with the older concern with morphology.

When the Society for the Study of Human Biology established its own new journal, the Human Biology Council was formed to support *Human Biology* and accepted that journal as its official organ. After I had been editing it for more than thirty years, some members wanted to see the editorship turned over. Francis E. Johnston, who had just retired from a successful period of editorship of the *American Journal of Physical Anthropology,* was on a short list I had suggested, and he was appointed editor.

There was an accumulation of problems, some of them left over from my term as editor. The Wayne State University Press established policies, such as not issuing reprints, that went against the wishes of the council. The press was falling behind in the dates of appearance of the journal, and subscriptions were not being promptly entered. Johnston had a very favorable relationship with the commercial publishers of the journal he had previously been editing, and he supported their effort to take over *Human Biology.* This brought the council into conflict with the Wayne State University Press. Perhaps if I had been more central to some of the discussions, I might have been able to mediate. However, I did report to the officers of the council what I thought would be involved in establishing another new journal with a different publisher, even though I would have preferred to keep *Human Biology* going. In the end, the council helped establish the *American Journal of Human Biology.*

I think that one journal covering a wide range of topics and appearing monthly would serve the profession better than two necessarily more specialized bimonthly ones. If there were to be two journals, however, it seemed best if each became somewhat specialized in different aspects of human biology, and I thought about who could give a suitable focus to *Human Biology.* The directions I had in mind were epidemiology or anthropological genetics. Anthony Way, one of the PhDs who gave Penn State such a high reputation for the graduates from Baker's programs, advised me that anthropological aspects of epidemiology were better served by other existing journals.

Michael Crawford, who had conceptualized anthropological genetics as a subfield when he and Peter Workman published *Methods and Theories of Anthropological Genetics* in 1973, therefore seemed the logical choice for editor-in-chief of *Human Biology.* His own research interests are very different from those of Johnston, who remained the editor for the journal of the Human Biology Council. Furthermore, Crawford had a reputation as a very hardworking researcher with the will to make a success of his undertakings. That some people thought he might be too headstrong was not a handicap, since decisiveness is a necessary characteristic for a successful new editor. Crawford was appointed and has been effective in his relationships with authors and others. He has continued as a leader in the organization as well as continuing research on the biology of human populations that includes consideration of the genetic dimension. When I think of how naive I was when I first started editing, and how rapidly Crawford and Robert Malina (the present editor of the *American Journal of Human Biology*) adapted to their roles, I think the two serial publications will prosper.

The third journal with the phrase *human biology* in its title, the *Annals of Human Biology* published by the Society for the Study of Human Biology in England, has recently had a change of editors and will need their leadership to continue to serve the profession well; its authors and readers are among the leading human biologists in many countries, and if that status can be maintained, its prospects are also promising. Of course, human biology is a very broad field, and there are many journals that serve different aspects of it. Scores of other journals are cited frequently in *Human Biology*. Among them, I remain on the editorial board of the *Journal of Biosocial Science* and have started to serve *Antropologia Fisica Latinoamericana* and *Annals of Human Biology*.

I remained as editor of *Human Biology* with one brief hiatus for thirty-five years. During the last few years of my teaching career, we

Michael Crawford, the editor-in-chief of *Human Biology*. His books and research reports on anthropological genetics are largely responsible for its recognition as a discipline.

Robert Malina is the leading exponent of the introduction of anthropological methodology into the study of sports physiology.

were asked to fill out time and effort reports. In mine, I estimated that the editing represented about a third, research a third, and teaching gross anatomy a third, so the anatomy department provided a substantial subsidy in my salary. The Department of Anatomy, now Anatomy and Cell Biology, continues to support my anthropological activities. I have long been involved in editing. My wartime experience with *Biological Abstracts* and postwar effort with the *Yearbook of Physical Anthropology* were important learning experiences.

When I took on *Human Biology*, Spuhler edited the *Yearbook* for a year. However, the foundation established a new *Yearbook of Anthropology* and used my departure and the new *Yearbook* as an excuse to suspend publication of the one in physical anthropology. Actually, only one issue of the general yearbook appeared, and then a still different program replaced it.

Ten years later, in 1962, Santiago Genoves in Mexico City reestablished the *Yearbook of Physical Anthropology* with help from his institution and again from the Wenner-Gren Foundation. I edited a catch-up issue covering the missed years and assisted Genoves for several years more.

In the last years of Genoves's editorship, John ("BJ") Buettner-Janusch wrote a scathing review of the 1965 *Yearbook* and published it in the *American Journal of Physical Anthropology* (1967). The *Yearbook* was still useful to physical anthropologists in countries like Mexico where Genoves worked. In such places, only a few of the journals were received, and the reprinting of a selection of what were considered the more important articles continued to be useful. In the United States, however, copying machines had become almost universal, and the university libraries, despite their complaints about budgets, had much expanded resources for subscriptions to journals. Buettner-Janusch's complaints certainly had some justification from that North American point of view. The American Association of Physical Anthropologists, which was the sponsor of the *Yearbook*, rewarded BJ with the editorship and a budget several times greater than Genoves had been allowed. The sponsorship by the AAPA and distribution to dues-paying members as a benefit of membership continue, but the free distribution to others ceased, and the *Yearbook* is now a regularly appearing publication distributed by a commercial publisher.

In the early years of the *Yearbook*, it recognized important trends in the science. It reprinted virtually everything important that was published about the *Australopithecus* fossils except articles appearing in the *American Journal of Physical Anthropology*. The *Yearbook* editors felt

Santiago Genoves, a Mexican physical anthropologist, revived the *Yearbook of Physical Anthropology* after it had suspended publication for ten years.

At sea, as quartermaster during the voyage of Thor Heyerdahl's primitive craft the *Ra II*, on the second of Santiago's three crossings of the Atlantic from Africa to the Caribbean by raft. Genoves used these dangerous adventures to examine social stress among the very diverse members of the crews confined together for months on end. So close to the sea with his feet sometimes in the water, he also recorded the extensive pollution.

On land, in 1994. (Photographs courtesy of Dr. Genoves.)

that it would be a duplication to reprint from the association's journal. Those early issues of the *Yearbook* also recognized and republished almost all the key papers about the sickle-cell trait and its inheritance. The role of this example of genetics in anthropology, in reference to balanced selection in particular, seemed important. Almost nothing was then being published in the field of nonhuman primate behavior, but the *Yearbook* tried to find and give further voice to what there was. In retrospect, most of today's trends in physical anthropology were recognized, and the change in orientation of physical anthropology from pre-World War II to modern biological anthropology was already reflected in the first seven issues of the *Yearbook*. The present interests in reproductive physiology and molecular anthropology still largely lay in the future, however.

Besides the journals, I should say a word about several series of books. The Society for the Study of Human Biology holds annual symposia that are subsequently published in book form. The themes of these meetings show the strong tendency of the field to turn to subjects of direct relevance to human welfare. The 1996 symposium, "Human Biology and Social Inequality," was organized by S. S. Strickland. Participants for 1997's "Urbanism and Human Biology" were invited by Stanley Ulijaszek, who has been very active in the study of such practical questions as the relationship of food intake to growth and reproduction in human populations. The 1998 symposium, "Health and Ethnicity," is being planned by Helen MacBeth of Oxford Brookes University.

Oxford University Press published a series of books in biological anthropology that were devoted to studies of the people of various regions, areas, and locations. Some of the volumes show continuity with an old tradition in anthropology, but I understand that the series is being suspended. Cambridge Studies in Biological Anthropology, on the other hand, has been devoted to books on general questions. *The Anthropology of Modern Human Teeth* by Christy Turner II and Richard Scott (1997), which thoroughly covers tooth morphology on a global basis, continues a traditional theme. Roy J. Shephard and Audris Rode's *The Health Consequences of Modernisation* and Lyliane Rosetta and C. G. N. Mascie-Taylor's *Variability in Human Fertility*, however, are about applications to concrete human problems of the present and the future.

In the fall of 1958, we had just returned to the United States from a fourteen-month sabbatical leave in Peru. I was aware that there were virtually no up-to-date works about human evolution. The well-written books by Hooton and Howells were increasingly out of date. I wanted to contribute but did not want to write a textbook. A publisher's contract would require me to write to the curriculum, so without one, I decided to write a book for the general reader.

My father gave the manuscript to the person at Henry Holt and Company who had edited one or two of his books. The response was negative and not encouraging. However, I asked Jack Pickering, an old friend from Harvard days, to show it to the trade book editor at the Stanley Rinehart Company, where he was an editor in the college department. The eventual reply came that the trade editor had told Pickering to "tell the professor he can't write," but Pickering added: "We think that if you make some revisions, it would make a book for our department." Pickering also assisted with the editing for the college audience. By the time it appeared under what would now be considered a sexist title, *The Evolution of Man*, the Rinehart company had been merged with Holt, so the two publishers who had said no wound up publishing it after all. In terms of number of copies sold, it was a publishing success.

Holt, Rinehart and Winston then wanted from me a course textbook, and after toying with many possible titles, I used the kind of solution Alfred Kroeber resorted to when he called his textbook *Anthropology* and called my much revised and extended version of the earlier work *Physical Anthropology*. From the beginning, I had tried not to be influenced by anyone else's textbooks, but inevitably I leaned on what I had been taught. Pickering challenged me on why I had put racial classifications in the earlier book after arguing against their validity, and one of the improvements was to omit any such classification from the later book. After two editions, the publisher suggested a new edition with a joint author who taught the course as I did not. That edition therefore fitted the usual course syllabus better. I still enjoyed writing a new introductory section on the question of whether chimpanzees have culture, adding a new chapter on demography and making revisions, but I did not find it as satisfying to emphasize consensus views on some contentious issues. Furthermore, there had been a shortage of satisfactory textbooks on the subject when I started, but now there were a considerable variety of good alternative textbooks, so I have not been interested in continuing.

13

Bernice "Bunny" Kaplan

I first worked with my wife, Bernice Kaplan, when we edited the *Yearbook of Physical Anthropology* following the first Viking Fund Summer Seminar. Bunny says that we had met earlier, at the meeting of physical anthropologists in Cleveland in the spring of 1946. I had only half remembered it, if at all, and she had formed an unfavorable opinion of me then. Apparently, a group of students were sitting around gossiping, and I had joined them and tried to talk seriously. What we both most remembered about that meeting was not each other but the enthusiasm of Stan Garn, just beginning his professional career, vaulting over the backs of several rows of seats in the auditorium to mount the stage and give his paper on human hair form. Several months later, at the summer seminar, Bunny and I worked closely on the *Yearbook*, and I came to appreciate her more and more. I had a car, and after work, I would drop off some of the participants and manage to make Bunny's apartment the last stop.

Bunny deserves a biography of her own, but this brief chapter will have to suffice here. She was born in New York City in 1923. Her father was from Libau (now Liepaja), Latvia. Her mother, Marie Antoville, was born in St. Petersburg. Bunny is a real New Yorker; that is, she was born in New York County, which is the borough of Manhattan. She is an only child, but her numerous uncles and aunts also migrated to New York City, and Bunny has many cousins who

Bernice "Bunny" Kaplan, Professor of Anthropology at Wayne State University, has contributed to most areas of anthropology: social anthropology, applied anthropology, biological anthropology, medical anthropology, and the teaching of anthropology.

were born and lived there. Bunny's mother descended from one of two brothers who, to avoid being conscripted into the tsarist army, pretended to be only sons of different families and hence exempt. One took the surname Antovilsky and the other Antokolsky. One of the Antokolskys was a well-known sculptor who worked for the tsar.

Melville Herskovits once told us a story that resonated, because the violin virtuoso Mischa Elman lived with Bunny's maternal grandparents in St. Petersburg when he was a student at the conservatory. The family owned a factory and a home large enough to house both the family of fourteen children and the Finnish factory workers. Music students at the St. Petersburg Conservatory boarded with the family from time to time. It was one of the few places a Jew could stay outside the pale of settlement.

According to Herskovits, one day, his friend Elman said, "I had a dream in which I was to play a concert, but I couldn't play. Funny thing, when I woke up, you know, I felt good."

Herskovits said that he replied, "That's simple. You really don't like to play."

Elman, obviously less familiar with Freudian ideas than Herskovits, naively asked, "How did you know that?"

Elman's brother, a pianist, also lived in Bunny's grandmother's house in St. Petersburg, and her mother always said that Mischa Elman had an unhappy childhood, as his brother forced him to practice at all hours.

In New York City, various of the Antovilles entered the art and antique business, and when Bunny's mother married, her husband learned the framing and restoring business and worked in his wife's gallery. In fact, his name was Meyer Kaplan, but his customers and many friends called him Kappy Antoville, and he answered to that name. When Bunny was three, her father developed a severe gastric ulcer and had to have the first of several operations. Her mother had to look after the shop, so Bunny was cared for by an Irish nursemaid. Bunny's interest in anthropology began by reading books and being taken to the American Museum of Natural History by the Irish nanny, who used to meet her boyfriend there. When Bunny was a junior at Hunter College in 1942, she started to work as a volunteer in the anthropology department at the American Museum of Natural History. When she graduated, she got a full-time job there while attending Columbia University on a part-time basis. She stayed on at the museum after hours and served as manuscript typist for Franz Weidenreich while he was writing about the *Gigantopithecus* fossils. Subsequently, Bunny entered the PhD program at the University of Chicago and worked in the anthropology department at the Chicago Natural History Museum.

In 1946, Bunny was taken on as a teaching assistant at the University of Wisconsin. There were so many returned veterans and other students taking introductory anthropology courses, however, that her appointment was promptly raised to instructor, and she was given eleven discussion sections of the course to teach. She completed her master's degree at Chicago in 1947 and went with me to Mexico for fieldwork in April 1948. After our return to the United States, Bunny taught anthropology at Hobart and William Smith Colleges in Geneva, New York, during the 1948–49 academic year. We were married in July 1949. Her dissertation was completed and the degree awarded in 1953. Bunny has been part of all my subsequent research and writing.

Bunny had obtained a job in the sociology and anthropology department at Wayne State University, but when we married, the university cited a rule against nepotism and tried to convert Bunny to part-time status at a very greatly reduced salary. Spuhler was in charge of hiring for the summer school session at the University of Michigan, and he recruited Bunny. Later, when the department at Wayne learned that Bunny would be teaching at Michigan and unavailable for part-time work, they quickly decided that the nepotism rule did not apply to a couple in different colleges of the university and hired Bunny back full-time. She remains Professor of Anthropology there, albeit with somewhat reduced teaching responsibilities.

As is true of most successful female scholars of her generation, she has been chiefly responsible for raising our family, and furthermore, much of her academic work is credited to others such as her students and myself.

Bunny has seen our three children through school and university. Robert Alexander, the oldest, works in the university in an institute for developmental disabilities; he is an artist with a specialization in metal working. Edward Meyer, the second child, is a musician with a master's degree in improvisation, and he also repairs pianos professionally. Anne Titania, our daughter, is in private law practice. Unlike her parents, she became completely fluent in Spanish and has helped serve the Hispanic community as a disc jockey on a local Spanish-language radio station and as a teacher of English as a foreign language.

Bunny's research interests have been somewhat opportunistic, since she has been with me wherever I've gone. In addition to both acknowledged and unacknowledged collaboration in all that I have been doing, Bunny has been engaged in interests of her own. In Canada, she once showed me how to work on an archaeological dig.

In Mexico, she was concerned with cottage industries but also found time for investigating social organization and even dance. Bunny's study of the craft industry in Paracho was reported in her University of Chicago PhD dissertation and in an article in *Alpha Kappa Deltan* (1960). She found the spirit of enterprise to be the dominant theme. The experience of the men who had been in America did not in itself make a great difference, since most of them had worked on the railways or in the beet fields largely in the company of other Mexicans. However, money earned in America was invested in Paracho, in housing and in establishing and mechanizing woodturning and guitar-making activities. Some women who in 1948 had been weaving on a pre-Columbian type of loom strapped to their backs were embroidering blouses in 1952. The people were always on the lookout for profitable self-employment.

Bunny also did general ethnology and took copious notes on all that we saw and heard. One study, of a dance that was supposed to be Indian but may have been a peasant version of an early European court dance, was published in the *Journal of American Folklore* (1951). In the evenings before Christmas in 1960, it was so cold at eight thousand feet altitude that we stayed inside, but our five-year-old son visited houses where there were parties and reported back on the *Posadas*, the celebration of the Holy Family's staying at inns.

In Peru, Bunny provided our joint studies with ethnographic background. In Italy, she collaborated in our studies of surnames. In England, she studied the response of Asians to the national health system and made a number of studies with C. G. N. Mascie-Taylor of the epidemiology of childhood asthma. And in the United States, she looked at various aspects of culture, especially some that would capture the interest of her students. For instance, she challenged students to help her find out why such a useful adjunct to personal hygiene as the bidet had found so little acceptance here. By the time her students had become involved, one plumber reported to a journalist for *Time* magazine that he had more inquiries about bidets in the last year than in all his prior experience.

14

Fieldwork in Mexico

In the anatomy department at Wayne, F. Gaynor Evans, who organized the gross anatomy course, resigned and went to the University of Michigan. I offered to take over responsibility for the course, but the head of the department, Ernest Gardner, who was on the verge of writing a textbook on gross anatomy, decided he could do that better if he took over Evans's role himself. The textbook, by Gardner, Gray, and O'Rahilly, is an excellent work in part because the illustrations are from actual specimens dissected by Gardner and in part because it documented the sources of the information, a feature that was lacking in the previous English-language textbooks of gross anatomy.

Since I was not asked to become more deeply involved in teaching gross anatomy, I concluded that although I would do my share of the teaching in the medical school course, my main professional identification would continue to be as an anthropologist. That is the basic reason I accepted requests to edit biological anthropological publications and looked for an opportunity to do anthropological fieldwork. My colleagues in anatomy have been supportive. During the forty-two years that I was editor, first of the *Yearbook of Physical Anthropology* and then of *Human Biology,* the anatomy department provided secretarial and other services for the journals and helped when I held office in an anthropological society. One chairperson,

Harry Maisel, had taken his medical degree in South Africa, where so many anatomy professors, including Phillip Tobias, who taught him anatomy at Witwatersrand University in Johannesburg, have done significant research in anthropology. Nevertheless, when some of my other colleagues were asked about me, they tended to say good-naturedly, "Lasker? He is a very distinguished anthropologist. Of course, we don't know what he does."

The medical school once had a professor of neurosurgery who came to the anatomy department to collaborate with my colleague Evans in research on how much force it takes to fracture skulls. Whenever he saw me, which was often, he would ask, "Have you measured any skulls today?" No matter how much I tried to explain the other things that anthropologists do, he would always repeat that question. It was probably just his way of learning more about anthropology, because he insisted that all his residents spend a year full-time in anatomy, and several of them took a reading course in physical anthropology with me.

My studies in China, before I had any formal training in anthropology, involved reviews of the literature rather than fieldwork. My research for my thesis had been done in the United States. Thus, when I received my degree, I had no experience of foreign field research. In 1948, it was time to change that, so I wrote a proposal for the study of returned emigrants in Mexico, and the Viking Fund provided the money. I wanted Bunny to go with me, of course, but Shapiro had asked her to go to Puerto Rico to conduct a study of migrants there. In view of the earlier experiences of Lessa and Hulse with Shapiro, Bunny stipulated that before accepting his offer, she would need to clear a dissertation topic with her advisers at the University of Chicago. She waited from August until December 1947 to hear whether Shapiro's project had been funded and, not having heard, agreed to go with me to Mexico instead. Frederick Thieme got his PhD at Columbia University, nominally under Shapiro, but he was a self-starter and sought advice wherever he could find it, including from Washburn, who was then still in New York. Thieme went to Puerto Rico, and the results of his part of the work were analyzed and published much later not by Shapiro but by Thieme, after he had joined the faculty at the University of Michigan.

In Mexico, money was scarce, and people often scrambled to get it. When we arrived in Mexico for the first time, the immigration doctor at the border in Nuevo Laredo extracted twenty dollars from me in lieu of medical examinations he said we needed. The female clerk, however, said that we did not need the visas that the consul had insisted on issuing, and the chief officer at the border post phoned the consul, shouted at him that he was a *burro,* and arranged for us to enter on tourist cards. As we finally drove on, the doctor ran after us. Bunny said, "Don't stop, he wants more money." I stopped, however, and as the doctor arrived waving the twenty-dollar bill, he was repeatedly saying, "Not necessary, not necessary," as he handed it back. In due time, we also got the fee for the visas back in the form of a personal check from the consul. So there were some officials on the take, but others were trying to clean things up.

In Mexico City, Daniel Rubin de la Borbolla saw to it that we met the other anthropologists there. Everyone always seemed anxious to help. Before we left Mexico City for Michoacán, some two hundred miles to the west, we had met Manuel Gamio, author of the first community study in Mexico, that of the village of Teotihuacan at the foot of the famous Pyramid of the Sun, and Juan Comas, who was, I think, the first professionally trained physical anthropologist in Mexico. From them, we learned about their Indianist Institute, a major effort by anthropologists to attend to the welfare of their subjects. Comas remained a friend whom we met many times thereafter. He and several other members of the faculty in anthropology at the Autonomous University of Mexico (UNAM) were Spaniards who had republican sympathies and were refugees from the civil war in Spain. Comas wrote many books and papers and was a staunch opponent of every tendency to misuse biological anthropology in the service of racism. He was also very concerned with his status as professor, in the European sense. He wrote a textbook and histories of anthropological institutions including formal lists of appointments and publications. By contrast, he had scant tolerance for amateurism in physical anthropology and vigorously attacked every little detail of any attempt by those outside the profession to dabble in anthropometry. At one point, Comas unleashed his criticism against his colleague Santiago Genoves, a fellow Spaniard, who had apparently overstepped the role of subordination to the professor that Comas thought was his due. One time, when someone from a U.S. university, where departments have multiple professors, had apparently given Santiago the title of *Professor* in correspondence or possibly even in a publication, I received an anonymous postcard that evidently came from Comas, saying of Genoves, "Professor of what? Chair where?" Genoves had studied at Cambridge University and had a superior knowledge of English, which gave him an advantage in dealing with English-speaking anthropologists, and some *gringo* anthropologists quite naturally turned to him for assistance with their activities in Mexico.

Genoves and I became good friends when we collaborated in editing the *Yearbook of Physical Anthropology*. He has always had enormous personal drive. On three occasions, he crossed the Atlantic from Africa to the Caribbean by raft. When one enters the museum devoted to the Ra expeditions in Oslo, Norway, the first thing one sees is a huge photograph of Santiago Genoves before the mast of the flimsy craft. Comas's interest in *indianismo* is more than matched by Genoves's interest in world peace. Genoves is also an advocate of conflict resolution at lower levels, and he used the crew's isolation from the outside world on the rafts as a laboratory for studying the interpersonal relationships among the diverse members. His work in English, *The Acali Experiment: Five Men and Six Women on a Raft across the Atlantic for 101 Days*, describes his third such voyage. More recently, he has been writing and speaking out for peace all over the world. Despite Comas's open complaints about him, I never heard Genoves say anything derogatory about Comas.

In the environment of Mexico City, Comas had to struggle to fill what he considered should be the role of a full-time professor. Other Mexican anthropologists have had to put several activities together to make a career. Rubin de la Borbolla became director of the Museum of Popular Arts and Industries and, besides anthropology, had to concern himself with promoting the best in folk art, in part through sales of work by selected artisans who were striving to maintain top quality. Genoves had to branch out and become a TV personality with a science program. Luis Vargas also has excellent command of English and therefore has been able to spend his leaves of absence teaching anthropology in the United States. His wife, Leticia Casillas, is a medically qualified pediatrician and has maintained her status in two professions. Under the circumstance of so little opportunity for full-time employment in anthropology in Mexico, one should not be surprised that some of the themes of research lack great originality. Quite the contrary, one is amazed that anthropology is accorded such high standing.

In Mexico, the declaration that one is an anthropologist receives respect from everyone. When they learned that we were anthropologists, the shoeshine boys in the street wanted to talk with us about our work, and a former anthropology student of Bunny's who became president of Ford Motor Company of Mexico found that his knowledge of anthropology and an ability to talk about it helped his personal relationship with the president of the country.

Our field party in Mexico in 1948 consisted of F. Gaynor Evans and his wife, Harriet, and Bunny Kaplan and me. Later, Pablo Velasquez, Beatriz del Castillo, and other Mexicans assisted. In Mexico City, Daniel F. Rubin de la Borbolla entertained us at a sumptuous dinner and agreed to arrange for our fieldwork. For some while, nothing happened, however, except that we saw the tourist sites, visited some possible villages for the work, and, no doubt, improved slightly on our deficient Spanish.

Before we left the United States, we had corresponded or talked with many individuals to try to prepare ourselves for work in Mexico. We had a memorable meeting in Texas with George Engerrand, who had left France because of the Dreyfus affair, had lived in Mexico, and knew so much of interest about it. Both Ralph Beals and George Foster had said that we might work in the villages they had studied: Cheran and Tzintzuntzan, Michoacán, respectively. Norman Humphrey provided an introduction to someone in a village in Jalisco, where he had spent time. After we had been in Mexico City for nearly a month, we became impatient and decided to strike out for Michoacán or Jalisco to follow one or another of these leads on our own. When we told Borbolla, he picked up the phone, talked with the bishop and with the director of the museum in Morelia, and arranged for Pablo Velasquez to take us to Paracho. The very next day, we drove to Morelia and visited the museum and the ruins of the Yacata (a prehistoric temple) in Tzintzuntzan. A day or two later, we went to Paracho with Pablo.

Our first sight of Paracho was the plaza where the bus stopped. The shops and homes of the leading citizens, the most successful merchants, faced the plaza. So did the former church, seized by the national government during the revolution and converted into a boarding school for Tarascan Indian boys, two from each village. The new church, still under construction, also faced the plaza, and there was a so-called hotel, actually an inn where muleteers and their animals formerly stayed overnight. The government building ("mayor's palace") and the jail also faced the plaza, and at the moment we arrived, some pigs had entered the plaza, and several men with lassos were "arresting" the pigs and putting them in the jail to be held until the owner paid a fine to redeem the hostages. There was a market next to the plaza; although there was a butcher's stall and some food stands on other days, the full operation of the market was limited to Sundays and special fiestas.

Beyond the market, we came to the house of Pablo's godparents, Don Cesario Sosa and Doña Maria Caro. Like all the better houses near the plaza, it was of whitewashed concrete, and only blank walls and a heavy wooden gate faced the street. Rooms on all four sides faced an inner *solar,* or courtyard, with a few fruit trees. Unlike most houses, it had a latrine and a wooden dugout "canoe" for the storage of rain water, but there was also a well, one of only six in the town. Other people bought their water from a man who came from the great well on the outskirts with a donkey carrying four large earthenware pots on its back. Don Cesario's well was very deep. While we stayed there, whenever I woke up cold in the morning, I would warm myself by facing the well with my back to the rising sun and hauling up buckets of water arm over arm. The surprise that first evening was that Don Cesario, living in what we thought of as a rural village, plied us with questions in passable English about affairs of the world, such as "What is going on in the Soviet Union and in Israel?"

Paracho was oriented toward the outside world, which was a market for its crafts. The town has no arable land of its own, so there were few farmers, and the main source of income was craft work. The chief industries for men were the manufacture of guitars and woodwork turned on a lathe. Women wove *rebozos,* the huge, dark blue cotton shawls that were ubiquitous in the region. Making them involved hard labor on a belt loom strapped to a woman's back. All these crafts led to secondary specialties: for women, varnishing guitars or tying the fringes on the scarves; for men, making guitar strings and, especially, traveling all over Mexico to sell the products of the others. Many were entrepreneurs on the lookout for new products. Some years later, we asked after the son of one of the businessmen. His wife explained that he was in Japan scouting for new ideas.

Doña Maria spoke Tarascan as well as Spanish and some English, and she was in constant demand as a letter writer, especially by people from the surrounding agricultural villages. Such people were always very courteously invited to come in for a free drink of water from the well. Don Cesario spoke easily in the very expressive English he had learned when working in the United States. He told us many tales of his youth and his trips there. He first went in 1908 at the age of fourteen in search of his brother, who had gone before to a place he thought was San Bernardino. Mexicans who worked on the

Doña Maria Caro (standing at right) and her two god-daughters, Marilu (lower left) and Gregoria Galvan (lower right), with Gabriel Lasker and Bunny Kaplan in Paracho, Mexico, in 1952.

traque, as they called the railway, helped Don Cesario along his way. They would feed him and let him ride the handcars and, eventually, persuaded the Italian foremen that he was older than he was so he could get work.

Since I once spent a week working on the track of the Virginia and Truckee Railroad in Nevada, I can imagine what it was like for the young Cesario. My Nevada crew consisted of two Washoe Indians and an Italian-American foreman. We replaced only the most dangerous of the damaged ties, those at the end of a rail or at a "frog" where a switch led to a siding. The other three members of the crew called me "the kid," and they would relieve me of the heavy lifting for a while by sending me on errands.

Many other men from Paracho had been going to the United States to work on the railway in earlier years and then to work in beet fields and at other agricultural jobs. Even a few women went, including Doña Maria once. She could not stand the food and lived mostly on Coca-Cola until she could return home.

During the revolution of 1910–1920, the exodus was general. In 1917, Paracho was sacked and burned twice. The small home defense guard fled to the hills. A few men joined Zapata's army; others reached the United States. Many people actually starved. In 1933 and 1934, during the depression in the United States, many of the emigrants returned to Paracho.

One result of the migrations was the considerable worldliness of the people. For instance, when we were in Peru in 1957–58, there was a series of postage stamps with pictures of the Eiffel Tower, and some of the university students we asked had no idea what it was. When next we were in Paracho, we asked some high school students, and they all had a clear notion about it. More than a score of households in Paracho were receiving a daily newspaper. Besides our hosts, many of the people in Paracho had interesting experiences abroad. The policeman had been in France with the American Expeditionary Force during World War I. Another man said he had been fishing for salmon in Alaska and had spent the winter "underground [in a semi-subterranean house] with some Eskimos." One difficulty of our research was the trouble we had in finding enough nonmigrant men to compare with the migrants. The nonmigrant men we did measure included youths who said that they had not been to the United States "yet." Working in the nearby provincial city, Uruapan, Evans had somewhat less trouble of this kind with his part of the research.

Paracho, Michoacán, Mexico, in December 1960. Isauro Castillo and Marilu Galvan entertained Lasker's sons Rob and Ted with Bunny and the aid of two burros in front of Isauro's family's home and shop. Isauro's usual occupation was traveling all over Mexico to sell guitars, chief product of the town. Marilu, like her sister and many other daughters and sons of Paracho, is a teacher.

Pablo Velasquez came from a village called Charapan, not far away. He had been educated in a normal school and also in the United States and was dedicated to *indianismo,* what would now be called ethnic identity. Through his constant companionship for the first part of our stay, we came to think of Paracho as very Indian. Of course, he tended to select survivals of ancient ways to show us, and he sometimes used names for them in Tarascan. We only gradually became more aware of signs of modernity and departures from a timeless peasant society that Pablo, with his strong commitment, tended to describe as remaining unchanged since before Cortez's conquest of Mexico in the sixteenth century.

For instance, at the festival of Corpus Christi, there was a dance of the *Huananchas* that Bunny has described in a folklore journal. Pablo called it "Indian," but in form it was more a peasant version of a Renaissance court dance.

The women who wove *rebozos* formed a sisterhood and met to drink in a hall called *Guataperra,* which may have been a survival of an Indian custom but was not much different from the brotherhoods and sisterhoods, organized to serve a particular saint, found elsewhere in Latin America and Europe.

Evidence of how little traditional Tarascan had survived was illustrated by a parade on one of the national holidays. The schoolchildren were supposed to be dressed up as Indians but were in fact costumed as Aztecs, their traditional enemies.

When Cortez attacked what was to become Mexico City, the Aztecs sent emissaries to the Tarascans to ask for their support as allies. The Tarascans, however, killed the would-be ambassadors.

Bunny often complained when I would say that something or another was "just like in China." Years later in Peru, I would remind her about it when she would find things there that seemed to her "just like in Mexico." What we were both observing were the worldwide characteristics of peasant societies. There were frustrating episodes doing research in Mexico, of course, and the inevitable incidents of diarrhea.

During our first period of field study, the time came for the Viking Fund Summer Seminar in New York. We were needed there to help, so we went by train and stayed for several weeks. The people in Paracho apparently could not believe that we were coming back, and several came by at the last minute to be measured, saying, "You have not measured me yet." Leaving and coming back was useful in a situation where some people were finding excuses to delay their participation. When we finally did leave Paracho, Don Cesario, who was the director of the village orchestra, had them come to serenade us at a farewell party, and we felt a sense of belonging that brought us back many times in subsequent years. In fact, our daughter, Anne, maintains a friendship with the two adopted daughters of Doña Maria and with the next generation, too. We also became good friends with several Mexican anthropologists.

Paracho always seemed peaceful and safe, but our friends there would warn us not to go to this or that place for the fiesta because "the people there would kill you." Actually, when I checked the records of deaths in the town office twenty-one years later, five of the 298 men I had known and measured had been killed by gunshot. Reading the records reminded me of incidents of violence while I had been there, but these were always explained away: "He was drunk," or "He was with the other man's woman." Among the 182 women I had measured, five had subsequently died in childbirth, and there were numerous records of deaths of infants. During an epidemic of whooping cough, we repeatedly heard the explosion of fireworks that accompanied the funerals of "little angels." A four-year-old boy in our own household came down with the disease and was treated by rocking him in a swing and feeding him donkey milk.

On our second visit to Paracho, a few days before the fiesta of Corpus Christi, I was in the plaza on the way to visit some of my study subjects when I heard the priest call over the loudspeaker in the church tower for a *junta,* or gathering of men. I saw a dozen or so men on a flatbed truck and thought that they were going to the forest to get timber to build a corral in which to fight bulls at the fiesta. I would have liked to join them, but I had my work to do. When I returned that evening to the house of Doña Maria, there was a gathering of old men talking and drinking. One of them was a senator from Mexico City. He was as European-looking as I am, but he was holding forth about how he was going to solve the problem peacefully, and "we indigenous people from this place must stick together." What I had mistaken for a search for suitable lumber was an armed war party dispatched to defend the town's ownership of a part of the forest claimed as Paracho's common land, a claim disputed by the next village, whose men had been cutting wood there.

We spent two weeks with Charles Leslie, a medical anthropologist, and his wife, Zelda, in the field in Mitla, Oaxaca, in 1953, when

Charles was gathering data for his dissertation. Bunny was interested in cottage industries, and the industry there was the distillation of mescal. The kind best known outside Mexico is distilled legally and is called tequila. When we first arrived in Mitla, someone was having a fiesta, and at Leslie's suggestion, I bought and took a Coyotepec black pottery flask of mescal for the host. Later, the man who had sold it saw me and upbraided me. He had assumed a *gringo* would take it away with him. If he had known that it was to be drunk locally, he would not have wasted money on a tax stamp!

After a morning of fieldwork in Mitla during which I was obliged to test the products at several stages of manufacture, it was difficult to return to the mayor's office in the afternoon to collect the data on migration from the marriage records for a little project of my own. Doing intensive studies in a single community at a time, as Elsie Clews Parsons, a colorful anthropologist well remembered in Mitla, had done when she was there collecting material for her *Mitla, Town of the Souls,* published about 1935, was the usual method for ethnologists. Restudying a community intensively, as Charles Leslie was doing, was then a new idea. Collecting comparable data on a few demographic variables in order to reach a general conclusion, as I was trying to do, was at that time thought of by some as outside the range of what anthropologists should do. Physical anthropologists, being more accustomed to survey methods than ethnologists, were more often the ones interested in ethnic demography.

In Mitla, we witnessed a "horse race." The men on horseback milled around at the starting place. At a signal, two of them dashed toward an overhead line from which metal rings hung by strips of rotten cloth. Each horseman carried a wand in lieu of a lance and tried to spear one of the rings. The first one to reach the line set the whole apparatus bobbing so the second one had no chance to succeed even if the first one missed. If either succeeded, however, the mayor conducted him to a row of young girls, one of whom presented him with a colored ribbon. Spearing a ring is comparable to, and must be the origin of, catching the brass ring at an old-fashioned merry-go-round. Both are no doubt derived from tilting. The young girls represent the virgin ladies for whom knights of chivalry fought. The ribbons, and also, of course, the blue ribbons at county fairs, represent the silk kerchiefs from ladies' hats that were given to their victorious champions in the tilting lists in ancient times.

In places like rural Mexico, one encounters surviving cultural practices from medieval Europe. For instance, we were told that Tarascan Indians learn English faster than Spanish speakers. One example that was cited was that the Spanish word for candle is *vela*, but the Indian word is *candela*. No doubt, the Indians had learned it in an earlier century from a European priest who used a Spanish synonym that is a cognate of the English.

We have endeavored to maintain links with Mexico over the years. We returned for a further period of fieldwork in 1960 and subsequently participated in the first four Coloquio Juan Comas with the Mexican Association of Biological Anthropologists, in 1980, 1982, 1984, and 1986.

My share in the work we did in Mexico, whatever its short-comings, is the best research I have done. In 1948, I measured and observed 480 adults while Bunny recorded the results and answers to questions. In 1952, one or the other of us conducted interviews in all 810 households to obtain demographic and economic data. In those sexist days, it is perhaps not surprising that in the households Bunny visited, more economic activity of women was recorded than in those I visited. On those trips and in 1953, we also collected small amounts of special data of several kinds. We published the results of these and of some related investigations elsewhere in Mexico in a series of articles in *Human Biology* (1952, 1953, 1954, 1974, 1976, 1985, 1990) and in the *American Journal of Physical Anthropology* (1954, 1961, 1969), as well as in other journals. Indeed, we have in some ways overexploited a rather small database. I think our work has illustrated a number of important aspects of human biology.

Our original plan had been to follow the research strategy of Franz Boas's study of immigrants as Marcus Goldstein had done in his 1943 monograph. We had hoped to see if there were significant differences in stature and other measurements of the body, head, and face between men who had never left Mexico and their brothers who had migrated to the United States and returned. When we found that brothers tended to migrate together, we had to content ourselves with comparing groups of individuals who were not necessarily related. Even so, we found that relatively few men had never been to the United States, and some of them, when asked, said, "Not yet." Among the women, only a few had gone. Thus, the study was too small for definitive answers to some questions.

Of the various results, I shall therefore refer in detail only to stature. It is a good indicator of general size, and the measurements are more accurate than those of other dimensions. The 23 women who had lived in the United States were 2.1 centimeters taller on average than the 157 who had not. Among the men, the 126 who had gone before the age of twenty-seven were 1.9 centimeters taller than the 111 nonmigrants on average, and the 59 men who were twenty-seven or older when they first migrated were not significantly different from the nonmigrants in this respect. In fact, they were 0.4 centimeter shorter.

We concluded from this that the migrants who went when they were young were taller because they lived in the United States, presumably because of better nutrition. However, we were able to further discount the possibility that migrants are physically much different from nonmigrants. When we inquired who had been to the States in the intervening four years since we had measured them, we found that, after allowing for prior experience, they were only 0.5 centimeter taller than the 229 men who did not go during those four years.

The population of Paracho, like that of most of Mexico, is of mixed origin, so there are differences on that account. Thus, the average stature of men who described their parents as indigenous was 1.1 centimeters shorter than that of those who described their parents as white or mixed. The average difference was only 0.2 centimeter among the women, however, and in two articles in *Phylon* in 1953, Bunny and I found almost no differences in biological characteristics between the two groups. Hair color and form and even the characteristics of the upper front teeth that are considered hallmarks of the American Indian were not greatly different. The chief difference was that older individuals tend to think of their parents and themselves as "natives" of the place, but young people think of themselves as members of the general Mexican population, which is mixed, and this is the way they described their own parents. In a parallel study in Peru, we found essentially the same thing; there also, race was not primarily biological. Physical characteristics were virtually useless in discriminating ethnic origins of individuals.

However, there were some differences between local populations. In 1952, we conducted a study using, we believe for the first time under field conditions, a photoelectric reflection meter for recording skin color. We found that in the boarding school where there were supposed to be two boys from each Tarascan Indian village, skin color averaged somewhat darker than boys of the same age in the village schools.

On a subsequent trip, we collected urine specimens and tested for a substance (an amino acid, BAIB) that occurs in higher concentrations in American Indians. The proportion of high excretors in Paracho was somewhat higher than reported for people of European origin, but it was lower than in two nearby more "Indian" villages and lower than in the more "Indian" Mexican state of Oaxaca.

As we became interested in different problems, we often turned to the Paracho data for an example. For instance, when we thought to use surnames for studying inbreeding, we found that in Mexico, women who should use their own fathers' and mothers' surnames would, in some cases, substitute their husbands' names for one of their "normal" surnames when speaking to a foreigner. In any case, we tried to examine inbreeding by looking at marriages of people with the same parental surnames and found some suggestion of a slight effect in the offspring. But we tried the same approach with a larger set of data we had collected in Peru, and there was no hint of any such effect. If there is some small influence of biological effects of moderate degrees of inbreeding, it will probably take very large studies of diverse populations to establish, because we also did not see it in a comparison of those whose parents were both from the same place with those whose parents came from different places.

In still another study using our data, we tested to see if there was a relationship among any of twenty-five measurements we had taken and each of four criteria of Darwinian fitness (genetic survival). The criteria were (1) number of children born, (2) number of surviving children, (3) number of brothers and sisters ever born, and (4) number of surviving brothers and sisters. Ten percent of the comparisons were suggestive. One of them that may be interesting enough for further study is that some survivors had larger head dimensions. Of course, it is well known that better-nourished individuals tend to be larger in most dimensions and that the more affluent tend to live longer and, in societies like that of Mexico where contraception was not practiced, to have more offspring.

Today, anthropology is more specialized, but when we were in Paracho, both of us were interested in all sorts of things. On days when we could not measure individuals, our field assistant, Pablo Velasquez, sometimes took us to examine archaeological sites that had not been investigated. On the side of the mountain to the east of the town, the former *Yakata*, or temple mound, had been raided by fortune hunters, but on the surface we found broken prehistoric tools made of obsidian, the black volcanic glass of the region, and one broken piece from a very fine pot of plumbate ware that must have come from Central America. There was also one broken human figurine, also from a late pre-Columbian epoch. Where there had been a well west of the town, we also found some interesting shards on the surface and also at the original site of Paracho, south of the town on a hill where it had been located before the Spanish arrived and forced the people into a town of Spanish design.

15

Peru

*I*n 1957, I received a letter inviting me to apply for a Fulbright Research Fellowship in Peru. It was the first year of the Fulbright program in Peru, and a major project was in archaeology. The invitation asked for someone to study excavated skeletal material. I

Fieldwork in San José, Lambayeque, Peru, in January 1958. This fishing and boat-building village had no harbor, so the boats were launched into the surf by the crew, as in this picture, and beached on their return.

did not want to do that and was about to decline, thinking that they probably wrote a great many invitations like the one I had received. The department chairman, Ernest Gardner, suggested that I phone and find out how many letters they had sent out. When I did so, the person in Washington, D.C., who had issued the invitation was surprised by the question, as mine was the only letter he had written.

Under those circumstances, we prepared a counterproposal. Bud Newman, who had been spending a year at the Cornell University project at Vicos in highland Peru, made some suggestions about where we might go and what we might do. We decided to study the living population of some of the so-called Mochica villages on the north coast of Peru. We later learned that Newman was the one who had suggested us at first and then, when we counterproposed, the one who persuaded the program to accept us.

We arrived with our two young sons by sea at Callao, the port of Lima. The secretary of the Fulbright commission in Peru, Dr. Eduardo F. Indacoechea, and his wife met us on board ship, and he handed me an envelope with what he described as "samples of the denominations of Peruvian currency"—actually, enough money to get by on until we opened a bank account. Then he took us to Pension Morris, where virtually every foreign anthropologist used to stay for rest and recreation.

Paul Baker, in his autobiographical sketch in *Annual Reviews of Anthropology*, refers to his pleasure at staying there. When we arrived, Marge d'Andrade, the English hostess, saw to everyone's needs. Later she was succeeded by her sister Nora and Nora's daughter Olga. We met Alan Holmberg of Cornell University, who had started an applied anthropology experiment by buying the hacienda of Vicos and turning it over to the community. We also got to know William Mangin and his family. Mangin was and still is doing ethnographic studies of the slum squatter settlements called *barriadas* in Lima. The main thrust of the Fulbright program in Peru was archaeology. When we arrived, several archaeologists were already there. David Kelly was in the garden deciphering Maya glyphs from Mexico and Guatemala. Dwight Wallace was there with his wife and children, and we used to play a game called *sapo* in the garden of Pension Morris. It is rather like quoits or horseshoes, but in *sapo,* one tosses small, heavy disks at the bronze statue of a toad in order to get the disks in the mouth or in other holes in the box on which the toad is mounted. Playing in the garden, the best *pisco* sours in Lima to drink, and the conversations made the Pension Morris the mecca loved and now much missed by Peruvianist anthropologists.

Newman had told us of the difficulties of working at altitude, especially of living there with our young children. Even on the coast, our younger son (only three months old when we went) had enough health problems to keep us worried. We never did visit Vicos, and our forays into the Altiplano were limited to a day trip up the Rio Rimac with the Mangins and a three-day touristic visit to Cuzco and Machu Picchu. On the flight to Cuzco on a DC3, our two-year-old son (the younger one was left behind) made a constant fuss. When we reached altitude, he passed out. The pilot made oxygen available to the passengers, and Bunny put an outlet tube under Rob's nose. I said, "Don't give him too much, or he'll come to." In Cuzco, I had altitude sickness and felt cold the whole time, too tired in the afternoons for anything except going along with others in a car. The cathedral had no pews—worshipers would stand—and when we visited it, I was struck by the sight of young boys playing soccer on the open floor.

On the north coast, we had trouble finding suitable housing in any of the villages. In the end, I found a suite of six rooms in a very large eighteenth-century house in the sleepy town of Lambayeque, which had once been a capital of the province. When we were there, the population was only about thirteen thousand. The house was run by a lady who lived there with her adult son and who served the townspeople as a sort of lawyer without degree, fixing every kind of business. It proved lucky for us because she was able to arrange the rental of furniture, the acquisition of servants (her goddaughters) so Bunny could work, and a variety of other useful contacts. She always said, "I know everyone in this country, from the peons in the field up to the president of the republic."

It happened one day that the prime minister was coming to dedicate a new electric power station, and the mayor saw me in the street and gave me an invitation to the dinner that was to follow at a military and civilian club. Just before dinner, the distinguished guest and the hosts paraded to the power house up the freshly repaved street in front of our palatial old house. Only men were invited to the dinner and were in the entourage, but the women, including our landlady, Bunny, and the maids with our children, watched from the doorways. As the prime minister passed the house where we lived, the landlady rushed into the street and hugged him. After that, whenever she repeated her mantra, "I know everyone in this country, from the peons in the field up to the president of the republic," she would add, "Remember how the prime minister left the parade to embrace me in the doorway!"

The secretary of the Fulbright commission, Indacoechea, and I got along well. Among the many things I needed for my research, he always sought to get me what I most wanted, especially if he saw mutual advantage in it. For instance, I do not know of other Fulbright scholars who ever had the use of a late-model automobile. However, for Indacoechea, it was a way of tying up Fulbright commission counterpart funds, which had to be spent in local currency, in something whose value depreciated less than the inflating currency itself. Thus, Indacoechea negotiated for me to contribute a small amount from my incidental allowances toward the cost of a two-year-old Chevrolet that had been imported into Peru for a diplomat who was leaving. I affixed a Wayne State University College of Medicine sticker to the car, and for some years afterward, visitors to Lima told me that they had seen that car in Lima, identified by the sticker, with the secretary's son driving it.

During our yearlong stay on the north coast of Peru, I made anthropometric measurements and observations with Bunny's assistance in several different communities to show some of the variation within a small region. I was thus also able to approach some of the same problems I had looked at in Mexico, but since there had been virtually no international migration, that most important aspect of my earlier work on Chinese and Mexicans could not be included. However, we undertook some additional studies. I collected samples of blood for blood group studies, and we found that two individuals had the sickle-cell trait, the first demonstration that this genetic condition of presumably African origin occurs in populations of mixed ancestry in Peru.

Many people of African descent had been brought to Peru, and Saña, a nearby town, was well known in the area as being heavily populated with people of mixed African ancestry.

It was in San José, Peru, that I noted the high frequency of a few surnames, concluded that it resulted from isolation and inbreeding, and collected lists of names for the specific purpose of studying the genetic structure of populations. Subsequently, I borrowed or devised a number of approaches to the use of surnames in analyzing population structure and applied them to data from Peru, Mexico, England, the United States, Italy, and Denmark.

Toward the end of our stay in Peru, Indacoechea asked me for suggestions about who might come the following year. Paul Baker had done his research up to then on heat stress in American soldiers in the United States. It occurred to me that he was at a stage in his career when "real" anthropological fieldwork would appeal. He turned out to be just the right kind of person and the proposed place of research, Cuzco, just the right university to sponsor it. Indacoechea had dealings with every Peruvian university except that of Cuzco, and it was difficult for him to deal with the rector there, because Indacoechea had once been secretary of education in the regime of a conservative dictator, and the rector of the University of Cuzco had a reputation as a radical. However, the rector was a physician who had once published a paper on an ancient skull, so we could be considered as having a mutual interest in physical anthropology.

Left to right: Bunny Kaplan, Gabriel Lasker, Paul Baker, and Thelma Baker, 1996. Paul Baker is one of those most responsible for the development of human adaptation studies. His numerous former students at Pennsylvania State University also have gone on to prominence in research of physiological variables of humans in different environments. Thelma and Bunny are professional anthropologists much of whose work was carried out at a time when it was largely credited to their husbands. (Photo by Mark Weiss.)

This served as an excuse for Indacoechea to get us together. The real purpose, however, was to arrange a setting for Baker's work. The opportunity was apparently right for Baker, too. He was in a position to supplement his Fulbright grant with substantial funds that would allow him to train students in high-altitude physiology in the Andes in Peru.

It was through my many experiences with Baker, Michael Little, Roberto Frisancho, and the others who had been with Baker in Peru that I came to feel so much at home with the Penn State group. That led to subsequent associations with some of their graduates, such as Alice James and Douglas Crews, with both of whom I have collaborated in research.

During our year in Peru, we were based on the north coast, hundreds of miles away from the capital, and our associations with Peruvian anthropologists were limited. On a Fulbright exchange in Chile, we lectured at the National University but were there only for two weeks. Thus, my experiences with anthropologists in these countries and elsewhere in South America are largely the result of reading their work. That is enough to give me the impression that there are individuals who are eager and hard at work but generally laboring under the same limitations as I have mentioned in respect to Mexico.

16

Meetings and Congresses

The Wenner-Gren Foundation bought an eleventh-century castle, Burg Wartenstein, in Austria. It was part of the string of fortresses and fortified churches built to defend Christendom from the Mongol hordes. The inner court was medieval, and the dungeon had walls several meters thick at the base, but much of the old fortress had been updated repeatedly over the years, in the nineteenth century with walls of rounded stones and more recently with battlements of cinder block covered in concrete. The foundation equipped it for international conferences by converting the stable block into sleeping rooms. The great hall was decorated with armor. Paul Fejos acquired the armor at the national pawn shop where, he said, old families would pawn heirlooms that they could not bring themselves to sell outright. I went to conferences at the castle on three occasions: in 1960 to discuss the teaching of anthropology, in 1964 to found the International Association of Biological Anthropology, and in 1975 to discuss molecular anthropology when that concept was first being introduced. At those conferences, one got to know many of the other participants well. The participants were together all their waking hours for a full week and not just the limited hours of formal sessions.

There was ample to drink at the cocktail hour and at dinner. Once, Paul Fejos complained bitterly to me when someone had taken a bottle from the bar to the dormitory in the former stables. I told him that he was responsible for the atmosphere that fostered such behavior by being so liberal with drinks at the times and in the places of his choosing.

The foundation imposed a rigid structure on the meetings. Time for recreation such as an operetta in Vienna or a walk in the mountains was tightly controlled, and the hosts took exception if members absented themselves at other times, such as for a walk to drink beer in the Gasthaus in the nearest village.

Family members were not welcome except for one festive evening when there was a gala dance with a few musicians in traditional Tyrolean costume.

Participants who were attending a conference during their university holiday as part of a longer family summer excursion had to leave their families in the village of Glognitz at the foot of the mountain. There was really nothing to do in Glognitz. When Bunny was there with our children, she took the occasion to improve her German by sitting in front of the TV at every meal—a good way to learn a language. An exception in living arrangements at the castle was made for one distinguished English social anthropologist, Meyer Fortes, who was on his honeymoon and was allowed to stay in the dungeon with his new bride. When Morris Goodman, who is on the faculty of the Wayne anatomy department with me, organized the conference on molecular anthropology with Richard Tashian, a University of Michigan geneticist, I advised them to make Tashian's wife the recorder, so she was able to be at the castle with her husband and serve as managing editor for the book of proceedings.

I always enjoyed small conferences such as those I attended at the castle. On the other hand, I did not find the big international congresses, such as the International Congress of Anthropological and Ethnological Sciences or the International Congress of Americanists, as rewarding. Once, at an International Congress of Human Genetics in Paris, I was the last person on the program. The chairman did not even call on me for my paper, and I had to stand up, introduce myself, and say that I had a paper on the program and had come to deliver it. The few people left in the auditorium paid scant attention. Other anthropologists have complained of similar disappointments at large international meetings.

At an International Congress of Americanists in Philadelphia in 1956, the hosts had thoughtfully arranged to have a barrel of beer on tap in a convenient lobby of the University Museum. It was an inexpensive gesture, relative to other items on the budget, and proved to be a very successful focus for conferees to get to know one another and come to grips with professional questions without having to be on guard and show off what they know, as happens at the formal presentations of too many prepared papers. That was the first anthropological congress in the United States that Soviet anthropologists attended, and the three of them there were the center of much attention. At that time, I could not have imagined that American researchers of my acquaintance, such as Michael H. Crawford, would one day be working effectively with colleagues in Siberia, for instance.

On another occasion, Sol Tax and Margaret Mead arranged a huge Congress of Anthropological and Ethnological Sciences in Chicago and instructed participants not to read their papers, which were to be printed in advance. At the congress, we were only to discuss the papers. Fortunately, again with some aid from the Wenner-Gren Foundation, Elizabeth Watts and Frank Johnston organized a precongress conference on biological anthropology in Detroit, and I arranged for the participants to give their papers there and get to know one another in an informal atmosphere. Many of the delegates reported that the three days in Detroit were more rewarding than the week in Chicago. Since all the papers were published in preliminary form and distributed beforehand, the sessions at the congress in Chicago were to be given over solely to discussions. Many of the foreign delegates were upset by this and felt committed, some by the terms of their travel grants, to "giving" their papers.

I chaired the last biological anthropology discussion session on the final evening of the congress. We were supposed to discuss nearly sixty papers in the one hour and were provided with simultaneous translations in four languages. After telling the Americans that they were hosts and that only the papers of foreign guests would be discussed, I went to each of the foreign delegations and asked it to select one paper for discussion. At the beginning of the hour, it took me some minutes to assist William Stini, who was in the chair for the previous hour, to stop one of his speakers who was trying to say everything she had come to say. Of course, in the time left, I had to cut off almost all the speakers in my session after a mere five minutes each. In the end, I was able to adjourn the session to a television studio that a friend of Margaret Mead's had established. Television was still

something of a novelty, and some of the delegates who otherwise
would have had no opportunity to speak were proud to be able to do
so in front of the camera, but in fact I do not think the program was
ever aired.

After Paul Fejos's death, his widow, Lita Osmundsen, became
director of research of the Wenner-Gren Foundation, and she carried
on the conferences. I greatly admire what the foundation accomplished under her direction. Eventually, however, running the hotel
functions became too burdensome and expensive, the castle was sold,
and conferences now are held at different venues. The School of
American Studies in Santa Fe has facilities for small anthropological
conferences, and one I attended there was well managed. However,
organizers of conferences there have to find their own financing.

Even very small grants from the Wenner-Gren Foundation served
extremely well. For instance, I once obtained about a hundred dollars
to pay for some beer and soft drinks to smuggle to my hotel suite,
where I had to greet more than a score of foreign participants the
evening before the scientific session of a meeting. Even for more
serious grants, the speed of decisions and the flexibility contrasted
with the burden of obtaining money from federal agencies, which,
as a result of the grant-making processes, often eventually require a
larger budget for a comparable benefit.

The belief that meetings like the old summer seminars are the
best has stuck with me. One time, I wrapped a three-week intensive
course in methods for advanced graduate students around the dates
of the annual meeting of the American Association of Physical Anthropologists and invited some distinguished presenters, including
my friends Geoffrey Harrison, James Tanner, Derek Roberts, and
Frank Johnston, among others, to come early for that meeting or
to stay afterward for several days. Morris Goodman made the arrangements for a variety of laboratory demonstrations and exercises.
Many of those who attended made permanent associations with one
another and with some of the teachers who had come, notably with
those from Britain. The late Elizabeth Watts, during a distinguished
career at Tulane University doing research at the primate center there,
always included that three-week course in listing her educational
attainments. She kept in touch with the others who had attended,
visited those who had come from England, and for many years after
served the Society for the Study of Human Biology, which has headquarters in Britain, as liaison officer for North America. A student in

that course who came from England was Anthony J. Boyce, who has since been a key member of the faculty of biological anthropology at Oxford University and also manages a position of great responsibility in one of the oldest Oxford Colleges, St. Johns.

There were about thirty-five students, and, with very few exceptions, they went on to careers in research and teaching of some aspect of human biology. A few examples will suffice. Roberto Frisancho is Professor of Anthropology at the University of Michigan and a mainstay of the Growth Center there. Ralph Garruto rose through the ranks of researchers at the National Institutes of Health, is a member of the National Academy of Science, and is now starting a career as a university professor. Robert Halberstein, who was then a student of Michael Crawford, with whom he published repeatedly, is Professor of Anthropology at Miami University. Moses Schanfield, who was a student at the University of Michigan, has had a scientific career largely outside academia; he runs a molecular genetics company, his scientific research continues, and he is one of the founding forces behind the establishment of an Anthropological Genetics Association. And Mark Weiss, who was a student at the University of California, returned to Wayne State, where he is Professor of Anthropology when not on leave as a program officer of the National Science Foundation. I ran into Theodora Tsongas at the 1996 meeting of the American Anthropological Association. She is back in academia after a gap, in a program in environmental sciences and regional planning at Washington State University, and she had kept in touch with several others she met at the course, including Lowell Sever, another anthropologist who left academia for the larger world beyond the universities.

The course on methods in human biology was viewed as such a success that despite my general reluctance to get involved in administrative matters, I tried again. In 1974, Brunetto Chiarelli, who is now Professor of Anthropology at the University of Florence, had been named director of the School of Human Biology in Erice, Sicily. Chiarelli, one of the most effective organizers of human biology in Europe, is very experienced at managing the mechanics of conferences, and I volunteered to deal with the curriculum, staff, and recruiting some of the students for a course in Erice. The topic selected was "Demographic Aspects of Human Biology," and the National Science Foundation and the science education arm of NATO helped with funds. Again, there were very worthwhile associations among the presenters. For instance, Kenneth Weiss, now one of the most prominent authorities on the evolutionary biology of human disease, and Ryk Ward, a distinguished New Zealand geneticist who is now Professor of Biological Anthropology at the University of Oxford, got together to write a book. I came to know better and appreciate several of the presenters, notably Henry Harpending, who later made important contributions to human evolutionary genetic theory in Ken Weiss's department at Penn State and is now at the University of Utah. At Erice, he helped me keep my little Fiat car running; I gathered that in his fieldwork in Africa, he was the member of the expedition who was the vehicle mechanic. It is nice to know that a theoretical geneticist can be so practical. Of most significance to me was establishing relationships with some of the student participants, such as Pamela Raspe and David Coleman, with both of whom I subsequently conducted joint research in England.

The meeting at Erice was not without mishaps, however. Donna Leonetti's car was stolen, with all her PhD thesis material in it. Fortunately, she had the courage to finish and has been doing interesting studies of diabetes mellitus among Japanese living in America.

Henry Harpending and Gabriel Lasker. Harpending is a molecular anthropologist and a member of the National Academy of Sciences. He has applied ingenious models using timing and population sizes to try to determine to what extent modern human beings replaced or mixed with earlier populations.

Also in Erice, we misplaced our daughter, Anne. At age fourteen, she did not want to hang around while we worked, so we arranged for her to take in a series of two-week holidays for English youngsters. The first was on a sailboat near Portsmouth, the second a college course in calligraphy at York, the third a dramatics program near Abington, and the last one a youth hostel trip up the Rhine with English schoolgirls. She managed all the transfers, although at one point she took a train to Scotland by mistake and another time ran out of cash and had to borrow from a stranger. However, when she was supposed to arrive at the airport at Palermo in Sicily to join us at Erice, she was not on the plane, and she was not there the next day. On the third day, she was the last person off the plane, proud that she had sent an (undelivered) telegram to explain that we had not left her enough time to get to Brussels for the plane on which we had booked her. Fortunately, we had with us our second son, Ted, who had been with an archaeological party in Italy and who reassured us that Anne could manage, as, fortunately, she did.

17

Personalities

Rumors about John Buettner-Janusch were always a stock in trade. He seemed to stimulate antagonisms. No doubt, he had his friends, and he ingratiated himself with others, but there were many he rubbed the wrong way, and, of course, they talked about him to anyone who would listen. One was an orthopedic surgeon named Charles Goff of Hartford, Connecticut, who was interested in anthropological problems. Stan Garn describes Goff as "an ex-cavalry officer married to a Russian princess who got the Swann tool company to build el cheapo anthropometers." Anthropology's cast of characters was always colorful, but a less expensive substitute for Swiss tools of the trade was a very down-to-earth contribution to the profession.

William C. Boyd was among the first effectively to apply blood group immunology in anthropology. At one time, he took bone specimens of cadavers of individuals of known blood group, buried them for a while, and then attempted to type the blood groups of the individuals from the bone specimens. He did not succeed, but P. B. Candela took pieces of the specimens and succeeded in typing them all. While Buettner-Janusch was a student at the University of Michigan, Charlotte Otten, Marjorie Gray, Frederick Thieme, and some others, possibly including Buettner-Janusch, worked on the technique. Later, Buettner-Janusch was at Yale, at the same time that Goff had an appointment there. On a trip to the Dominican Republic, Goff had persuaded some high official, perhaps a patient of his who was close to the dictator, Trujillo, to let him take a sample of bone from the skeleton alleged to be that of the brother of Christopher Columbus, and Goff asked Buettner-Janusch if he could blood-type it. He agreed and took the specimen. Goff was keen to have an answer and pestered Buettner-Janusch for the results. Buettner-Janusch finally told him the type, but Goff was subsequently appalled to find the specimen package still unopened on a shelf in Buettner-Janusch's office.

Buettner-Janusch apparently also had other detractors at Yale, and he left after about seven years. He seems to have had no love for Yale, because when he published his textbook, it included a brief account of his career in which he even mentioned a job at Wayne University, where he had taught an evening course while he was a student at Michigan, but there was no mention of his many years at Yale.

Those who spoke favorably of Buettner-Janusch cited his accomplishments. He and his wife, Vina, did much to show that developments in laboratory science might usefully be applied to some of the problems in primatology. For instance, I was surprised to learn from Garn that Buettner-Janusch had run a conference at which one of the most important speakers was Morris Goodman, who had recently changed jobs from the Michigan Cancer Institute to the Department of Microbiology at Wayne State University. He presented the first immunological evidence that human beings, chimpanzees, and gorillas are more closely related to one another than any of them are to orangutans, gibbons, or rhesus monkeys. Soon after I met Goodman for the first time, I arranged to publish some of his findings in *Human Biology*. I later served on a committee that advised the dean to transfer Goodman's appointment to the anatomy department, where he remains a valued colleague with whom I still often discuss such topics as primate taxonomy.

Buettner-Janusch had a reputation for imaginative budgeting. It is said that in 1952, when he had been in charge of an archaeological party as a student, the other students complained of the interminable diet of beans, while Buettner-Janusch paid his wife well for cooking the beans and ended the summer with the program's car. When he was in charge of the local committee for an annual meeting of the American Association of Physical Anthropologists in Durham, North Carolina, the registration fee was two and a half times that of the previous year.

143

Morris Goodman, one of the
first to apply the methods of
molecular biology to primate
systematics, in his laboratory at
Wayne State University, 1997.

Later, Buettner-Janusch was charged with and convicted of man-
ufacturing and selling illegal pychoactive drugs from his laboratory at
New York University. While he was out on parole, the judge who had
presided at his trial received some candy in the mail. The judge's wife
sampled it but survived the attempted poisoning. Several different
poisonous substances were identified in the candy. It seems to me
that a clever person, if he is in his right mind, would know that each
additional poison would make it easier to identify the perpetrator. He
was convicted of the attempt and eventually died in the penitentiary.
Part of the tragedy is that Buettner-Janusch was a pioneer in stress-
ing the importance of modern genetics and primatology in physical
anthropology.

The history of physical anthropology is full of accomplishments
by physicians in various branches of medicine who were self-trained
in anthropology. Ales Hrdlicka, considered to be the father of physical anthropology in America, comes immediately to mind. It was
Hrdlicka who founded the AAPA and, largely with his own funds,
the *American Journal of Physical Anthropology*, still the most important
periodical in the field. Hrdlicka was so convinced that a medical education was essential to being a physical anthropologist that he paid
to send several recruits for the field through medical school. Of them,
T. Dale Stewart is the only one who remained an anthropologist, and
Stewart was fully appreciative of Hrdlicka and his accomplishments
in anthropology.

There is no doubt that his lifetime of long days in the field and in the bone lab also led to Hrdlicka being the first to report several aspects of bone and tooth morphology. For instance, he was the first to provide a useful description of shovel-shaped incisors. But he was dogmatic, and some of his interpretations are controversial. Hooton once likened Hrdlicka to Horatio at the bridge, figuratively defending the Bering Strait and holding off attempts of humans to cross from Asia to America. He published rebuttals of each claim for the early appearance of humans in the New World. Many skeletons unearthed in the Americas that were claimed to be old were neither documented as being so nor different in any significant way from more recent American Indians. The ability to date specimens has been revolutionized since Hrdlicka's death, and with it our knowledge of the peopling of the Americas, but many of his interpretations have been confirmed.

Hrdlicka had strong views on other aspects of the science. At a meeting of the American Association of Physical Anthropologists, he once stated that "statistics will be the ruination of the science." In 1929, Raymond Pearl started another journal, *Human Biology*, to accommodate types of articles that fell outside the range that Hrdlicka thought appropriate for the journal he edited. Hrdlicka thought that the proper study for physical anthropologists concerned the morphology of bones themselves, and he was said to have destroyed significant cultural context by the way he removed skeletons from archaeological sites in the Aleutian Islands. In the Smithsonian Museum, he sorted the femora, pelves, skulls, and so on, separately in such a way that his successors there have found it difficult to reassemble skeletons for holistic study such as paleopathology projects. Unlike Hooton, or even Boas, Hrdlicka had little impact through students. Dale Stewart was a real disciple, but among others, I know only that Paul Gebhard and Marcus Goldstein spent time with Hrdlicka at the museum, and William Laughlin was with him in Alaska.

Laughlin has one other distinction: he is, insofar as I know, the only professional physical anthropologist who was a student of Ashley Montagu. Some, including Straus, used to run Montagu's work down, because he spent little time on a research project before publication, and his work was considered slipshod. However, recently, Montagu has received recognition for his contribution to the realm of ideas and their dissemination to a wider public. C. Loring Brace, Professor of Anthropology at the University of Michigan, spoke appreciatively about Montagu when he was presented the

Darwin Prize of the American Association of Physical Anthropologists in 1997.

Brace himself writes well and has a knack for selecting a few variables, such as two dimensions of teeth, and using them to explicate much about the whole of human evolution. Brace's colleague at the University of Michigan, Frank Livingstone, has the same ability with quite different variables, especially the hemoglobin variants. Together with other colleagues such as Spuhler and Thieme in the early days and Garn, Frisancho, and Milford Wolpoff more recently, they have made the University of Michigan a major center for physical anthropology.

During the first few years of the Viking Fund Summer Seminars, I worked very closely with Sherry Washburn editing the *Yearbook*. For

A get-together at the home of James Silverberg during a meeting of the American Association of Physical Anthropologists in Milwaukee. Robert Meier (left) is known for his studies of fingerprints. When used for identification of individuals, emphasis is placed on the patterns on individual fingers, but Meier (as well as Derek Roberts and others) placed emphasis on the relationship of the pattern on each finger to those on all the others. Silverberg (second from left) is a cultural anthropologist who has furthered applications of anthropology to welfare. C. Loring Brace (second from right), one of the last students of E. A. Hooton, is also one of the few physical anthropologists who has studied the history of ideas in the field. Through measurements of huge numbers of teeth, he also has shown that there has been a gradual evolutionary trend to reduction in the size of human molar teeth. Lasker is on the right.

some reason, in 1948, I was in charge of sending out the invitations to the seminar. It was the year Le Gros Clark came, and it was the first time some of the Americans had heard him. Jim Tanner, then in Alice Stewart's famous Department of Social Medicine at Oxford University, heard about it and wanted to come, so the Viking Fund invited him, too.

Others who came to one or another of the seminars included Kenneth Oakley and Raymond A. Dart. When Solly (later Lord) Zuckerman came, he said something about *Australopithecus* that we thought untrue. Bunny had recorded it in her shorthand notes and reported it in the proceedings. Zuckerman was annoyed and, after the *Yearbook* published it, stated that he never said it.

The one important figure in physical anthropology of the time whom I did not meet was Robert Broom. He had been in the United States during the war, and Bunny had heard him speak at Hunter College in New York, but he had not gone to any of the American Association of Physical Anthropologists meetings that I attended. Once, he was in the United States at the time of a meeting of the AAPA in Philadelphia. I was secretary, and the executive committee met the evening before in the home of Carl Coon, a member. Broom had just conducted successful fieldwork under the sponsorship of Wendell Phillips, and someone, presumably Phillips, offered to have Broom come to the meeting to talk about the new finds.

Phillips himself had a bachelor's degree in anthropology. During the war years, he was exempt from military service because of handicaps from childhood polio. He had a reputation as a slick persuader and is said to have excavated Yayoi graves in Japan right after the war and to have used a military plane to send the objects to the United States while veterans with their priority numbers for discharge from the Army were waiting for the same transport. While doing anthropological work in Arabia, Phillips is reported to have negotiated oil leases so valuable that the seven leading oil companies combined to acquire them from him.

During the war, Coon served in the OSS. He obviously was sent to North Africa or the Arabian Peninsula, because he once boasted and laughed about booby-trapping toilet seats and hams since no Arab would use either and only Germans would trigger the fuses. Perhaps Coon and Phillips crossed paths then, or perhaps Coon had some interest in the oil or in friendship with the sheikhs Phillips was courting. In any case, at our committee meeting, Coon stated that we should not invite Broom because of his relationship with Phillips, and if we did, he (Coon) would resign. The executive committee was then an old boys' club, many of them former Hooton students, and we assumed that Coon had good reasons and agreed. Broom was told that the program had been completed in advance, which was true. However, George Barbour, a geologist who had also been in South Africa, was given time at the end of a planned session, and he showed slides of sites and prospective sites seen on his trip. He had lots of slides and took more time than those on the program were allotted.

In 1962, when he had just published *The Origin of Races*, Coon was the president and I was the vice president of the AAPA. Some reviewers found Coon's book offensively racist, especially the introduction. Furthermore, Carleton Putnam, then president of Delta Airlines, had just published a scurrilous pamphlet about race and attacked Ashley Montagu by name and also other Jews for their leadership and support of the movement for racial equality. From the details in Putnam's pamphlet, it was clear that he must have had help from someone who was in on all the rumors that went around among physical anthropologists about Montagu's education. It must have been Coon, because he was given to broad offhand statements and, if phoned, perhaps in the middle of the night, might have said those things. Furthermore, Coon and Putnam shared the name Carleton and were assumed by some to be cousins. Putnam may have presumed upon some real or assumed relationship. Be that as it may, Coon told the executive committee, "He's no relative of mine." I do not recall any direct denial of his having talked to Putnam, but that was the implication, although now it is known that they corresponded. The next day at the business meeting, Edward I. Fry proposed a motion on race, but as there was a discussion of the wording, Coon adjourned the meeting and appointed Fry, Garn, and Josef Brozek to word a resolution to present to a special business meeting convened to act on it. The motion condemned such writing as "Race and Reason" (the title of the Putnam pamphlet). Only Coon spoke against the motion. Marshall Newman was the incoming vice president, and, recalling that Coon had once before threatened to resign, I took Newman aside to remind him that if that happened, I wanted no confusion. Under the terms of the bylaws, I remained in office as vice president until the close of the business meeting, and I would assume the chair.

The vote for the resolution was something like ninety-one "aye" and one "nay." Other anthropologists no doubt agreed in part with

Coon's opinions about race, of course. Coon, Garn, and Birdsell had written a book about races that describes human geographic variation, and Edward E. Hunt Jr. assisted Coon with data for a later book, but nobody joined Coon in the vote against the motion, and Coon stormed out of the room. Larry Angel went out after him. Angel was a Quaker and was always in favor of resolving disagreements. Furthermore, he was the only one of my former fellow students who seemed never to give up entirely on racial types as a way of organizing human biological variation. Angel brought Coon back in, but Coon went to the front and simply stated, "I resign," and left again. He never came to a meeting of the association again. In fact, I have been told that he never went back to the anthropology department at the University of Pennsylvania. He left Philadelphia, retired to his home in Marblehead, Massachusetts, and lived there the rest of his life. Nineteen years ago, I proposed making a book out of some lectures I had given. A publisher sent my proposal out for review, and one of the reviewers was Coon. He did not like my approach and the fact that points were not backed up with scores of supposedly supportive references, as in his own works.

Coon was a person with a great store of memory. For years, there was a television program called *What in the World?* with odd artifacts from the storage vaults of museums presented for identification by the panelists. Archaeologists are concerned with material culture, and Frol Rainey also participated. Coon was a star and was able to identify all manner of oddments. Ralph Linton was good at those identifications of cultural materials, too. Most anthropologists now have little museum experience in their training, and an interest in material cultures, usually limited to local areas, is left for archaeologists.

Race and racism were always among my concerns. In 1954, while I was secretary of Section H (Anthropology) of the American Association for the Advancement of Science, the annual meeting was scheduled to be held in Atlanta, Georgia, in hotels that were segregated and for whites only. Provisions had been made for "Negroes" only for the scientific sessions. Bunny persuaded me that I should neither attend nor organize the program for such a meeting. The one African American of recognized standing in anthropology was Montague Cobb, Professor of Anatomy at Howard University. I wanted to get him involved, and someone nominated him for chairman of the section. As such, he would also be a vice president of the association. There were several candidates, and it took two or three ballots for him to get a majority. I had thought that virtually all anthropologists would favor full integration of the meetings and that with a black officer, our course would be persuasive. I wrote to the executive director of the association stating that some of our members (initially, that was Bunny, but there were many later) would not attend a meeting where informal gatherings of all members would be impossible in the official hotels, and that I would not organize an anthropological program. He counterproposed that the anthropology section meet at Morehouse, a college for Negroes (as African Americans were called at the time) in Atlanta.

Margaret Mead was on the executive board of the AAAS, and I wrote a similar letter to her. To my surprise, she did not back me up. She replied that she would look into it, and later she wrote me that she had talked with five prominent Negroes and that four of them thought we would do more good by attending. Cobb would not say that he would not go, but I do not think he did. One of the concerns of the executive director was whether the officers' dinner could be held in the segregated hotel, as he would have preferred, or whether it should be moved to Morehouse College so Cobb could attend.

A resolution never to meet again at a place where all the members could not participate fully in both formal and informal activities was presented to the council of the AAAS during the Atlanta meetings, probably not by an anthropologist but by Dr. Plough, secretary of the botany section. I recently learned that Cobb had graduated from Amherst, a small college where Plough was one of the professors and would almost certainly have known all the students in his courses. The council decided not to vote on the resolution while the association was a guest in Atlanta but to submit the resolution to all the fellows. Following the Atlanta meetings, it was circulated as a mail ballot and passed decisively. This was reported in the *New York Times* and perhaps locally in Atlanta. The Atlanta convention industry wanted the end of racial segregation in the hotels. Shortly afterward, that happened, and the hotels in Atlanta were integrated well before the civil rights movement integrated hotels, restaurants, and other public facilities throughout the rest of the South.

18

Associates

One way for me to explore personal influences is to review associations with some of those with whom I have done joint research and to think about those we have sought out (or who have sought us out) at the three or more professional meetings we attend each year. I notice that in recent years, an increasing proportion of my publications are with joint authors. There are three reasons. First, there is an increasing tendency toward collaborative research in all fields of science. Second, I am more aware than formerly of the significance of the role of others in whatever I do. And third, I am more dependent on others, especially for the collection of data.

Since my university appointment has been in an anatomy department, I have not been directing PhD students of anthropology. Nevertheless, I have been involved in joint work with some students. Roy Fernandez was a tragic dropout from society who had bouts of mental illness. He did a research project involving the ability to taste PTC, a substance some people can taste at very low concentrations and others, presumably with a hereditary different taste capacity, do not taste even in concentrated dilutions. In 1972, I also gave some of the PTC to my son Robert so that he could test some schoolmates by the serial dilution method, and two years later, my son Edward retested some of the same students. The results seemed to indicate that some tasters may become nontasters over time, and vice versa. The ability to taste PTC has always been assumed to be a strictly hereditary permanent condition, but from my sons' experience, I think that the assumption should be examined by a longitudinal study testing the taste ability of children and youths over a period of years.

I also have done bits of research with students at other universities than my own and have attempted to encourage and have been stimulated in turn by young (virtually everyone now seems young) anthropologists elsewhere. Pamela Raspe was a student at Cambridge University, but was under the supervision of Tony Boyce at Oxford, when we first looked at some data of hers in 1978, and she made an analysis of population relationships from surnames of the population of the Scilly Isles. Although she is now interested in important problems of child development, we continue to work together on aspects of surname isonymy when we have a chance. She has a skill I lack: she writes the computer programs to answer the questions that arise.

Raspe's thinking sometimes outdistances my ability to follow. Recently, James F. Crow devised a formula that allowed us to make inferences about the probable past movements of related individuals from the distribution of surnames. Raspe then sent me the results of an application to British data and a comparison with other methods expressed in formulas with different mathematical symbols, and I had the task of writing up the results. I complained to Bunny that it was hard to write a paper about something I did not quite understand, and she had us both laughing by pointing out that I had been doing that all my working life. It brought to mind the time when I wrote abstracts for *Biological Abstracts* in every field of biology whether I knew much about it or not, and also the time Charles Windsor added an appendix that I could not understand to a paper of mine that he published.

It is hard to believe, but C. G. N. Mascie-Taylor, the head of the Department of Biological Anthropology at Cambridge University, had not yet submitted his thesis when we first worked together on one of the more than thirty projects on which we have collaborated. He is a person of enormous energy and has the capacity to keep multiple research projects with different sets of coworkers all going forward simultaneously.

When I was studying surnames, a number of other people also came forward with data to apply to resolving questions about the genetic structure of populations. Besides researchers in London and

Oxford, and Raspe and Mascie-Taylor in Cambridge, they included cultural anthropologists such as R. K. Wetherington and Robert Van Kemper; physical anthropologists with an interest in historical problems, such as Theodore Steegmann Jr. of SUNY at Buffalo; Alice James, then a student at Penn State; and an English genealogist, D. A. Palgrave. Eventually, Mascie-Taylor arranged for me to publish a synthesis, *Surnames and Genetic Structure.*

As for those I have looked forward to seeing at the annual meetings of the American Association of Physical Anthropologists, the American Anthropological Association, the Central States Anthropological Society, the Human Biology Council (now the Human Biology Association), the American Association for the Advancement of Science, and others that have not been an annual routine, the numbers are large. Not counting brief pleasantries, in meetings some ten days a year for fifty years, I must have conversed at some length with six or more people a day. Many of those three thousand or more conversations have been with the same few people, but others involved introductions to new people and new ideas. We always tried to share a meal with Fred and Leone Hulse and often with Fred and Jean Thieme. I had visited Larry and Peggy Angel while I was in Civilian Public Service as a conscientious objector and feeling the need of moral support. Bill Pollitzer is always asked to give the reports of resolutions committees, because he lards them with puns on the members' names and with many jokes. More important, perhaps, those of us who know him well count on him with his constant good humor to try to defuse the kinds of petty disagreements that inevitably arise as these kinds of institutions grow.

Over the years, we enjoyed many a quiet lunch or a drink with Sherry Washburn, and we would discuss the state of the science and the directions and prospects for the future. He and I have agreed on most of the issues that have faced physical anthropology over the years: the problem with "race" as the unit for organizing human biological variability and the value of organic evolution for understanding temporal variation. However, our attitudes toward editing are somewhat different. Washburn does not like to publish views that he thinks are wrong. On two occasions, he advised publishers against publishing books that promoted ideas with which both Sherry and I disagreed but which I thought should be published and he did not. On my recommendation, both were published. One thoroughly summarizes and winds up a subject that I think has run its course.

The other is a Freudian approach to the origin of human culture. Whatever their impact on trends of thought, both were publishing successes, and one of them was a book club selection.

When Washburn was the editor of the *American Journal of Physical Anthropology*, he found it somewhat frustrating to be in charge of a refereed journal whose content was largely determined by the nature of the manuscripts submitted and the opinions of reviewers. Washburn would have preferred a more proactive role, commissioning accounts and good photographs of every significant paleoanthropological find. I know he went out of the way to get Raymond Dart to submit the important articles describing Dart's fossil finds at Makapan in South Africa to the *American Journal of Physical Anthropology*. Washburn once said that the field of physical anthropology should have two journals, *Human Evolution*, which he would edit, and *Human Biology*, which I would. He never realized his wish, but I got mine and continued as the editor for a long while.

Sherwood L. Washburn, professor emeritus, University of California. His emphasis on function in mammalian anatomy and primate behavior largely determined the direction of physical anthropology after World War II. It would be difficult to overestimate his influence on his contemporaries in the profession.

19

Biological Anthropology in Britain

*A*s a boy of fourteen, I had been taken to Europe to visit relatives. I did not go again for a long while, but Bunny was very interested to go, and in the 1960s and since then, we have traveled to Europe many times. On one trip, we visited Bunny's nursemaid in a tiny village, Killofin, Labasheeda, on the tidal River Shannon in Ireland. Across the road from the house was a creamery, and beyond the creamery lay the river. What impressed me was that the farmers who clattered down the street with their horses and carts to wake me each morning must have been poor, because each one had only one or, at most, two cans of milk. Finally, one came with a tractor pulling a trailer with ten or more cans. At breakfast, I remarked to our hostess about this one apparently affluent man with a herd of cows. "Oh, no," she replied in her broad brogue. "That man goes around and collects milk from those families who have only one cow and not enough milk to spare to be worth taking to the creamery themselves."

As editor of the *Yearbook of Physical Anthropology*, I had been receiving reprints and reading journals from England and elsewhere throughout the world, and I felt that I knew many of the authors even before we met in person. When we went to England, Kenneth Oakley, at the British Museum, showed me the Rhodesian skull from Broken Hill. There seems to be so much variation among the fossil human skulls from Africa that it still presents something of an enigma.

Derek F. Roberts and Gabriel Lasker in an English park. Roberts's indefatigable energy in research in human biology and genetics has resulted in many major findings, beginning with his early work on the world distribution of human traits that showed their functional significance relative to climates.

Geoffrey A. and Elizabeth Harrison. Geoffrey has conducted many studies of local populations in England and abroad, including pioneering studies of the biochemistry of stress in ordinary populations. He created an important training and research institute of biological anthropology at Oxford University.

My first trip to Oxford was particularly rewarding. I met Joe Weiner, whom I later came to admire for his leadership in the inter-disciplinary use of physiological variables in anthropological studies, something I had wanted to do but never accomplished. W. E. Le Gros Clark spent much of a day with me in the Department of Anatomy. His works on embryology, primatology, and human paleontology stand up well in the face of all the subsequent improvements in methods and vast expansion of studies. I also met Derek Roberts. He was always interested in furthering the research of others and serving the international fraternity of biological anthropologists, so I added him to the editorial board of *Human Biology* in 1961. Roberts has many skills, such as use of foreign languages and mathematics, that complement his knowledge of anthropology and genetics. On the editorial board and in other editorial capacities, Roberts takes great pains to correct the defects in manuscripts, especially of those for whom English is not the first language and those by students. During this period, I also met Geoffrey Ainsworth Harrison. Like most other graduates of Oxford and Cambridge I have known, he writes easily understood and gracious English prose. He once confided in me that part of the share of the work his coauthors always relegate to him is the writing up of their reports.

The contribution of British biological anthropologists to the definition of the field may be exemplified by an experience I had during a Wenner-Gren Foundation conference in 1964 at its Austrian castle, Burg Wartenstein, to consider the organization of an international society. Harrison and Weiner were there, and Weiner spoke up for the British contingent, which was the most effective one. To get away from sterile subjects such as race and toward more meaningful topics, the British were adamant that the science be called *human biology* rather than *anthropology*. The continental Europeans tried to argue that the terms are synonymous, but the latter suggests the older interests in "racial" origins. Santiago Genoves from Mexico and Paul T. Baker from the United States wanted a designation that would identify transdisciplinary breadth. In the end, since the title should be in the two UNESCO languages, English and French, I suggested that the French term for human biology could be slightly different from the English one; it was agreed to call it *human biology* in English and *anthropobiologie* in French.

During World War II, a group of anthropologists in the Department of Anatomy at Oxford University were engaged in projects applying anthropometry to problems of military equipment design. The Laboratory of Anthropology continued after the war until Professor Le Gros Clark retired. The incoming professor of anatomy at Oxford, G. W. Harris, a neuroscientist, apparently had no interest in the continuance of anthropological research, and the significant work begun there by Weiner and Roberts ceased. Weiner took a post

Chapter 19

at the London School of Hygiene and Tropical Medicine, and Roberts accepted a post at the University of Washington in the United States. It was only later that Geoffrey Harrison came from the University of Liverpool and established in Oxford a separate Department of Biological Anthropology, of which he became professor. He carried on research on a variety of different problems, including fieldwork in several continents, and has an enormous fund of knowledge as a result and a more comprehensive view of human biology than the numerous more narrowly specialized professionals.

Among various research accomplishments, Roberts had written a very important article in the *Journal of the Royal Anthropological Institute* on basal metabolism, race, and climate that pioneered studies relating human variations to climates, but his experience in trying to initiate a research program in America was unfortunate. He apparently had expected more support from the university for his research, whereas they had expected him to undertake a heavy teaching load as well as to support his research through outside grants. In addition, Roberts came to have a low esteem of physical anthropology in America in general, and he wrote a very critical article about it in the *American Journal of Physical Anthropology*. Fortunately, the general response was to try to do better, but after a year, Roberts returned to England, where he has had a distinguished career as the head of the largest university human genetics department, the one at Newcastle upon Tyne. While Roberts was still in the United States, in 1960 or 1961, he visited us in Berkeley, California, and in that informal setting and on a trip to the Napa Valley to sample wines, we became friends.

I should mention that having come of age during Prohibition, I had shockingly limited discrimination about wine. Association with Roberts and other friends who served on the wine committees of two Cambridge University colleges has improved my taste only moderately. But the association with Roberts has provided other more important lessons. He is now engaged in editing a history of biological anthropology in many countries, and I am sure he will be looking for the worthwhile studies in the enormous volume of publication in the field. We have been serving together as editors of a series of books on biological anthropology along with Robert Foley and Nicholas Mascie-Taylor of Cambridge University, and I find that I still learn of developing areas of study in the discussions of proposals and manuscripts.

Facilities for biological anthropology in England have always been limited. For instance, when I first visited Nigel Barnicot at

Margaret Mascie-Taylor and Charles Guy Nicholas Mascie-Taylor, 1998.
He heads the Department of Biological Anthropology at the University
of Cambridge. Among his numerous publications are thirty-some books,
chapters, and articles reporting collaborative research with Lasker.

University College in London, he urged me to come in on a Saturday,
since he worked on weekends when he could borrow equipment
from the Department of Biochemistry. Others assembled materials
for study at museums, the London Zoo, and the Royal College of
Surgeons.

In 1976, Bunny and I spent a summer in London, started some
research, and, despite an extraordinarily hot season, enjoyed our stay
in the Finchley flat of Julie Flowerday, a former student of Bunny's.
Bunny began a study of the medical experiences of Asian immigrants
in Britain. I was looking for something useful to do. The faculty in
biological anthropology at University College was young and very
enthusiastic, and one of its members, David A. Coleman, had some
raw demographic data from three registration districts that he offered
for joint research with me and, eventually, a mathematician from
the City of London Polytechnic, Wendy Fox. Thus, when Bunny

and I returned to England at the beginning of 1977 for a full year's sabbatical, there was something for me to begin immediately. Derek Roberts indicated that I would be welcome at Newcastle if I wanted to be headquartered there, but I had an invitation from Geoffrey Harrison to go to Oxford, and Roberts thought I would find that congenial. Indeed, it was, since Bunny was to continue her research on the health care of Asians and nonimmigrant English in London, and we could get together for three-day weekends in Oxford, whereas Newcastle would have been too far from London for such frequent commuting.

Geoffrey Harrison and his wife, Elizabeth, put me up in their own home when I first arrived and then arranged for me a guest membership in the senior common room, the social center for members of his college, Linaker College, and housing in a flat in North Oxford. The Department (now Institute) of Biological Anthropology is located in a Victorian house some distance from the center of the university. The Department of Social Anthropology occupies a similar building across the street, but at the time Rodney Needham was its head, relations between the two departments were poor. Members of the two departments rarely visited across Banbury Road. When Bunny came to visit me in Oxford, she went over to the social anthropology department and met some medical anthropologists with whom she had mutual interests. However, the members of the two departments even drank their ale in two different pubs that faced each other across a nearby street, the North Parade, which in that inimitable British manner, is south of the South Parade. At Oxford, anthropology is a subject only for graduate study; the two departments, however, do contribute to an undergraduate program called human sciences, as do sociology, demography, and other departments.

Harrison asked me to give a series of lectures at the university. The lectures did not go well. I had not been teaching anthropology, and even when there are few of them in the room, English university students do not expect to enter into discussion as I would have preferred. However, Harrison also asked me to tutor two biochemistry undergraduates who had requested permission to do an extra "paper," as such a course is called, in biological anthropology. I took them on, since they would not have been allowed to study anthropology if I did not agree. That turned out to be a welcome experience that really introduced me to the Oxford educational system, and I am happy to report that they did well on the examination. In Oxford and

Cambridge, the college tutor prepares the students in the subject, but the one and only examination is set by a different member of the university faculty, who grades it with an outside faculty member from a different university, and the college tutor has no influence in the determination of the grade.

Harrison and his colleagues had engaged in an intensive multi-phased anthropological study of the human biology of the population of several villages near Oxford (summarized in Harrison's 1996 book, *Human Biology of the Otmoor Population*), and they provided me with data on surnames from these communities. The Otmoor is a low-lying swampy area on which the surrounding villages had ancient common rights to graze their animals. In the previous century, the duke of Marlborough started to drain and fence it for agricultural purposes. The villagers, who were considered backward and isolated, joined together and met this with violence. In recent times, people from the outside who commute to Oxford to work have moved in. Some students and faculty members at Oxford joined me in exploring what can be learned about the breeding structure of the populations from the distribution of surnames. From a number of such studies of surnames there, we were able to show the effect of the close association of the populations of the "Seven Towns of the Otmoor" and more inbreeding than is usual in rural England.

Harrison's office door was always open for me, no matter how busy he was. He and his associates were conducting the first studies of lifestyle and stress in the general population by measuring hormone levels. Although we did not work closely on the same research, we would sometimes get together at six o'clock when the local pub opened and would walk down to the North Parade to have a beer.

In the evenings, there was often music at the university or in one of the colleges, and I saw most of the historic buildings of Oxford by going to such events rather than as an ordinary tourist. One cannot help reflecting on English history when listening to classical music in the Hollywell, a small auditorium designed by Christopher Wren, the architect of St. Paul's Cathedral, London, or in the university church, with a nick in one column where a platform had been built for Cranmer to stand in the dock at his trial for heresy before he was burned at the stake.

From Friday through Sunday, Bunny would join me in Oxford, and we would go to recitals together. We noticed one man who was

161

always there sitting near the front center. Bunny whispered, "I think he is the music editor for the Oxford daily paper."

"You know," I replied, "he thinks I am the music critic for the paper."

On a trip to Cambridge to attend a seminar at the Centre for the Study of the History of Population and Social Structure, the librarian introduced me to one of the graduate students, David Souden, who volunteered to provide some historical data to give time depth to my studies of population structure through the analysis of surname distributions. The collaboration was great fun in another way. I had a car, and when we traveled anywhere with Souden, such as back and forth between Oxford and Cambridge, he always knew all the byways and the buildings of historic interest and what had happened where. By using alternative routes, I learned more about English history than I had ever learned in school. In the following eighteen years, we stayed part of each year in Cambridge. Souden was still there for the next several years, and we explored many more places together. I think that in that way, I now know more about the history of England than I do of America. One of Souden's subsequent activities, based on his knowledge of all those historic places, has been to find sites for "on location" shooting of scenes in TV productions and in movies.

By 1978, Pamela Raspe was the demonstrator in the Department of Biological Anthropology at the University of Cambridge. I first met her in 1974, when I met Coleman at the intensive course on demographic aspects of physical anthropology that Brunetto Chiarelli and I had organized at Erice in Sicily. Pamela was working on her doctoral thesis in 1977 when I met her again, and she suggested that we come to Cambridge the next summer and work with her to analyze a small part of her data. She arranged an apartment for us at Wolfson College in Cambridge, and we spent part of the summer there and part in Oxford. When he saw what Raspe and I were doing, Mascie-Taylor devised a project and invited us for the following summer. Then, the summer after that, David Souden put us up in a house belonging to Emmanuel College (the college where John Harvard had been a student before he gave his books and his name to the college in the American Cambridge).

By then, I was involved in a number of projects with Mascie-Taylor, and Bunny was working with him on a series of longitudinal studies of the epidemiology of asthma, the most important childhood disease in Britain. When I retired from teaching anatomy and Bunny had another sabbatical, we were made fellow commoners at Churchill College, with which we have been associated ever since. Fellow commoners were originally people, such as sons of the nobility, who were students but had too much status to dine with the other students in the colleges. In return for the privilege of dining at high table with the fellows (the members of the faculty who govern the college), the fellow commoners contributed silver to the college. I think that calling members of the nobility "commoners" is a very English twist. At one time, fellows were elected for life, but that had become a problem when some became doddering, so now a retirement age is usual. Since I was deemed to be too old to be a visiting fellow, my title was "fellow commoner with the privileges of fellow." The Mascie-Taylors are close friends, and Bunny and I both find useful professional opportunities in research with Nick. We have been going to Cambridge when Bunny is free from her teaching duties at Wayne State University in the summer or is eligible for a half-sabbatical. Nick is engaged in a number of big epidemiology projects in Great Britain, Sudan, Bangladesh, and elsewhere abroad that turn out masses of data in need of analysis. Furthermore, he is a very skillful data cruncher. One of those databases is the National Child Development Study (NCDS), a collection of many hundreds of variables on every child born in England, Scotland, and Wales in one week in 1958. Detailed information was collected at the time of their birth and periodically later when they were seven, eleven, sixteen, twenty-three, and thirty-three years of age. If we have a question that can be approached using that sort of data set, we try to tease the answers out. There are difficulties with survey data in which the questions have been set by others and not necessarily followed consistently over time, but sometimes the questions and data mesh. Furthermore, unlike many other kinds of studies, the samples are huge and random to the extent that one birth cohort is representative.

Mascie-Taylor and I have been able to study the effect of internal migration on the distribution of blood groups; the distributions were already relatively homogeneous, so subsequent migrations made only a little difference.

We also examined the relationship of social class to heights and weights and the influence of changes in social class. The social class differences are established early, by age seven, and maintained into adulthood. Those moving up the social scale tend to be taller than the average of their old social class but shorter than the one they are moving into. Those moving downward show the reverse tendency. However, socially mobile families were probably not culturally typical of the social classes to which they belonged.

Mascie-Taylor is heavily engaged in lecturing, running the department, and supervising graduate students (and helping other students with statistical problems), as well as with research and editing, but he manages to get it all done. Often, if I have a question about the relationship between variables in a data set, he takes the problem home and the next day comes in with the partial regressions. Since work is such a large part of his life, I hope that he continues to get pleasure from research, as I do, and satisfaction from the fact that the department he chairs has received the highest rating level, five, given by the British government agency that monitors universities.

20

Other Countries

So far, this account has been mostly about my relationships with other American anthropologists and with British colleagues. When I was in China and looking for some area in which I could make a career, the American consul in Tientsin suggested that I consider the diplomatic service. I think that I am too blunt to have made it a success. Of course, when I had to deal with diplomatic issues, such as when I was president of the American Association of Physical Anthropologists and we were meeting in Mexico City, I felt no shame about looking for strengths in Mexican anthropology. For instance, I called attention to the quality of the museum presentations as symbolized by the magnificent National Museum of Anthropology. I did not choose such occasions to complain about weaknesses resulting from the dearth of adequately compensated jobs available to anthropologists in the country.

The problems of anthropology in European countries may not be so very different from those in Latin America. The corruption of anthropology during the Nazi period left a legacy of distrust for anthropology that was not immediately overcome. That is, the liberalizing influence of scientific comparative studies of population biology may have been partially offset by a history of misuse of anthropology in the service of ethnic and racial distinctiveness. Nevertheless, the trends seen in the United States are at least partially seen also in work emanating from Poland, France, and elsewhere on the continent.

Gabriel Lasker in conversation with Jesper Boldsen, a Danish anthropologist, at the Rose Cottage on the Cam River at Fen Ditton near Cambridge. On summer weekend afternoons, Lasker and others often went there for the substantial "set tea" of sandwiches and cakes, and to watch the eight-oar shells practice. At the May bump races, in which more than a thousand students row, they preferred to watch with the crowd on the other bank of the river, where the coaches on bicycles on the towpath hurry to keep up with, and urge along, their college boats.

Through our mutual connections with the University of Cambridge, I have become friendly with and have done some collaborative research with Jesper Boldsen, a Danish anthropologist with an appointment in a department of social medicine of one of the Danish universities. He has a very keen mind and loves to construct biological history by following a series of facts and logical inferences about skeletal biology. Just as so much skeletal material elsewhere is being reburied and lost to the application of science to human welfare, the Danes are codifying information on tens of thousands of excavated skeletons and advancing the study of paleo-demography. However, I understand from Boldsen that there is (or was) not a single chair in biological anthropology in the whole of Denmark. The situation may not be much better in some other European countries. As a consequence, what can be accomplished is being done by individuals with primary responsibilities in other kinds of departments, and that may limit the scope. My lack of adequate language skills prevents me from making a fair appraisal of the extent and originality of much that has been done, and that inhibits me from saying more about it.

Because of my poor command of languages, most of my European experience has been in England. The only other European country where we have done any anthropology is Italy. I had always assumed that North Americans invited to attend conferences in Europe would be expected to find their own travel funds. I was therefore surprised when a feeler from Brunetto Chiarelli, then professor at the University of Turin, about my willingness to participate in a conference was followed with instructions to go to the Pan Am office and pick up my air ticket. In fact, I had just gone to Mexico without planning to make the Italian trip, and there was barely time to go home, sleep overnight, and return to the airport. Whenever I have been in Mexico, I have suffered from Montezuma's revenge, and I missed some of the sessions at that conference in Italy because of the continued effect of the earlier trip. Chiarelli was very considerate of my well-being, and we became friends. We worked together on several subsequent projects, including the course at Erice on demography in anthropology, described earlier.

In 1971, Chiarelli had a program of research in the Alps on the Italian side of the border with France. Bunny and I spent a short period in the village of Bellino (*Blins* in the local dialect, langue d'Oc). Again, we turned to a study of the distribution of surnames to provide information on the structure of a region of Alpine villages. Even a brief field experience there and touristic visits to Alpine villages in Switzerland, including one where anthropologists Robert Netting and Walter Ellis were working, give one a sense of the nature of the special cattle-herding culture that was present in all the Alpine countries of Europe before skiing became the chief industry. Before World War II, the men of Bellino had been organized into Alpini defense units by Mussolini. During the early years of the war, Italy was at war with France, and the front line lay at the crest of the mountain just above Bellino. The people in Bellino spoke French and were suspected of French sympathies, so the Alpini units were sent to the Russian front instead of being used for the defense of their valley. Many members were killed in Russia, and very few returned. Since there were so many widows and spinsters in the village, the local priest organized them into an order of nuns, and they set to doing men's work, caring for cows, making hay, and so on, to support themselves. Other families also had too few male workers. One such family had no men or boys to take the cattle to the high pastures for the summer, but an English anthropologist, Sandra Wallman, and her Caribbean entomologist husband had a school-age daughter who had observed local customs and was drafted to herd the cows.

Once, the mayor of the village was going up to his cattle in the high summer pasture and taking a donkey. Our young son Ted loved the mountains and went along with his camera. The mayor moved so fast, however, that although Ted had repeatedly scrambled to get ahead, the mayor passed by him each time, and Ted took a whole series of snapshots of the Alps with the back end of the donkey ahead on the trail. Ted reported that the food at the summer shelter consisted of pasta served with pounds of newly made butter.

Chiarelli had invited so many outside investigators into the little hamlet where we stayed in Bellino that we could not imagine how any of the traditional types of anthropological investigation, such as the social anthropological studies that Sandra Wallman was carrying on there, could succeed. However, Chiarelli instituted a practice that deserves consideration by others faced with similar problems. He asked each of his visiting scientists to give a seminar for the villagers. When my turn came, I went to the church on a Sunday to talk. Two of the ladies of the town had donned fancy traditional peasant costumes for the occasion. I held forth about the values of anthropological study of the kind being undertaken, and Melchiorre Masali, of the University of Turin, acted as my translator. He had lived on the Isle of Jersey and has excellent command of English, and I could follow well enough to know that he did a good job of interpreting. However, when the time for questions arrived, the issues departed far from what I had tried to present. One gentleman asked, "Why is it that we are smart and the people down in the lower valley are so dumb?"

I answered as best I could: "You have this wonderful environment here in the beautiful mountains with all you know about the natural environment and the life of herding your cattle. How could those people down in the plain know all this?" It apparently satisfied everyone. The priest, who also spoke a few words of English and was fluent in Spanish as well, cordially invited me to his place to hear more about the University of Turin project and to share with me a drink of liqueur, Rossi Anticci.

I first became aware of the high quality of population genetics in Italy through reading. I had met Adriano Buzzati Traverso at Cold Spring Harbor in 1952 but became better acquainted when, after a stint as consultant to *World Book Encyclopedia*, I joined him on an advisory panel to the encyclopedia's annual supplement, *Science Year*.

This was written by distinguished scientists, beautifully and amply illustrated in full color, and well printed and substantially bound at a modest price (then only $5.95). It was sold as a continuing subscription, mailed and charged to subscribers each year unless they wrote to discontinue. At one time, about 1972, we were told that publication probably would have to be suspended because the publisher could not afford to sell each issue separately and the method of sale by continuing subscriptions might be prohibited. In fact, this did not happen. However, it was expected, and I was surprised to find that the fees of the consultants had been greatly increased. That taught me something about business; I reasoned that the staff, under threat of unemployment, was investing the publisher's money to their own possible future advantage, their relationship with the outside authors and others who made it possible for them to produce popular works on scientific subjects.

I know other Italian human geneticists through correspondence, and in recent years, I have worked with Gianfranco Biondi of the University of Rome, La Sapienza, an anthropologist who works on genetic problems. We get together when both of us are at Cambridge University at the same time, and I appreciate Biondi's careful attention to details of the research.

In my work for the encyclopedia, I found that only about 10 percent of articles are revised for each edition and that efforts to deal with a group of articles therefore might take years. I made it my business to try to improve the references to human biology in the sections called "The People" in the numerous geographic articles by substituting information about specific variables for the general and often misleading racial categorizations that appeared in some of them. For *Science Year*, there was an interest in anthropology because it provides a good source of material accessible to younger and other less sophisticated readers than is generally true for such sciences as chemistry and physics.

21

Human Biological Variation

My chief professor, Hooton, believed that genetics was predominant in the human state, in criminal tendencies, illnesses, and abilities. He also believed that human morphology was determined genetically, and therefore morphology marked character. Hooton published a book on the physical characteristics of American criminals based on the study of a large number of mug shot photographs. The book was severely criticized by those who had studied social influences on criminal behavior. One devastating review was by sociologist Robert Merton jointly with anthropologist Ashley Montagu. At just about the time that the review was published, there was a meeting of the American Association of Physical Anthropologists, and Ashley Montagu had presented a title and abstract of a paper concerning the human pyramidalis muscle and its homolog in marsupials. The pyramidalis is a small muscle in the lower abdomen of humans that had been referred to as an atavism going back to opossumlike ancestors, because there is such a muscle in kangaroos, for instance, in the pouch on the abdomen into which the embryolike infants crawl soon after birth to be held close to the maternal nipples.

When the time came for Montagu's paper, he did not discuss this but announced that he had changed his report's title to "Men, Apes, and Anthropologists." This was a takeoff on the title of another Hooton book, *Men, Apes, and Morons,* and the inference was that some anthropologists, including Hooton, were morons.

Later at the same meeting, Hooton, who was much sought after as a speaker, gave a featured address. He started out ironically: "Unaccustomed as I am to public speaking" (pause for effect). "I wondered what I should speak about" (another pause and "er" for emphasis). "I thought perhaps I should talk about the pyramidalis muscle, huh?" That was his only reply that I know of to all the criticisms.

I did not agree with Hooton's hereditarianism, of course. My interest in human biology began with the study of human genetics, but the work I consider my most important has been to show the limitations of simple genetic determinism, especially when it has been extended from individuals to supposed races and other types.

William H. Sheldon, the constitutional psychologist, developed the concept of somatotypes, individual inherent characteristics maintained throughout life which determine each individual's temperament and can be identified in the individual's bodily configuration as seen in standardized nude photographs. Hooton was a great fan of Sheldon.

Ancel Keys at the University of Minnesota conducted a major human experiment in which volunteers who were conscientious objectors underwent six months of partial starvation and another six months on only slightly higher caloric intake. The object was to evaluate strategies for recovery from the wartime famine conditions in Europe and Asia of 1944 to 1945 with only slightly improved food resources. Josef Brozek, one of the senior researchers on that project, had taken standardized nude somatotype photographs of the thirty-six volunteers before the start of the project, after six months, and again at the end. Brozek made the photographs available to me, and I was able to show enormous changes in morphology expressed as somatotype. Furthermore, Hooton permitted me to send the photographs to him to be somatotyped by trained technicians working for him on a large somatotyping project. Without knowing that there were two sets of pictures of each individual (before and at the end of the period of partial starvation), the technicians assigned a usual range of scores to the before pictures, but the pictures taken after six months on less than seventeen hundred calories per day were rated as much more *ectomorphic*, the term used to describe "constitutionally" scraggly individuals. That is, working "blind," the technicians identified the same marked change in somatotypes that I had.

Theodosius Dobzhansky was much impressed by somatotyping and invited Sheldon to participate in the Fifteenth Cold Spring

Harbor Symposium on Quantitative Biology held June 9–17, 1950. Washburn, who was arranging with Dobzhansky a panel of biological anthropologists for that meeting, asked me to come and talk about somatotypes and starvation. I had published my paper "The Effect of Partial Starvation on Somatotypes" and had nothing further to add to that discussion, so I gave a paper on hereditary traits of the teeth. Those at the meeting who were interested in genetics of dental traits had been trying to deal with the complex etiology of dental measurements, and I attempted to present information on somewhat simpler categorical traits. Sheldon, however, felt obliged to deal with the problem of varying somatotypes that I had addressed in my published paper. He did it by dividing somatotype into a morphophenotype which is subject to change and an underlying ideal morphogenotype. There is no way to measure or observe the latter, so the concept is not scientifically useful, and this idea was not taken up by others. Many young biological anthropologists were at the meeting, as were distinguished geneticists, and perhaps the discussions, at least the informal ones, set somatotyping in its appropriate, but limited, place. At least, after that, I do not recall any papers by geneticists about the inheritance of constitutional types. Physique has implications for success in sports, of course, and a physical educator, Lindsay Carter, and a former associate of Sheldon's, Barbara Honeyman Heath Roll, have recorded the history and made the best case possible for the use of somatotyping in their definitive book on its development and applications.

In our 1948 study of Mexican migrants to the United States who had returned to their native village in Mexico, we found that those who had spent more of their youth in the United States tended to be bigger than those who had come here only when adults or not at all. The design of the study thus built on that used by Franz Boas in his study of Jewish and Italian migrants and, more specifically, that of Boas's student Marcus Goldstein. He had studied Mexican immigrants and their American-born adult children in Texas, compared them with parents and adult children in Mexico, and found that the difference in environments had a large effect on the dimensions he measured in the adults. In addition, F. Gaynor Evans went to Mexico and made measurements of adults in Uruapan, a provincial Mexican city, comparable to those I had made in Paracho. We analyzed them, and the results were similar in the two places. These and other studies of migrants demonstrate that under different conditions, individuals grow somewhat differently. The nature of some environmental influences on the most studied variables such as stature are now well known: under improved conditions, people grow taller. However, when I entered anthropology, stature was described as a racial characteristic. Individuals of any genetic constitution grow up under the influence of environmental circumstances, so the relationship between what Galton called "nature" and "nurture" is always relative to the genetic variation among the individuals and the degree of differences among the environments. Among genetically very different individuals in consistent standardized conditions, the genetic element appears to be important. Among genetically similar populations living in different environmental circumstances, the genetic factor appears much smaller.

However, once again, some geneticists seem to believe that an individual's DNA is all that constitutes that individual, and they have extended that notion to groups of people. The concept of "pure race" is not true of any group of people today. There is no evidence that any group of people was ever genetically isolated for long, certainly not any large group of individuals in the thousands of generations since human beings first made boats and crossed open waters. So the concept is only a hypothesis about an even more remote past and quite likely never occurred. Therefore, we have been skeptical about race and about overemphasizing genetic influences on morphology and behavior. We still need further studies to explore the role of environmental factors during human development on genetic predispositions. For instance, because dermatoglyphics, once established, are permanent, some investigators have viewed them as purely genetic. Of course, we know that if there were any fingers to print after mothers had taken thalidomide during pregnancy, the finger prints would be radically affected. Hand prints are apparently affected by fetal alcohol syndrome. I wonder if maternal smoking could also affect them. There are still many questions concerning the biological mechanisms of development and growth. The answers may help us to deal with the variety of factors that influence formation of desirable and undesirable traits.

Recent work in human population genetics has depended heavily on mitochondrial DNA. Since this is inherited as a clone, from mother to child, it simplifies many types of analysis. But mitochondrial DNA contains only a tiny fraction of human genetic material. It is therefore

173

more important to learn about the past patterns of migration that dispersed specific sequences in the much more abundant nuclear DNA that is subject to recombination each generation. In a species such as ours, which can carry water and food and make long treks and voyages, the gene pool is shared by all. Hundreds of generations of long-distance travels have produced a situation in which we are all certainly related in terms of distant lines of descent. Douglas Crews and I have adduced evidence to support these ideas, but more information is needed or, at least, needs to be considered.

During a lull in fieldwork in Peru in 1957, I began to collect data on surnames because of a vague sense that the distribution of surname frequencies could be used as an index of isolation. Before I published anything, I encountered the sophisticated models of inbreeding coefficients being devised by two brilliant geneticists, James F. Crow and Newton E. Morton. They were both students of Sewell Wright, whose many studies of population genetics anticipated much of the work that has been done since. A chief attraction of surname genetics has been that data are easily obtained and they very readily permit testing of theoretical ideas about population genetics. Some of the leaders in human population genetics from an evolutionary point of view, besides James Crow and Newton Morton—for instance, L. L. Cavalli Sforza and Robert Sokal—have also used surnames in this way. One thing that attracted me, however, is that the basic logic is so simple and materials so easy to acquire that anyone, potentially even high school students, can be introduced to scientific method by doing an original study using surname data. Instead of merely learning about the results of science, they can, in a small way, do research the outcome of which is unknown in advance.

Besides human genetic models, one also can demonstrate something of the nongenetic component of names by comparing surname analyses with pseudo-genetic analyses of appropriate sets of given names that lack a genetic component. Nevertheless, analysis of surnames in human biology is primarily in relationship to genetic structure of populations. Although such studies represent a large fraction of my publications in recent years, I do not count them as being as significant as my efforts to study the relationship of environmental and genetic determinants of human morphology. Nevertheless, the study of surnames has given the agreeable opportunity to work with others.

Sometimes, when I have had a bright idea, I later am likely to find it passed off among other ideas in an earlier paper by Newton

Morton. Morton is a fine theoretician. Crow, whom I also consulted, is also very perceptive, but his papers are more leisurely in style, not quite so dense, and hence easier for someone like me, not too adept at symbolic thinking, to grasp. Many ideas, for instance about genetic linkage, that are only now being explored by laboratory methods were previously examined theoretically and statistically by Crow and Morton. The use of data on surnames lends itself to some theoretical considerations about inbreeding and, especially, about the breeding structure of populations. For instance, historical changes in average amounts of inbreeding in populations (especially the general populations of large areas such as whole countries) can be studied using surnames but would be difficult using pedigrees and nearly impossible using genetic markers. Crow and Morton were the first to interest me in such studies and have continued to guide me from time to time.

Playing with surname data (it is a mistake to take it too seriously in detail, because the assumptions necessary to match surname genetics with biological genetics are not fully met) has brought me in close touch with other fascinating people, only some of whom are mentioned in these pages. I want here to record my pleasure in both the intellectual and the social aspect of these collaborations, a happy element of my life, especially since I retired from teaching seventeen years ago.

22

Major Changes in the Field

During the years that I have been active in biological anthropology, there were, in my opinion, two revolutions in the field. The first of these involved the overthrowing of the idea of typological races that dominated the discussions at the Viking Fund Summer Seminars in the years immediately after World War II. The second was the turning away from a concern with race altogether as attention was refocused on questions of biological function in human populations. The Human Adaptability Project of the International Biological Program during the late 1960s led this second revolution. Financial support for the changed directions of research interests was a factor in both cases. I have already referred to some of the people and events involved, especially in the first of these periods.

The concept of a typological race is derived from an idealized set of characteristics (a particular shape of the head and features of the face, color of the eyes and hair, form of the hair, and so on) which are believed to be inherited and presumed to characterize a people, often some past group of people who are assumed to have had these characteristics in "pure" form. There are a number of flaws in this concept.

Although the traits are inherited, at least some of them are also much influenced by the circumstances in which the individuals grew up.

As the inheritance of such characteristics is not controlled by the same part of an individual's DNA, the traits are more or less independent of one another.

Because of the independence of traits, only a few individuals have all of the traits. This is true even if the number of described "races" is not three or six but is very numerous, with many "mixed" and subtypes described.

Even if the parents are of the same type, the children may not be.

With the accumulation of evidence, each former claim of a pure race in some past population fails. The more material there is available, the clearer it becomes that there was always considerable variation and that physical traits in ancient populations were nearly as diverse as in most populations now. Behavioral characteristics that are strongly influenced by external psychological and cultural conditions are sometimes gratuitously assumed to be genetically tied to the types.

Constitutional types share some of these misconceptions, but no such type is thought to have ever been universal in some past population; they are thought of as inherited in the individual but not necessarily shared in the family. Indexes that considered two traits simultaneously and types that considered many traits simultaneously had a certain utility in descriptions. However, the computer allows one to use multivariate forms of analysis in which one can easily examine the interrelationships among a number of traits, so types are no longer even useful for that limited purpose.

Although his own interests in 1946 were in experimental functional anatomy and later in nonhuman primate behavior, it was Sherwood Washburn, through his organization of the Viking Fund Summer Seminars in Physical Anthropology, who brought about the first revolt against the assumptions of the concept of racial types then prevalent.

Of course, Ashley Montagu had been arguing the case against the concept of race earlier. His insistence that in talking about "race" we were dealing with ethnic groups, defined by culture and not by biology, was addressed largely to social scientists and to the general public rather than to physical anthropologists, even after 1952, when Montagu was involved with many respected scientists in formulating the UNESCO Statement on Race. Thus, Montagu was not taken very seriously by most professionals of the time, because his publications, scattered over diverse subjects, were viewed as superficial. My wife,

Bunny, notes that there is an antipathy on the part of stuffy scholars toward anyone who deigns to write for the general public. Montagu does popularize. He is an avid reader and writer of book reviews. He has made many interesting statements but was often not the first person with the idea. For instance, in about 1935 and within a year or so of the first clear indication that tobacco smokers had shorter life expectancy than nonsmokers, Montagu had published that conclusion. However, he did not provide any additional new evidence.

At the summer seminars, Washburn's approach to the subject of race was crucial. (One should also mention the contribution of Paul Fejos at the Viking Fund for his financial support of Washburn's activities.) Washburn was conducting experimental studies on rats that showed that some of the kinds of features of the skull that in humans had been taken to be hallmarks of race, or atavisms surviving from earlier fossil progenitors, are in fact responses to muscular stress and subject to modification by disuse of specific muscles. The approach was generalized in Washburn's *New Physical Anthropology,* which called for a move away from repeated standardized measurements based on an unsubstantiated theory of race and toward devising research methods to answer particular problems.

At the same time, the revolution of scientific thinking against the old race concept was furthered by those who knew some modern human population genetics, such as Marshall Newman and James Spuhler. Basically, they saw most human breeding populations as being at least somewhat open, and they knew that most genes are independent of one another rather than being closely linked. Therefore, true breeding racial or constitutional types could not persist; indeed, they could not exist. Those senior anthropologists who held a contrary view, such as Hooton, Coon, and the constitutional psychologist William Sheldon, attended the seminars, but only for a day, while the "young Turks" were there talking for the duration. Of the younger typologists, Georg Neumann did not attend the seminars and remained uninfluenced by them. Lawrence Angel made some published references to types, but that seems not to have influenced others, and the works for which Angel is best remembered are in other areas. Joseph Birdsell's position is a puzzle; he seemed to accept the argument against types, but he continued to publish material on Australian Aborigines that had been collected on a typological basis. He continued to talk about migrations of aboriginals to Australia in terms of with which wave of migration they were associated. He also accepted a genetic approach and talked about p (for "putative") genes.

On the subject of race, Washburn's contribution, like Montagu's, was his influence on wider audiences. Surprisingly, after World War II, some of the senior figures in human genetics (such as William Boyd on race and Theodosius Dobzhansky on constitution) continued to believe that inherited types were a useful concept, but the Fifteenth Cold Spring Harbor Symposium in 1952, again organized by Washburn with Dobzhansky, saw the idea effectively refuted, and the notion of racial types began to disappear from scientific publications. In 1962, Washburn was asked by the executive board of the American Anthropological Association to devote his presidential address to the subject of race, and he gave a clear exposition which was published in the *American Anthropologist* and has been reprinted widely.

The notion of racial types survives among the ill-informed and some who have been isolated geographically from mainstream thinking, such as in eastern Europe until recently. Of course, discredited ideas about racial superiority and even Nazism itself are resurrected repeatedly by extremists and need repeated attention in every generation to be critically reanswered whenever they do.

The second revolution, away from any interest in race as a useful approach to human variation, was already apparent in the work of some American anthropologists, but the leader on the international scene was Joseph Weiner at Oxford University. Weiner was skeptical of established "science." He was the first person to declare Piltdown Man a fraud. Someone had cleverly disguised pieces of a human skull and an ape jawbone and planted them to be discovered in an early geological site. As a student, I had been required to read the works of Sir Arthur Keith describing them and, like everyone else, never thought of the possibility of deliberate fakery. However, Weiner's curiosity led him to see if he could make a fake that looked like one of the pieces, and when that succeeded, he sought help from Le Gros Clark and Kenneth Oakley, and the three of them showed that the original was also a fraud. But who perpetrated it? There have been numerous whodunit books on the subject. Some thought the Jesuit priest Teilhard de Chardin might have suspected a fraud. He had actually found one of the teeth and was a firm believer in human evolution. Although the pope has now taken a similar position, at the time of his writings, Teilhard de Chardin must have had complex motivations as a Catholic theologian and evolutionist.

It is still not certain who was responsible. The most common assumption is that it was Charles Dawson, the discoverer himself. In any case, I think each of the three scholars who did expose the Piltdown fraud have made other, more important contributions to physical anthropology. Le Gros Clark recognized early the importance of *Australopithecus* and successfully synthesized data on human evolution; he had a thorough understanding of the anatomy and embryology of the nonhuman primates and used it in interpreting the fossils. Oakley developed the fluorine dating method for old bone which led the way to improved chemical and physical methods of dating fossils. Weiner's publications show the highly important nature of the change he led. He pursued issues other than race and focused on applied physiology, the topic that had first interested me in biological anthropology. I never mastered that subject, however. On my first trip to Mexico, I took a spirometer to study vital capacity in subjects at high altitude, but I could not motivate the subjects to inhale maximally. Weiner made many observations on work capacity. His colleague at Oxford, Derek Roberts, also worked on physiological variables. However, it is Weiner's role in organizing the Human Adaptability Project of the International Biological Program on a worldwide basis that I think has changed biological anthropology enormously. Although many authors published in the IBP-HAP volumes, it was largely Weiner who was responsible for the shift in paradigm.

In many countries, funds were made available to biological anthropologists for studies that dealt with human responses to heat, cold, altitude, and other environmental challenges, and race was nowhere in the forefront. In the United States, the direction had already been established through applied research on work physiology with potential military and peaceful applications. Anthropologists who had become involved in this way, notably Paul Baker, allied themselves with Weiner in expanding the focus onto the general question of the biology of human adaptation.

Other biological anthropologists who did applied work for the U.S. military establishment after the war, such as Robert M. White, Edward Hertzberg, and Francis Randall, did not publish contributions to general theory. The material for Hertzberg's dissertation on eye color was lost, and he did not complete his PhD. Randall was killed at an early age in the crash of a passenger airplane hit in midair by a military aircraft. White wrote several strong defenses of the importance of applied anthropology.

I had mixed feelings about the Human Adaptability Project at first. In the United States, a small group including James V. Neel, Paul Baker, Dimitri Shimkin, and some Arctic anthropologists had structured the American effort so that funds from the National Science Foundation would flow to their own research. That was desirable to the extent that the funds were new ones, but it seemed likely that the money would also come at the expense of small independent one-off projects of the kind that I tend to favor. Nevertheless, when, at Paul Baker's instigation, the editor of *Science* asked me to submit an article on human adaptation, I wrote a piece in which I tried to define the subject and cover a variety of studies that the organizers of the project had proposed. The chief point was that some adaptation is prompt and reversible, such as sweating when it is hot; some is acquired during life, such as immunity to a childhood infectious disease; and some is inherited in the population, such as, in all probability, some advantage of dark skin color in equatorial climates. Thus, I tried to give the project a boost, because I saw the turning of attention to a different set of important issues as tending to leave the sterile topic of race in the dust of scientific progress. I regret to say that racist thinking dies hard, and cultural terms such as *ethnic group* have been co-opted into its service. We need as much as ever scholars who understand human genetics, as it is so rapidly developing, who can also understand why an individual's DNA is not the totality of his humanity, and who can teach the relationship convincingly, not only in an academic setting but also at other levels of discourse.

After the International Biological Program ended, I was one of the editors of a dozen or so books on the American contribution to that effort. Neel's group never produced a volume, but the papers that were published add knowledge of the genetic structure of some of the last peoples to be almost untouched by global society. The volumes summarizing the other components of Weiner's Human Adaptability Project manifest valuable new insights into human biological responses to various ecological stimuli by hundreds of researchers in many countries. The altitude volume, *Man in the Andes,* edited by Paul Baker and Michael Little, summarized a mass of research, much of it produced by Baker's former students. Baker and some of his students went on to study the relationships to the very different climate of Samoa of various factors of human biology and disease, and Little and his students and associates conducted studies under still other contrasting physical and cultural conditions among the Turkana of the savanna in Kenya. It was clear that Baker, with Little and the others, had established the "school" of physiological anthropology that I thought necessary when I first became interested in anthropology in 1936. Pennsylvania State University became the leading center for graduate training of this kind.

Frank Blair, one of the editors of the American segment of the International Biological Program, contributed a book, *Big Science: The US/IBP*, which deals with the frustrations of working on such organized efforts on an international scale. Issues of diplomacy sometimes had to take precedence over scientific issues. One might think that such a big scientific effort on the subject of ecology would influence public policy toward the solution of ecological problems. However, there was little of that, at least in the short run. The books we edited were too technical. As is usual among scientists, most of the hundreds of researchers directed their contributions at an audience composed of others like themselves.

By contrast, Barry Commoner's concern with the environment had a strong impact. Commoner, who had already spread the alarm about pollution of the Great Lakes, was a member of the first Committee on Social Responsibility of the American Association for the Advancement of Science. Presumably, it was Commoner who had suggested my name to the chairman of the committee, Ward Pigman. Our report, which dealt with the many threats to the environment, was not only published in both *Science* and *Scientific Monthly* but was also published in its entirety in the *New York Times*. The report itself may have been the result rather than a cause of the interest, but the subject of the deterioration of our physical environment has been much in the news ever since. Indeed, the idea of a "natural environment" that does not include the human cultural component is purely imaginary. Bunny reminds me that anthropologists interested in human ecology define *Homo sapiens's* natural environment as encompassing the cultural component.

One of my own chief interests has always been migration. Mascie-Taylor and I edited a book about it in 1988. There are two aspects of migration. One is the adaptations that take place when people move into different environments. The other is that migration moves people of different genetic constitution to places where they breed and interbreed and change the human genetic geography. The old approach was to write speculative histories on the basis of interpretations, often biased by preconceptions based on linguistic, ethnic, and other nonbiological considerations. Modern methods and large data sets have refined results. Nevertheless, Douglas Crews and I published an article in *Molecular Phylogenetics and Evolution* in which we pull together some evidence that before the discovery of agriculture, marriage was probably frequently intertribal. That is, the lattice or trellislike geographic pattern of intertribal descent lines in pedigrees was denser than it became among settled agriculturalists. Because migrations are episodic, the situation is complicated, and there is a temptation to overinterpret by arbitrarily selecting explanations that fit some attitude about races or nationalities. The best one reliably can do is to be content with a general picture of the average result of so much intermarriage. Over many generations, it interrupts all isolates and also exposes their descendants to the likelihood of genetic accretions from throughout the species.

Whatever the case with neutral mutations, the migratory episodes over any appreciable span of time inevitably prevent the accumulation and maintenance locally of unusually low frequencies of genetically determined traits that would be beneficial in virtually all environments. Any genetic determinants of important mental abilities would have a strong tendency to become nearly universal. Thus, except for examples of disadvantageous rare, and presumably relatively recent, mutations, known genetic differences among geographic areas all seem to be either for selectively more or less neutral traits or, in some instances, for selective advantage only under the environmental circumstances of certain locations and periods of time. As the patterns of migration tend to become more intense, variation that has resulted from local selective forces or random processes is increasingly within, rather than between, areas.

I use the term *variation* to describe the pattern because, except to the extent that it means the same thing, the term *diversity* may be misleading. That term is used in ecology to describe the number of different species, genera, and so on, but within a species such as ours, there are no biological subgroups that can be counted, although, in the past, some tried to define such groups.

A very large and expensive research program, the Human Genome Project, has been established to determine the complete sequence of bases in human DNA. Quite appropriately, some researchers have pointed out that human beings are not identical. Some molecular geneticists and anthropologists have initiated a so-called Human Diversity Project. The anthropologists among them should be well aware of the kind of consideration I have described about diversity and its implications about sampling, but they have been reluctant to contradict flatly the well-meaning nonanthropologist supporters who operate out of a nineteenth-century paradigm of race. Thus, some work being performed in a current technical, genetic, and statistical environment is being polluted by phrases like "pure Caucasian." The researchers apply the term to small segments of DNA, but they do not mean that the DNA is pure; they assume that "races" were once pure, and it reminds one that Nazis who believed "Aryans" were once pure set out trying to purify them again. I fear that the public may be misled. The long-term benefit of human population genetic research directed to future health and welfare of the whole species requires a method of study designed to evaluate variation by use of sampling methods in which any individual (or, at least, each characteristic of the DNA of any individual) has some known likelihood, albeit perhaps small, of being studied for his or her benefit.

To the extent that there are local and regional genetic differences, migration places people of some genetic constitution in an environment different from that in which their relatives live. The kinds of influences that can be studied in such natural experiments are very varied indeed and have barely begun to be exploited. Results from research of this kind vary.

Among those engaged today in such research, Roberto Frisancho has been looking at one of the variables that first interested me in anthropology: blood pressure. Elevated blood pressure is well established as a common trait of poor African Americans and urban Africans in Africa. Frisancho's question was: Does this result from factors associated with their poverty or with the genetics of their African ancestry? He found a community in Bolivia where former runaway slaves had settled. The land and location are apparently suitable for growing coca. Even there, where the heads of families of African ancestry are the affluent landlords, their members tend to have elevated blood pressure, whereas the mestizos of European and American Indian descent who do all the hard work are less subject to hypertension.

A contrasting recent migration study, that of Barry Bogin, found that Maya children in the United States are taller, heavier, and more muscular than those in Guatemala, and the smaller size of the non-migrants cannot be interpreted as being genetically based but rather represents smallness as a response to chronic food shortages. The nonmigrants are not "small but healthy," but rather environmental influences, such as diet, affect child growth.

Causal interrelationships among individuals of various kinds in different settings are not simple, and analytic studies find both genetic and environmental components, which vary from one situation to another. There are traits common in some populations adapted to a specific environment, such as larger lung capacity at high altitude and color vision among hunters, but researchers do not find any sort of measurable "superiority" of any particular populations in adaptation to the human way of life in general.

In the shift in biological anthropology away from the issue of the origins of human morphological variation and Darwinian fitness to the more applied science of development of physical fitness, the role of exercise science in physiological anthropology has considerable importance. Physical educators began doing anthropometry in the nineteenth century, and in the twentieth century many, such as Jana Parizkova in what was then Czechoslovakia and Gaston Beunan in Belgium, have also measured physical performance. In American universities, sports departments needed to justify their existence in academic institutions and have found that anthropologists, Robert Malina conspicuously among them, are engaged in a science with other applied physiologists that is related to the immediate interests of athletics departments but is also fundamental to human biology: the growth and genetics of human physical abilities. As in other branches of anthropology, Malina uses comparative methods and has examined various ethnic groups in the United States and Mexico.

23

Looking Back

I am happy with the concern human biologists have for the betterment of the lives of the subjects of their studies. It is important, nevertheless, to look for general underlying principles. For that, biological anthropologists have to stay alert to the issues of physiological function, growth and development, and evolution. If the applied studies help with that, too, fine, but it takes something more for fundamental understanding, and clues are likely to be found in the works of those who went before.

Writing these memoirs makes me glow with pleasure as I think about my relationships with others in the profession. It has also raised in my mind the question of who has most influenced my career. My mother had a scientific background and curiosity. She made friends with all sorts of people, from the grocer's boys to the great biochemists of the time. My father had a different, more formal bent. He was an observer, reader, and synthesizer, not a statistical thinker. On the other hand, he knew many intellectuals, some of whom came to the house, and my parents demonstrated how to get on with and learn from such relationships. While they lived, both my parents read and edited whatever I wrote for publication. Ever since I went away to school at the age of twelve, my mother's letters would end with a list of the words I had misspelled and with the part I had misspelled underlined. Sorry to say, I never took advantage of it, and only after

I began to edit the work of others did I start to look words up in a dictionary and begin to pay attention. My wife, Bunny, used to correct spelling of her students, but she eventually gave it up, saying, "I know how to spell; the student does not." Ever since, she has warned students that she will take points off for misspelled words, but she indicates which words are misspelled, and if the student looks them up, corrects them, and brings the paper back, she raises the grade to what it would have been without those errors.

For the last fifty years, Bunny Kaplan has been a professional associate as well as being involved in every personal respect. She has often influenced the general direction of my thoughts on expressing professional matters to others, since she has a keen sense of the importance to wider audiences of what we may think we are addressing only to likeminded, aloof scientists.

Thelma Baker surprised me recently. The Human Biology Association was honoring me at its annual luncheon. If you reach my age and keep on working on projects of interest to other members of the profession, such honors are almost automatic. Ralph Garruto, the president, asked Michael Little, the president elect, to say a few words about my work. Thelma then requested the floor to talk about "moral leadership."

I have been just about as practical and manipulative as others in the profession. I have stood up for women and other sometimes disadvantaged groups, but only when I thought their work matched in importance that of others, and usually it has been Bunny who set the course, as in my contribution toward the racial integration in Atlanta before it became general in the South. If female anthropologists do not appear often in this account, it is because there were relatively few in the earlier years. Other than Bunny, Pamela Raspe is the only one I have worked with repeatedly over the years. She has come to my aid once more with editorial help with this work, but she has had to allow me to ramble as I pleased.

In the end, where do I think the progress in the science has come from, institutions or individuals? Individuals make a big difference, but they express it through institutions. Washburn stimulated me more than anyone else. He is probably at his best in his lectures and conversations rather than in print. Baker, at Penn State, built a powerful team, bridging a research methodology traceable to Boas at Columbia with attitudes of respect of students that gets the best out of them as his mentor at Harvard, Hooton, had demonstrated.

Ralph Garruto, State University of New York at Binghamton, has been a major figure at the National Institutes of Health, where he has helped introduce the anthropological perspective of comparisons of different kinds of people in many kinds of cultures into epidemiological studies.

Michael A. Little, right, president of the Human Biology Association, presenting a bust of Franz Boas to Gabriel Lasker. Little has studied human adaptation in the contrasting environments of the Peruvian Andes and among the Turkana of the savanna in Kenya. (Photo by Mark Weiss.)

Hooton's open-hearted welcome to all who were interested in the subject shaped physical anthropology for two generations. But it was also the ability of Harvard to place its students in positions with great opportunity that mattered. For instance, Edward Hunt and Stanley Garn worked at the Forsyth Dental Clinic. Hunt later wrote many interesting articles, and Garn has been the most productive researcher in those aspects of physical anthropology that he pursues. I had a year in the Department of Anatomy at Harvard that shaped my subsequent career. If I had to advise a prospective student with just a few words, I would say to pay attention to the reputation of departments only to the extent that they represent the presence of bright and helpful teachers and students and the ability and willingness to expose students to valuable research experiences both within and outside the department.

Appendix

Annotated List of Publications of Gabriel Lasker

1936 Margaret Lasker, M. Enklewitz, and G. W. Lasker. The inheritance of 1-xyloketosuria (essential pentosuria). *Human Biology* 8:243–55. My mother did most of the work.

1937 Review of Otto Klineberg, *Race Differences. Nankai Quarterly,* Tientsin, China. I was much influenced by this book, which is still worth studying.

1941 The process of physical growth of the Chinese. *Anthropology Journal of the Institute of History and Philology, Academia Sinica* 2:58–90. I left the manuscript behind in China in 1937 and did not receive proofs.

1941 The diet of infra-human primates, 253 pp. Manuscript report prepared under grant to Vilhjalmur Stefansson from the American Meat Institute. Based on published sources.

1942 Without a nation: Anthropology looks to the future. *Compass* 1(2):19–22. Youthful enthusiasm with overconfidence in applied anthropology.

1944 Review of Chauncey Goodrich, *A Pocket Dictionary (Chinese-English) and Pekinese Syllabary. Far Eastern Survey* 13:172.

1945 Physical characteristics of Chinese. Doctoral dissertation, Harvard. Unpublished. The thesis about migration is marred by the difference in mean age of the migrants and the American-born.

1945 Chinese physical development. *Far Eastern Survey* 14(18):260–62. Material from the dissertation.

1945 Observations on the teeth of Chinese born and reared in China and

America. *American Journal of Physical Anthropology* 3:129–50. Just looking in the mouths did not yield very good data.

1946   Bernice Kaplan, Elizabeth Richards, and G. W. Lasker. A seminar in physical anthropology. *Yearbook of Physical Anthropology* 1945:5–11.

1946   Migration and physical differentiation: A comparison of immigrant with American-born Chinese. *American Journal of Physical Anthropology* 4:273–300. Chief result of the dissertation.

1946   The inheritance of cleidocranial dysostosis. *Human Biology* 18:103–26. A review and analysis.

1946   S. Kilgore and G. W. Lasker. Cleidocranial dysostosis with psychosis. *Archives of Neurology and Psychiatry* 56:401–16. A case study.

1946   Review of M. F. Ashley Montagu, *An Introduction of Physical Anthropology. Social Forces* 224–25.

1947   Physical characteristics of Chinese: A study of physical differences and developments among Chinese at home and abroad. Summaries of thesis, 1943–1945. Harvard University Graduate School of Arts and Sciences, Cambridge, Mass., 27–31.

1947   Physical anthropology during the year. *Yearbook of Physical Anthropology* 1946:1–8.

1947   The effects of partial starvation on somatotype: An analysis of material from the Minnesota Starvation Experiment. *American Journal of Physical Anthropology* 5:323–42. Somatotypes change dramatically. The credit for this study belongs to the staff of the Minnesota Starvation Experiment and the volunteers.

1947   Penetrance: Estimated by the frequency of unilateral occurrences and by discordance in monozygotic twins. *Human Biology* 19:217–30. Under the assumption that such differences between the two sides in traits like tooth morphology are developmentally not genetically determined.

1947   Physical traits of the Chinese in America. *East Wind* 3(2):2-6. Addressed to Chinese-Americans about my study of them.

1947   Review of M. S. Goldstein, *Demographic and Bodily Changes in Descendants of Mexican Immigrants. American Anthropologist* 49:100–101. One of the best studies of the effects of migration.

1947   Review of Erwin Schrodinger, *What Is Life? The Physical Aspect of the Living Cell. American Journal of Physical Anthropology* 5:103–4.

1947   Review of E. A. Hooton, *Up from the Ape. Social Forces* 25:465–66.

1947   Review of R. G. Barker, B. A. Wright, and M. R. Gonick, *Adjustment to Physical Handicap and Illness: A Survey of the Social Psychology of Physique and Disability. Social Forces* 111–12.

1948   G. W. Lasker and H. H. Reynolds. A cicatrix of the neck associated with anomalous dental occlusion in one of a pair of monozygous twins. *Human Biology* 20:36–46. I now think they may have been a fraternal pair.

1949 Physical anthropology in 1948: A record of progress. *Yearbook of Physical Anthropology* 1948:1–21.

1950 The Fourth Summer Seminar in Physical Anthropology. *Bibliographical Bulletin of American Anthropology* 12(1):114–18.

1950 H. Archambault, R. Archambault, and G. W. Lasker. Choledochus cyst. *Ann. Surg.* 132:1144–48. The surgeons needed help searching the literature and writing up their case.

1950 Review of C. D. Darlington and K. Mather, *The Elements of Genetics*. *American Anthropologist* 52:422–23.

1951 G. W. Lasker, D. L. Opdyke, and H. Miller. The position of the internal maxillary artery and its questionable relation to the cephalic index. *Anat. Rec.* 109(1):119–25. A prior study reporting a relationship is suspect.

1951 Genetic analysis of racial traits of the teeth. *Cold Spring Harbor Symposia on Quantitative Biology* 15:191–203. I did not wish to rehash my study of somatotype change during starvation, so when invited to the symposium, I worked this up largely from published literature.

1951 Review of M. F. A. Montagu, *Statement on Race*. *American Anthropologist* 53:563–64.

1952 Some old hypotheses tested and some new theories developed: Publications in physical anthropology during 1950. *Yearbook of Physical Anthropology* 1950:1–23.

1952 Physical anthropology in 1951. *Yearbook of Physical Anthropology* 1951:1–25.

1952 An anthropometric study of returned Mexican emigrants. In Sol Tax, ed., *Indian Tribes of Aboriginal America*, Vol. III, Proceedings of the 29th Congress of Americanists, 242–46.

1952 Mixture and genetic drift in ongoing human evolution. *American Anthropologist* 54:433–36. Measuring migration versus isolation.

1952 Note on the nutritional factor in Howells' study of constitutional type. *American Journal of Physical Anthropology* 10:375–79. An application of results of one study to published data of another.

1952 Environmental growth factors and selective migration. *Human Biology* 24:262–89. Results of our Mexican migration study. Despite small sample sizes, I consider it my best paper.

1952 Torus Palatinus: An historical note. *Dental Record*, November:269–73.

1953 The age factor in bodily measurements of adult male and female Mexicans. *Human Biology* 25:50–63. Adequate to show some age differences, but it would take a longitudinal study to show age changes.

1953 Ethnic identification in an Indian Mestizo community. *Phylon* 14(2): 187–90. Shows that age of the respondent is the chief factor in ethnic identification in Mexico.

1953 Review of Donald Mainland, *Elementary Medical Statistics: The Princi-*

ples of Quantitative Medicine. American Journal of Physical Anthropology
11:239–41.

1954 The question of physical selection of Mexican migrants to the U.S.A. *Human Biology* 26:52–58. A small prospective study shows little if any selection for physique.

1954 Photoelectric measurement of skin color in a Mexican mestizo population. *American Journal of Physical Anthropology* 12:115–22. Probably the first field study using this objective method.

1954 Potential application of community censuses and genealogies. *Science* 120:902.

1954 Human evolution in contemporary communities: Southwest. *Journal of Anthropology* 10:353–65. Application of demographic data to opportunity to evolve by drift.

1954 Seasonal changes in skin color. *American Journal of Physical Anthropology* 12:533–58. Monthly records for a year, but missing two summer months.

1955 Review of Weston LaBarre, *The Human Animal. American Anthropologist* 57:377–78.

1955 Review of W. E. Le Gros Clark, *The Fossil Evidence for Human Evolution. Human Biology* 27:241–43. A classic of the time, but we now have so much more material.

1956 Anthropology in medical education. In *The Teaching of Anatomy and Anthropology in Medical Education: Report of the Third Teaching Institute, American Association of Medical Colleges*, October:25–31. Published as Part II of the *Journal of Medical Education*, October 1956. I helped organize the conference in which several anthropologists and anatomists with common interests participated along with other medical school educators.

1956 Barry Commoner, Gabriel Lasker, Chauncey Leake, Benjamin Williams, and Ward Pigman. Society in the scientific revolution. *Science* 124:1231.

1956 Ward Pigman, Barry Commoner, Gabriel Lasker, Chauncey D. Leake, and Benjamin H. Williams. Text of convention report on the Impact of Science and Social Forces. *New York Times*, Monday, December 31, p. 6. Also published in 1957 as: Social aspects of science: Preliminary report of AAAS Interim Committee. *Science* 125:143–47. And in 1957 in *Scientific Monthly* 84(3):146–51. I like to think that we helped start interest in applied ecology.

1956 Review of Erik Skeller, *Anthropological and Ophthalmological Studies on the Angmagssalik Eskimos. Human Biology* 28:385–87.

1957 G. W. Lasker and Marjorie M. C. Lee. Racial traits in the human teeth. *Journal of Forensic Science* 2:401–19. A survey of published geographic data on tooth morphology.

1957   Review of William L. Thomas Jr., ed., *Current Anthropology: A Supplement to Anthropology Today. American Anthropologist* 59:353–54.

1957   Review of Coenraad F. A. Moorrees, *The Aleut Dentition: A Correlative Study of Dental Characteristics in an Eskimoid People. Science* 126:567.

1958   Marjorie M. C. Lee and G. W. Lasker. The thickness of subcutaneous fat in elderly men. *American Journal of Physical Anthropology* 16:125–34. A small project for a hardworking postdoc.

1959   Recent advances in physical anthropology. *Biennial Review of Anthropology* 1:1–36.

1959   Marjorie M. C. Lee and G. W. Lasker. The suntanning potential of human skin. *Human Biology* 31:252–60. An experimental study with a sun lamp on a small area of the back. The potential varied greatly.

1960   Edited: *The Processes of Ongoing Human Evolution.* Detroit: Wayne State University Press. Reprint of articles that had appeared in *Human Biology.*

1960   Human evolution in contemporary communities. Reprinted in *Readings on Race,* Stanley M. Garn, ed. Springfield, Ill.: Charles C. Thomas. 152–65.

1960   Small isolated human breeding populations and their significance for the process of racial differentiation. *Selected Papers of the Fifth International Congress of Anthropological and Ethnological Sciences,* Philadelphia, September 1–9, 1956. *Men and Cultures,* ed. under chairmanship of Anthony F. C. Wallace. Philadelphia: University of Pennsylvania Press. 684–91. An effort to apply data to a theory about genetic drift.

1960   Migration, isolation, and ongoing human evolution. *Human Biology* 32:80–88.

1960   Comments on La antropologia fisica en Mexico, 1943–1959: Inventario y programa de investigaciones, Juan Comas and Genoves T. Santiago, *Cuadernos del Instituto de Historia, Serie Antropologica* 10:49–52, 58–60.

1960   Variances of bodily measurements in the offspring of natives of and immigrants to three Peruvian towns. *American Journal of Physical Anthropology* 18:257–61. There was a considerable difference among measurements of subjects within communities.

1960   Review of Genoves Tarazaga, *Diferencias Sexuales en el Hueso Coxal. Human Biology* 32:205–7.

1960   Review of S. M. Garn and Zvi Shamir, *Methods for Research in Human Growth. American Journal of Physical Anthropology* 18:241–42.

1961   *The Evolution of Man: A Brief Introduction of Physical Anthropology.* New York: Holt, Rinehart and Winston. I still included a classification of races although I did not believe it meant much.

1961   G. W. Lasker and F. Gaynor Evans. Age, environment and migration: Further anthropometric findings on migrant and non-migrant

Mexicans. *American Journal of Physical Anthropology* 19:203–11. This study in a nearby city largely confirms results of the study in Paracho.

1961 Review of Sol Tax, ed., *The Evolution of Life: Its Origin, History and Future.* *American Anthropologist* 2:382–83.

1962 Comments on Tadeusz Bielicki, Issues in the study of race: Two views from Poland, with discussion. (1) The racial analysis of human populations in relation to their ethnogenesis, by Andrzej Wiercinski; (2) Some possibilities for estimating inter-population relationship on the basis of continuous traits. *Current Anthropology* 3:31–32, 44, 45.

1962 Differences in anthropometric measurements within and between three communities in Peru. *Human Biology* 34:63–70.

1962 Review of Lytt I. Gardner, ed., *Molecular Genetics and Human Disease.* *Human Biology* 34:168–70.

1963 David G. Mandelbaum, Gabriel W. Lasker, and Ethel M. Albert, eds. *The Teaching of Anthropology.* American Anthropological Association, Memoir, 94. Also as: *The Teaching of Anthropology.* University of California Press. Many papers and points of view.

1963 David G. Mandelbaum, Gabriel W. Lasker, and Ethel M. Albert, eds. *Resources for the Teaching of Anthropology.* American Anthropological Association, Memoir, 95. Also as *Resources for the Teaching of Anthropology.* Berkeley: University of California Press. We collected a lot of data about practices.

1963 *Human Evolution: Physical Anthropology and the Origin of Man.* New York: Holt, Rinehart and Winston. A textbook at the high school level.

1963 Advanced courses. In *The Teaching of Anthropology,* 111–21. Physical anthropology beyond the first college course.

1963 A survey of catalog listings in anthropology. In *Resources for the Teaching of Anthropology,* 7–21.

1963 G. W. Lasker and Harold Nelson. Student enrollments and teachers of anthropology in California. In *Resources for the Teaching of Anthropology,* 23–35.

1963 Teaching aids in physical anthropology. In *Resources for the Teaching of Anthropology,* 63–68.

1963 Comments on Josef Brozek, *Quantitative Description of Body Composition: Physical Anthropology's "Fourth" Dimension. Current Anthropology* 4:22–23.

1963 F. R. Ellis, L. P. Cawley, and G. W. Lasker. Blood groups, hemoglobin types, and secretion of group-specific substance at Hacienda Cayalti, North Peru. *Human Biology* 35:26–52. We found two cases of sickling.

1964 Edited: *Physical Anthropology 1953–1961.* For the American Association of Physical Anthropologists by the Instituto Nacional de Antropologia e Historia and the Universidad Nacional Autonoma de Mexico.

Filled in the missing years of the *Yearbook of Physical Anthropology* by reprinting some important papers published during that period.

1964 Jack Kelso and Gabriel Lasker, eds. *Yearbook of Physical Anthropology, 1962.* For the American Association of Physical Anthropologists by the Instituto Nacional de Antropologia e Historia and the Universidad Nacional Autonoma de Mexico. The *Yearbook* still consisted largely of reprints.

1964 Similarities and differences between American and foreign articles published in *Human Biology.* Conference of Biological Editors Report on the Special Meeting of European and North American Editors. Ann Arbor, Mich. R. L. Zwemer and R. E. Gordon, eds., *Conference of Biological Editors,* University of Notre Dame, 59–63. Mimeographed report.

1964 G. W. Lasker and Bernice A. Kaplan. The coefficient of breeding isolation: Population size, migration rates, and possibilities of random genetic drift in six human communities in northern Peru. *Human Biology* 36:327–38. Application of data from demographic surveys.

1964 Review of D. R. Brothwell, ed., *Dental Anthropology. Eugenics Quarterly* 11:250–52.

1964 Review of Elizabeth Goldsmith, ed., *The Genetics of Migrant and Isolate Populations. Human Biology* 36:59–62.

1965 G. W. Lasker and Bernice A. Kaplan. The relation of anthroposcopic traits to the ascription of racial designation in Peru. *Homenaje a Juan Comas en su 65 Aniversario, Mexico* 2:189–220. Except for a small difference in some dental traits, the racial designations used on the Peruvian coast had little to do with biological differences. Older individuals were more likely to think of their parents as indigenous.

1965 Studies in racial isolates. In S. Vandenberg, ed., *Methods and Goals in Human Behavior Genetics.* New York: Academic Press. 17–28.

1965 The "new" physical anthropology seen in retrospect and prospect. *Centennial Review of Arts and Sciences* 9(3):348–66.

1966 Small isolated human breeding populations and their significance for the process of racial differentiation. Bobbs-Merrill Series in the Social Sciences. A-317. Reprint.

1966 Bernice A. Kaplan and G. W. Lasker. Review of Ralph L. Beals and Harry Hoijer, *An Introduction to Anthropology. American Anthropologist* 68:529–30.

1967 David G. Mandelbaum, Gabriel W. Lasker, and Ethel M. Albert, eds. *The Teaching of Anthropology.* Berkeley: University of California Press.

1967 The "new" physical anthropology seen in retrospect and prospect. In Noel Korn and F. W. Thompson, eds., *Human Evolution: Readings in Physical Anthropology,* 2nd ed. New York: Holt, Rinehart and Winston. 3–17.

1967 Comments on Donald S. Marshall, *General Anthropology: Strategy for a Human Science*, and Laura Thompson, *Steps Toward a Unified Anthropology*. *Current Anthropology* 8:84.

1968 Comments on Cesare Emiliani, *The Pleistocene Epoch and the Evolution of Man*. *Current Anthropology* 9(1):40.

1968 The occurrence of identical (isonymous) surnames in various relationships in pedigrees: A preliminary analysis of the relation of surname combinations to inbreeding. *American Journal of Human Genetics* 20:250–57. I had been trying to figure out a way to study population structure from the distribution of surnames when James Crow and Arthur Mange published one, and I applied it.

1968 Leakey, Louis S.B. *World Book Encyclopedia* L:141.

1968 Review of Victor A. McKusick, *Mendelian Inheritance in Man: Catalogs of Autosomal Dominant, Autosomal Recessive, and X-Linked Phenotypes*. *Human Biology* 40:418–19.

1968 Review of Sir Alister Hardy, *The Living Stream*. *American Journal of Human Genetics* 20:286.

1969 Gabriel W. Lasker, Jeffery Mast, and Richard Tashian. Beta-aminoisobutyric acid (BAIB) excretion in urine of residents of eight communities in the states of Michoacan and Oaxaca, Mexico. *American Journal of Physical Anthropology* 30:113–36. Mast, then a medical student, wanted an excuse to go to Mexico. He collected some of the specimens and did the lab work in Richard Tashian's laboratory.

1969 Isonymy (recurrence of the same surnames in affinal relatives): A comparison of rates calculated from pedigrees, grave markers, and death and birth registers. *Human Biology* 41:309–21. A test of different kinds of data.

1969 Human biological adaptability. *Science* 166:1480–86. I tried to outline the subject as consisting of three basic types depending on the duration of response: temporary, lifelong, and genetically fixed. I failed to cite plasticity through memory or antigens in blood sera.

1969 N. Wolanski, G. Lasker, E. Jarosz, and M. Pyzuk. Heterosis effect in man: Continuous traits in the offspring in relation to the distance between birthplaces of mother and father. *Genetica Polonica* 10(3–4):251–56. I would have withdrawn my name if asked; my only role was editorial.

1970 Physical anthropology: The search for general processes and principles. *American Anthropologist* 72:1–8. Reprinted 1973 as a Warner Modular Publication Reprint 302:1–8.

1970 L'adattamento umano alle condizioni ambientali. (Traduzione a cura di Donatella Testa.) Arnoldo Mondadori, ed., *Scienze & Tecnica 70*, Milan. 345–58.

1970 Physical anthropology and forensic medicine: Commentary. In O. von

Mering and L. Kasdan, eds., *Anthropology and the Behavioral and Health Sciences*. Pittsburgh: University of Pittsburgh Press. 221–23.

1970 First discussant and panel discussion, Symposium on Human Adaptation. *American Journal of Physical Anthropology* 32:259–60.

1970 Gabriel W. Lasker and Roy R. Fernandez. PTC tasting and dental caries. *Social Biology* 17:140–41. I am now dubious of any relationship.

1970 "Consanguinity." *Encyclopedia Britannica*.

1971 Human biological adaptability. In G. Nelson and J. D. Ray Jr., eds., *Biological Readings for Today's Students*. New York: John Wiley and Sons. Reprint.

1971 Pasado y presente de la evolucion humana. *La Gaceta, Mexico Nueva* May(5).

1971 Review of T. Dale Stewart, ed., *Handbook of Middle American Indians. Volume 9: Physical Anthropology*. The Americas: *Quarterly Review of Inter-American Cultural History* 28:121–23.

1972 *La Evolucion Humana: La Antropologia Fisica y el Origen del Hombre.* Mexico: Fondo de Cultura Economica. Brief and simple.

1972 The future of physical anthropology. *Yearbook of Physical Anthropology* 16:146–48.

1972 Physical anthropology: The search for general processes and principles. In J. D. Jennings and E. A. Hoebel, *Readings in Anthropology,* 3rd ed. New York: McGraw-Hill. 94–98.

1972 The potential relevance of studies of ancient Egyptian populations to the microevolutionary study of modern populations. *Journal of Human Evolution* 1(2):137–39.

1972 G. W. Lasker, B. Chiarelli, M. Masali, F. Fedele, and B. A. Kaplan. Degree of human genetic isolation measured by isonymy and marital distances in two communities in an Italian Alpine valley. *Human Biology* 44:351–60. A study based on vital records.

1972 Review of Francisco M. Salzano, ed., *The Ongoing Evolution of Latin American Populations. Anales de Antropologia* 9:285–89.

1973 *Physical Anthropology.* New York: Holt, Rinehart and Winston. A college textbook.

1973 Compiled: Bibliographies and Proceedings from Vols. 1 through 8. *Yearbook of Physical Anthropology.* University Microfilms, Ann Arbor, Mich.

1973 Human genetic distances and human mating distances. In M. Crawford and P. Workman, eds., *Anthropological Genetics*. Albuquerque: University of New Mexico Press.

1973 Morris Goodman and Gabriel W. Lasker. Measurement of propinquity and distance in anthropological studies. In J. F. Crow, ed., *Genetic Distances*. New York: Plenum Press.

Appendix

1973 Foreword to Daris Swindler and Charles Wood, *Baboon, Chimpanzee and Man*. Seattle: University of Washington Press.
1974 Tables of contents annotated with sources and cumulative index: *Yearbook of Physical Anthropology* Volumes 1–15 (1945–1967). *Yearbook of Physical Anthropology* 17:252–74.
1974 Demographic aspects of human biology. *Human Biology* 46:365–67.
1974 Gabriel W. Lasker and Bernice Kaplan. Graying of the hair and mortality. *Social Biology* 21:290–95. The positive results are probably due to the bias of inaccurate age responses.
1974 Gabriel W. Lasker and Bernice Kaplan. Anthropometric variables in the offspring of isonymous matings. *Human Biology* 46:713–18. Isonymy is not a good approach to inbreeding of individuals.
1974 G. Lasker, B. Chiarelli, and C. Bullo, eds. Report and Abstracts of the International School of Human Biology Workshop on Demographic Aspects of the Biology of Human Populations. San Rocco, Erice, Sicily, August 16–30.
1975 F. E. Johnston, Elizabeth Watts, and Gabriel W. Lasker, eds. *Biosocial Interrelations in Population Adaptation*. The Hague: Mouton. A selection of papers invited or contributed to the International Congress of Anthropological and Ethnological Sciences.
1975 Morris Goodman and Gabriel W. Lasker. Molecular evidence as to man's place in nature. In Russell Tuttle, ed., *Primate Functional Morphology and Evolution*. The Hague: Mouton. 71–102. I hoped to gain a wider audience for the results of Goodman's pioneering studies by contrasting them with generally accepted views based on morphology.
1975 Gabriel W. Lasker and Henry Womack. An anatomical view of demographic data: Biomass, fat mass and lean body mass of the United States and Mexican human populations. In F. E. Johnston, Elizabeth Watts, and Gabriel Lasker, eds., *Biosocial Interrelations in Population Adaptation*. The Hague: Mouton. 43–53. Measuring body fat in kilotons gives an idea of the scope of global nutritional needs.
1976 *Physical Anthropology*, 2nd ed. New York: Holt, Rinehart and Winston.
1976 Human biological adaptability. In P. Richardson and J. McEvoy, eds., *Human Ecology: An Environmental Approach*. North Scituate, Mass.: Duxbury Press.
1976 Gabriel W. Lasker and Rayner Thomas. Relationship between reproductive fitness and anthropometric dimensions in a Mexican population. *Human Biology* 48:775–91. Mixed results, probably not general.
1976 G. W. Lasker, B. Chiarelli, M. Masali, F. Fedele, and B. A. Kaplan. Grado di isolamento genetico misurato in base alle isonimia e alle distanze matrimoniali in Bellino. *Ricerce Antropologiche in Val Varaita*. Florence: Italiana Societa di Antropologia et Etnologia. We not only translated our paper into Italian; I also reported on it in the local church.

198

1977 What is molecular anthropology? In Morris Goodman and Richard Tashian, eds., *Molecular Anthropology*. New York: Academic Press. 3–12. Includes one line of evidence that the molecular clock does not always run at the same speed.

1977 A coefficient of relationship by isonymy: A method for estimating the genetic relationship between populations. *Human Biology* 49:489–93. I did not realize or remember at the time, but Newton Morton had the same idea previously.

1977 I've been thinking. Council of Biology Editors newsletter. 23:3. About the role of browsing in scientific communication.

1978 Human biological adaptability: The ecological approach in physical anthropology. In Michael H. Logan and Edward E. Hunt Jr., eds., *Health and the Human Condition: Perspectives on Medical Anthropology*. North Scituate, Mass.: Duxbury Press. 58–70.

1978 Gabriel W. Lasker and Rayner Thomas. The relationship between size and shape of the human head and reproductive fitness. *Studies in Physical Anthropology. Polish Academy of Sciences, Warsaw.* 4:3–9. A hint of Darwinian fitness of bigger heads.

1978 Increments through migration to the coefficient of relationship between communities by isonymy. *Human Biology* 50:235–40.

1978 Relationships among the Otmoor villages and surrounding communities as inferred from surnames contained in the current Registers of Electors. *Annals of Human Biology* 5:105–11. In studying the genetic structure of the British population from the distribution of surnames, I used many sources of data.

1978 Bernice A. Kaplan, Gabriel W. Lasker, and Brunetto Chiarelli. Communality of surnames: A measure of biological interrelationships among 31 settlements in Upper Val Varaita in the Italian Alps. *American Journal of Physical Anthropology* 49:251–56.

1978 David Souden and Gabriel W. Lasker. Biological interrelationship between parishes in East Kent: An analysis of marriage duty act returns for 1705. *Local Population History* 21:30–39.

1979 Gabriel Lasker and Henry Womack. An anatomical view of demographic data: Biomass, fat mass, and lean body mass of the United States and Mexican human populations. In William A. Stini, ed., *Physiological and Morphological Adaptation and Evolution*. The Hague: Mouton. 369–78. Reprint of 1975 publication.

1979 Christine Küchemann, Gabriel W. Lasker, and Douglas I. Smith. Historical changes in the coefficient of relationship by isonymy among the populations of the Otmoor villages. *Human Biology* 51:63–77.

1979 G. W. Lasker, D. A. Coleman, N. Aldridge, and W. Fox. Ancestral relationships within and between districts in the region of Reading, England. *Human Biology* 51:445–60. Coleman provided the first data for our study of English population structure—marriage records from three registers.

1980 Surnames in the study of human biology. *American Anthropologist* 82:525–38.

1980 Pamela Raspe and Gabriel W. Lasker. The structure of the human population of the Isles of Scilly. *Annals of Human Biology* 7:401–10. We exploited a part of Raspe's dissertation material.

1981 William H. Mueller, G. W. Lasker, and F. Gaynor Evans. Anthropometric measurements and Darwinian fitness. *Journal of Biosocial Science* 13:309–16.

1981 AAAS Committee on the Social Aspects of Science. Reprints from *Science* on Scientific Freedom and Responsibility (SFR-018).

1981 Classification of Races. *Funk and Wagnall's New Encyclopedia.*

1981 Review of Robert A. Day, *How to write and publish a scientific paper. Human Biology* 53:646–48. I recently gave my copy to Mascie-Taylor, who thinks it still would be good for his graduate students.

1982 Gabriel Lasker and Robert N. Tyzzer. *Physical Anthropology,* 3rd ed. New York: Holt, Rinehart and Winston. I added a chapter on demography, and Tyzzer improved the organization, but I enjoyed doing the earlier editions more.

1982 Veinte-cinco años de editor del *Human Biology.* In *Human Biology (1929– 1978): Ensayo historico-bibliografico.* Mexico: Instituto de Investigaciones Antropologicas. 15–18, 28–31.

1982 Genetic structure of the human population of Great Britain as revealed in the distribution of surnames. *Anthropological Studies in Great Britain and Ireland.* Anthropological Research Papers, Arizona State University, 27:19–26. Review of our studies.

1982 The two faces of physical anthropology. *Estudios de Antropologia Biologica.* Universidad Nacional Autonoma de Mexico. 13–24. Human biological processes and biological history.

1982 Autobiographical sketch. *Human Biology* 54:265–67.

1982 Gabriel W. Lasker and Derek F. Roberts. Secular trends in relationship as estimated by surnames: A study of a Tyneside parish. *Annals of Human Biology* 9:299–307.

1982 Review of *Yearbook of Physical Anthropology,* Vol. 23, ed. by Kenneth A. Bennett. *American Anthropologist* 84:155.

1983 G. W. Lasker and C. G. N. Mascie-Taylor. Surnames in five English villages: Relationship to each other, to surrounding areas, and to England and Wales. *Journal of Biosocial Science* 15:25–34.

1983 Gabriel W. Lasker and Bernice A. Kaplan. English place name surnames tend to cluster near the place named. *Names* 31:167–77. Although widely distributed, place-name surnames show a tendency to be more frequent near the place of the name.

1983 W. R. Fox and G. W. Lasker. The distribution of surname frequencies. *International Statistical Review* 51:81–87. The shape of the distribution is a Pareto curve.

1983 B. A. Kaplan and G. W. Lasker. The present distribution of some English surnames derived from place names. *Human Biology* 55:243–50. Tends to confirm our earlier study.

1983 The frequencies of surnames in England and Wales. *Human Biology* 55:331–40.

1983 C. G. N. Mascie-Taylor and G. W. Lasker. Geographic distribution of surnames in Britain: The Smiths and Joneses have clines like blood group genes. *Journal of Biosocial Science* 16:301–8. Maps of the two most frequent surnames.

1984 G. W. Lasker, R. K. Wetherington, B. A. Kaplan, and R. V. Kemper. Isonymy between two towns in Michoacán, Mexico. In R. Ramos Galvan and R. M. Ramos Rodriguez, eds., *Estudios de Antropologia Biologica*. Mexico: Instituto de Investigaciones Antropologicas, Universidad Nacional Autonoma de Mexico. 159–63. Any relationship of the present populations of the Tarascan Lake Patzquaro and Tarascan Sierra is little reflected by the surnames of Tzintzuntzan and Paracho.

1984 The morphology of human populations. In R. Ramos Galvan and Rosa M. Ramos Rodriguez, eds., *Estudios de Antropologia Biologica*. Mexico: Instituto de Investigaciones Antropologicas, Universidad Nacional Autonoma de Mexico. 145–57. Lines of descent viewed geographically form fascicles held together locally by inbreeding loops which are attached to each other by a network of outbreeding migrations. This view contrasts with traditional thinking about races.

1984 Anthropology journals: What they cite and what cites them. Comments. *Current Anthropology* 25:523.

1985 *Surnames and Genetic Structure*. Cambridge Studies in Biological Anthropology, no. 1. Cambridge: Cambridge University Press. I wanted to get the series started, and there was, and still is, no other book on the subject.

1985 G. W. Lasker and A. Theodore Steegmann Jr. Relationships among companies of the militia in the colony of New York in 1760 estimated by an analysis of their surnames. *Social Biology* 32:136–40.

1985 G. W. Lasker, B. A. Kaplan, and C. G. N. Mascie-Taylor. And who is thy neighbor? Biological relationship in the English village. *Humanbiologia Budapestinensis* 16:97–103. First attempt at a study of the fine structure of village populations by using surnames.

1985 G. W. Lasker and C. G. N. Mascie-Taylor. The geographic distribution of selected surnames in Britain model gene frequency clines. *Journal of Human Evolution* 14:385–92. Polynomial regressions on latitude and longitude.

1985 C. G. N. Mascie-Taylor and G. W. Lasker. Geographical distribution of common surnames in England and Wales. *Annals of Human Biology* 12:397–401.

1985 G. W. Lasker and B. A. Kaplan. Surnames and genetic structure: Repetition of the same pairs of names of married couples, a measure of subdivision of the population. *Human Biology* 57:431–40. An extension of isonymy to off-diagonal areas of the matrix of brides' by bridegrooms' surnames.

1986 G. W. Lasker, C. G. N. Mascie-Taylor, and D. A. Coleman. Repeating pairs of surnames in marriages in Reading (England) and their significance for population structure. *Human Biology* 58:421–25. An application of the RP method Kaplan and I had devised.

1986 G. W. Lasker and D. A. Palgrave. Genetic structure of human population interpreted from family-history records. *Journal of One-Name Studies* 2(8):201–3.

1986 J. L. Boldsen, C. G. N. Mascie-Taylor, and G. W. Lasker. An analysis of the geographic distribution of selected British surnames. *Human Biology* 58:85–95.

1986 Review of T. Bielicki, T. Krupinski, and J. Strzalko, *History of Physical Anthropology in Poland. Human Biology* 58:821–22.

1987 Application of surnames to the study of population structure. In A. J. Boyce and C. G. N. Mascie-Taylor, eds., *Mating Patterns.* Cambridge: Cambridge University Press.

1987 Migration as seen by physical anthropology. In Ma. Elena Saenz and X. Lizarraga, eds., *Estudios de Antropologia Biologica.* Mexico: Universidad Nacional Autonomo de Mexico. 249–54.

1987 C. G. N. Mascie-Taylor, G. W. Lasker, and A. J. Boyce. Repetition of the same surnames in different marriages as an indication of the structure of the population of Sandy Island, Orkney Islands. *Human Biology* 59:97–102.

1987 C. G. N. Mascie-Taylor and G. W. Lasker. Migration and changes in ABO and Rh blood group clines in Britain. *Human Biology* 59:337–44. Even the large prospective study of a one-week birth cohort is too small for definitive results.

1987 Review of P. S. Harper and E. Sunderland, eds., *Genetic and Population Studies in Wales. Human Biology* 59:989–92.

1988 C. G. N. Mascie-Taylor and G. W. Lasker, eds. *Biological Aspects of Human Migration.* Cambridge: Cambridge University Press. The two main aspects are the effects of people moving into different environments and the effects of intermating among different populations.

1988 G. W. Lasker and C. G. N. Mascie-Taylor. The framework of migration studies. In C. G. N. Mascie-Taylor and G. W. Lasker, eds., *Biological*

Aspects of Human Migration. Cambridge: Cambridge University Press. 1–13.

1988 Repeated surnames in those marrying into British one-surname "lineages": An approach to the evaluation of population structure through analysis of the surnames in marriages. *Human Biology* 60:1–9. Improves on our own previous method.

1988 Review of N. E. Groce, *Everyone Here Spoke Sign Language. Journal of Physical Anthropology* 77:139.

1989 G. W. Lasker and C. G. N. Mascie-Taylor. Effects of social class differences and social mobility on growth in height, weight and body mass index in a British cohort. *Annals of Human Biology* 16:1–8. The social class differences are established by age seven and maintained.

1989 A model for the study of sex-linked influences through the study of different classes of cousin pairs. *Annals of Human Biology* 16:467–72. Method based on first-cousin pairs, but it is difficult to get enough pairs to test.

1989 Genetics in the journal *Human Biology*. *Human Biology* 61:615–27.

1990 G. W. Lasker and C. G. N. Mascie-Taylor. *Atlas of British Surnames*. Detroit: Wayne State University Press. Maps of rare names. The techniques for making maps on computers has since greatly improved.

1990 G. W. Lasker, B. A. Kaplan, and J. A. Sedensky. Are there anthropometric differences between the offspring of endogamous and exogamous matings? *Human Biology* 62:247–49. Different studies yield inconsistent results.

1990 K. Gottlieb, P. Raspe, and G. W. Lasker. Patterned selection of mates in St Ouen, Jersey, and the Scilly Isles, examined by isonymy. *Human Biology* 62:637–47. Best examples of the best method (within lineages) of studying the recurrence of the same two surnames in different married couples.

1990 C. G. N. Mascie-Taylor and G. W. Lasker. Lack of an association between ABO and Rh blood group polymorphisms and stature, body weight, and BMI in a cohort of British women. *Human Biology* 62:573–76. Evidence of a high degree of homogeneity in a large sample.

1990 G. Biondi, P. Raspe, E. Perrotti, G. W. Lasker, and C. G. N. Mascie-Taylor. Relationships estimated by isonymy among the Italo-Greco villages of southern Italy. *Human Biology* 62:649–63. Biondi brought data to Cambridge University while I was there and asked me to help analyze. Added cases improve one's knowledge of the general structure of the populations of the species as a whole, but developing new approaches to a problem is more challenging.

1990 C. G. N. Mascie-Taylor and G. W. Lasker. The distribution of surnames in England and Wales: A model for genetic distribution. *Man* n.s. 25:521–30. Some maps of surnames.

1990 G. Biondi, P. Raspe, E. Perrotti, C. G. N. Mascie-Taylor, and G. W. Lasker. Inbreeding coefficients from isonymy in the Italian-Greek villages. *Annals of Human Biology* 17:543–46. The villages of ethnic minorities in Italy are much like other Italian villages.

1990 Review of H. F. Weisberg, J. A. Krosnick, and B. D. Bowen, *An Introduction to Survey Research and Data Analysis,* 2nd ed. *Human Biology* 62:447.

1990 Review of A. P. Mange and E. J. Mange, *Genetics: Human Aspects,* 2nd ed., *Human Biology* 62:577–78.

1990 Review of M. A. Little and J. D. Haas, eds., *Human Biology: A Transdisciplinary Science. Quarterly Review of Biology* 65:117–18.

1991 G. W. Lasker and C. G. N. Mascie-Taylor, eds. *Applications of Biological Anthropology to Human Affairs.* Cambridge: Cambridge University Press. Issues of health and welfare.

1991 Introduction to G. W. Lasker and C. G. N. Mascie Taylor, *Applications of Biological Anthropology to Human Affairs.* Cambridge: Cambridge University Press. 1–13.

1991 Pamela Raspe and G. W. Lasker. Relationships among given names in the Scilly Isles. *Journal of Biosocial Science* 23:241. Just to compare with surnames. There is an error in the formula; I should have let the senior author read the proofs.

1991 Cultural factors in the geographic distribution of personal names. *Human Biology* 63:197–202.

1992 Robert Sokol, Rosalind Harding, C. G. N. Mascie-Taylor, and G. W. Lasker. A spatial analysis of 100 surnames in England and Wales. *Annals of Human Biology* 19:445–76. Several approaches to mapping.

1992 G. W. Lasker and P. D. Raspe. Given name relationships support surname "genetics": A note and correction. *Journal of Biosocial Science* 24:131–33. A pseudo-genetic analysis of a cultural trait.

1993 G. W. Lasker and C. G. N. Mascie-Taylor, eds. *Research Strategies in Human Biology: Field and Survey Studies.* Cambridge: Cambridge University Press. Mostly case studies.

1993 Writing for publication. In G. W. Lasker and C. G. N. Mascie-Taylor, eds., *Research Strategies in Human Biology.* 186–200.

1993 Planning a research project. In: Lasker and Mascie-Taylor, *Research Strategies in Human Biology.* 1–19.

1993 Using surnames to analyse population structure. In David Postles, ed., *Naming, Society and Regional Identity.* Department of Local History, University of Leicester. In press. I read two sets of page proofs, and that is the last I heard. I do not believe this work was published.

1993 G. Biondi, G. W. Lasker, P. D. Raspe, and C. G. N. Mascie-Taylor. Inbreeding coefficients from the surnames of grandparents of the schoolchildren in Albanian-speaking Italian villages. *Journal of Biosocial Science* 25:63–71.

1993 G. Biondi, G. W. Lasker, and C. G. N. Mascie-Taylor. The use of surnames in evaluating inbreeding: Applications to Albanian, Croatian, and Greek speaking Italian populations. *Anthropologia Contemporanea*, 16:11–17.

1993 Revision: Datos sobre los apellidos hispanoamericanos en los estudios de biologia humana. *Annales de Antropología* 28:107–28. The Hispanic system of names lends itself well to the method, and I reviewed the considerable literature.

1993 Review of J. Cleland and A. G. Hill, eds., *The Health Transition. Journal of Biosocial Science* 25:565.

1994 The place of anthropometry in human biology. In S. J. Ulijaszek and C. G. N. Mascie-Taylor, *Anthropometry: The Individual and the Population.* Cambridge: Cambridge University Press. 1–6.

1994 B. A. Kaplan and G. W. Lasker. A. A. Dahlberg remembered. *Dental Anthropology Newsletter* 8(2):6–7. Obituary.

1994 The place of James Norman Spuhler in the development of anthropological genetics. *Human Biology* 66:553–66. Obituary.

1994 Review of Kenneth M. Weiss. Genetic variation and human disease. *Journal of Biosocial Science* 26:138.

1994 Review of C. Oxnard, J. Stone and P. White. Evolution, form, and geography. *Human Biology* 66:165–66.

1994 Review of James V. Neel, *Physician to the Gene Pool. New England Journal of Medicine* 331 (10):684.

1994 Review of M. K. Bhasin et al., *The Distribution of Genetical, Morphological and Behavioural Traits among the People of the Indian Region. Human Biology* 66:734–35.

1995 Evidence from surnames on the population structure of villages surrounding the Otmoor. In G. A. Harrison with a chapter by G. W. Lasker, *Human Biology of the Otmoor Population.* Oxford: Oxford University Press. I have done more on the subject since.

1995 The study of migrants as a strategy for understanding human biological plasticity. In B. Bogin and C. G. N. Mascie-Taylor, eds., *Human Plasticity and Variability.* Cambridge: Cambridge University Press. 110–14.

1995 G. W. Lasker and C. G. N. Mascie-Taylor. The effects of inter-regional migration on geographic variability in biological and social traits in Great Britain. *Human Biology* 67:629–40.

1995 G. W. Lasker and B. A. Kaplan. Demography in biological anthropology: Human population structure and evolution. *Human Biology* 7:425–30.

Appendix

1995 Review of M. Kimura, *Population Genetics, Molecular Evolution, and the Neutral Theory: Selected Papers. Human Biology* 7:544.

1996 M. Goodman, R. Tashian, and G. Lasker, eds. *Molecular Anthropology: Toward a New Evolutionary Paradigm.* Special issue of *Molecular Phylogenetics and Evolution.* San Diego: Academic Press. Papers from a conference.

1996 G. W. Lasker and D. E. Crews. Behavioral influences on the evolution of human genetic diversity. In M. Goodman, R. Tashian, and G. Lasker, eds., *Molecular Anthropology: Toward a New Evolutionary Paradigm.* Special issue of *Molecular Phylogenetics and Evolution* 5:232–40. Humans have carried fresh water and crossed open seas for a long time, and the criss-cross migrations and intertribal matings have tied the species together.

1996 G. W. Lasker and C. G. N. Mascie-Taylor. Influence of social class on the correlation of stature of adult children with that of their mothers and fathers. *Journal of Biosocial Science* 28:117–22.

1996 Jesper Boldsen and G. W. Lasker. Relationship of people across an international border based on an isonymy analysis across the German-Danish frontier. *Journal of Biosocial Science* 27:177–83. Some surnames are shared, but there is a break at a frontier because there are many more German than Danish surnames.

1996 C. G. N. Mascie-Taylor and G. W. Lasker. Further note on possible changes in the geographic distribution of ABO and Rh blood groups in Great Britain. *Human Biology* 68:473–78. Little change since the population was already nearly homogeneous.

1996 G. P. Biondi, P. Raspe, C. G. N. Mascie-Taylor, and G. W. Lasker. Repetition of the same pair of surnames in marriages in Albanian Italians, Greek Italians, and the Italian population of Campobasso Province. *Human Biology* 68:573–83.

1997 Census versus sample data in isonymy studies; relationship at short distances. *Human Biology* 69:733–38. Much of the relationship in a community is among people in the same residence.

1997 Potential for mischief. *Anthropology Newsletter* 38(7):2. Some molecular geneticists have been using terms such as "pure Caucasian" without realizing that there probably never were such people.

1997 Pamela Raspe and G. W. Lasker. Gst, a measure of gene diversity from surname distributions. Population subdivision in an area of England. *Revista Española de Antropologia Biologica* 18:19–24. James F. Crow proposed a method, and we tried it out and compared it to some other methods.

1997 Review of Richard Wragham and Dale Peterson, *Demonic Males: Apes and the Origins of Human Violence. New England Journal of Medicine* 336:969.

1998   Citations of human biology journals in human biology journals. *Human Biology* 70:140–41.

1998   G. Paoli, G. W. Lasker, et al. Changes over 100 years in degree of isolation of 21 parishes of Lima Valley, Italy. Accepted for publication. As compared with simple distance, relationships are hierarchical with neighborhood, village, valley, region.

1998   The hierarchical genetic structure of an urban town, Kidlington, Oxfordshire, examined by the Coefficient of Relationship to Isonymy. *Journal of Biosocial Science.* In press.

Bibliography

Adams, R. 1937. *Interracial Marriage in Hawaii*. New York: Macmillan.

American Association of Medical Colleges. 1956. The teaching of anatomy and anthropology in medical education, Part II. *Journal of Medical Education*.

Baker, P. T. 1996. Adventures in human population biology. *Annual Reviews of Anthropology* 25:1–18.

Baker, P. T., and M. A. Little (eds.). 1976. *Man in the Andes*. Stroudsburg, Pa.: Dowden, Hutchinson and Ross.

Baker, P. T., and J. S. Weiner (eds.). 1967. *The Biology of Human Adaptation*. New York: Clarendon Press.

Bertram, J. M. 1938. *First Act in China: The Story of the Sian Mutiny*. New York: Viking.

Birdsell, J. B. 1993. *Microevolutionary Patterns in Aboriginal Australia*. New York: Oxford University Press.

Bowles, G. T. 1932. *New Types of Old Americans at Harvard and at Eastern Women's Colleges*. Cambridge, Mass.: Harvard University Press.

Bowles, G. T. 1977. *The People of Asia*. New York: Scribner.

Brace, C. L. 1994. Ashley Montagu. *Proceedings of the Sixty-third Meeting of the American Association of Physical Anthropology. American Journal of Physical Anthropology* 95:456–57.

Buck, J. L. 1957. *Land Utilization in China*. 3 vols. Shanghai: Commercial Press.

Buettner-Janusch, J. 1967. (review) Yearbook of Physical Anthropology, 1965. *American Journal of Physical Anthropology* 27:403–5.

Chapple, E. D., and C. S. Coon. 1942. *Principles of Anthropology*. New York: Holt.

Cold Spring Harbor Symposium on Quantitative Biology. 1950 (1951). *Origin and Evolution of Man.* Vol. 15. Cold Spring Harbor, N.Y.: Biology Laboratory.

Comas, J. 1951. *Racial Myths.* Paris: UNESCO.

Coon, C. S. 1962. *The Origin of Races.* New York: Knopf.

Crawford, M. H., and P. L. Workman (eds.). 1973. *Methods and Theories of Anthropological Genetics.* Albuquerque: University of New Mexico Press.

Day (Bond), C. 1970. *A Study of Some Negro-White Families in the United States.* Westport, Conn.: Negro Universities Press (reprint).

Gardner, E., D. J. Gray, and R. O'Rahilly. 1960. *Anatomy: A Regional Study of Human Structure.* Philadelphia: Saunders.

Genoves, S. 1980. *The Acali Experiment: Five Men and Six Women on a Raft across the Atlantic for 101 Days.* New York: Times Books.

Goldstein, M. S. 1943. *Demographic and Bodily Changes in Descendents of Mexican Immigrants.* Austin: Institute of Latin American Studies, University of Texas.

Goodman, M. 1962. Immunochemistry of the primates and primate evolution. *Annals of the New York Academy of Sciences* 102:219–34.

Goodman, M., and R. E. Tashian (eds.). 1976. *Molecular Anthropology: Genes and Proteins in the Evolutionary Ascent of the Primates.* New York: Plenum.

Green, J. D. 1951. Comparative anatomy of the hypophysis with special reference to its blood supply and innervation. *American Journal of Anatomy* 88:225–312.

Hanson, H. E. 1939. *Humane Endeavor: The Story of the China War.* New York: Farrar and Rinehart.

Harrison, G. A. 1996. *Human Biology of the Otmoor Population.* Oxford: Oxford University Press.

Harrison, G. A., J. S. Weiner, J. M. Tanner, and N. A. Barnicot. 1964. *Human Biology: An Introduction to Human Evolution, Variation and Growth.* New York: Oxford University Press.

Hooton, E. A. 1931. *Up from the Ape.* Revised ed. New York: Macmillan.

Hooton, E. A. 1939. *The American Criminal: An Anthropological Study.* Cambridge, Mass.: Harvard University Press.

Hooton, E. A., and C. W. Dupertuis. 1955. *The Physical Anthropology of Ireland.* Papers of the Peabody Museum of Archaeology and Ethnology, Harvard University, 30 (1–2).

Howells, W. W. 1944. *Mankind So Far.* New York: Doubleday.

Hulse, F. S. 1963. *The Human Species.* New York: Random House.

Kaplan, B. A. 1951. The changing functions of the huanancha dance at the Corpus Christi festival in Paracho, Michoacán Mexico. *Journal of American Folklore* 64:383–92.

Kaplan, B. A. 1952. Environment and human plasticity. *American Anthropologist* 56:780–90.

Kaplan, B. A. 1960. Mechanization in Paracho, a craft community. *Alpha Kappa Deltan* 30(1):59–65. Reprinted in *Contemporary Cultures and Societies of Latin America*, ed. D. B. Heath and R. N. Adams. New York: Random House. 246–53.

Kaplan, B. A., G. W. Lasker, and B. Chiarelli. 1978. Communality of surnames: A measure of biological inter-relationships among 31 settlements in Upper Val Varaita in the Italian Alps. *American Journal of Physical Anthropology*, 49:251–56.

Kaplan, B. A., and C. G. N. Mascie-Taylor. 1997. Smoking and asthma among 23-year-olds. *Journal of Asthma* 34:219–26.

Klineberg, O. 1935. *Race Differences*. New York: Harper and Row.

Kluckhohn, C. 1944. *Mirror for Man: A Survey of Human Behavior and Social Attitudes*. Greenwich, Conn.: Fawcett.

Lasker, B. 1929. *Race Attitudes in Children*. New York: Holt.

Lasker, B. 1943. *Asia on the Move*. New York: Holt.

Lasker, B. 1944. *Peoples of Southeast Asia*. New York: Knopf.

Lasker, B. 1949. *Democracy through Discussion*. New York: H. W. Wilson.

Lasker, B. 1950. *Human Bondage in Southeast Asia*. Chapel Hill: University of North Carolina Press.

Lasker, M., M. Enklewitz, and G. W. Lasker. 1936. The inheritance of l-xyloketosuria (essential pentosuria). *Human Biology* 8:243–55.

Leslie, C. M. 1960. *Now We Are Civilized: A Study of the World View of the Zapotec Indians of Mitla, Oaxaca*. Detroit: Wayne State University Press.

Livingstone, F. B., 1985. *Frequencies of Hemoglobin Variants*. New York: Oxford University Press.

Macklin, M. T. 1935. The role of heredity in disease. *Medicine* 14(1).

Mandlebaum, D. G., G. W. Lasker, and E. M. Albert (eds.). 1963. *The Teaching of Anthropology*. Berkeley: University of California Press.

Martin, R. 1928. *Lehrbuch der Anthropologie*. 3 vols. Jena: Fischer.

Mascie-Taylor, C. G. N., and B. Bogin (eds.). 1995. *Human Variability and Plasticity*. Cambridge: Cambridge University Press.

Meiklejohn, A. 1932. *The Experimental College*. New York: Harper.

Pruitt, I. 1945. *A Daughter of Han: The Autobiography of a Chinese Working Woman*. New Haven: Yale University Press.

Reynolds, E. L. 1950. *The Distribution of Subcutaneous Fat in Childhood and Adolescence*. Monographs of the Society for Research in Child Development. No. 50.

Roberts, D. F. 1952. Basal metabolism, race and climate. *Journal of the Royal Anthropological Institute* 82:169–83.

Rowntree, B. S., and B. Lasker. 1911. *Unemployment: A Social Study*. London: Macmillan.

211

Shapiro, H. L. 1931. The Chinese Population in Hawaii: Preliminary paper prepared for the fourth general session of the Institute of Pacific Relations. New York. 3–29.

Shapiro, H. L. (with F. S. Hulse). 1939. *Migration and Environment.* New York: Oxford University Press.

Stefansson, V. 1932. *The Friendly Arctic: The Story of Five Years in Polar Regions.* New York: Macmillan.

Straus, W. L. Jr. 1949. The riddle of man's ancestry. *Quarterly Review of Biology* 24:200–223.

Thieme, F. P. 1957. A comparison of Puerto Rican migrants and sedentes. *Papers of the Michigan Academy of Sciences, Arts and Letters* 42:249–56.

Washburn, S. L. 1951. The new physical anthropology, *Transactions of the New York Academy of Sciences,* Series 2, 13:298–304.

Washburn, S. L. 1962. The study of race. *American Anthropologist* 65:521–32.

Washburn, S. L. 1982. Gabriel Ward Lasker. *Human Biology.* 54:171–73.

Watts, E. S., F. E. Johnston, and G. W. Lasker (eds.). 1975. *Behavioral Interrelations in Population Adaptation.* The Hague: Mouton.

Weidenreich, F. 1943. *The Skull of Sinanthropus pekinensis.* Chungking: Geological Survey of China.

Weiner, J. S., K. P. Oakley, and W. E. Le Gros Clark. 1953. The solution of the Piltdown problem. *Bulletin of the British Museum (Natural History),* Geological Series, 2(3).

Wiener, N. 1956. *I Am a Mathematician: The Later Life of a Prodigy.* Garden City, N.Y.: Doubleday.

Wittfogel, K. A. 1948. *History of Chinese Society: Liao (907–1125).* Philadelphia: American Philosophical Society.

Index

Acheson, Roy, on ossification, 100–101

Adams, Romanzo, 209; on social structure of Hawaii, 38

Aginsky, Bert, 32

Aginsky, Ethel, 32

Albert, Ethel M., 194, 195, 211

Angel, J. Lawrence, apt student of anatomy, 61, 75; did Stewart's work as treasurer of AAPA, 100; interest in paleodemography, 90, on race, 140, on types, 178; physical anthropology of Greece, 56; supportive friend, 56

Arensberg, Conrad, 47

Baer, Melvyn, 85

Baker, Paul T., 209; as teacher, 187; autobiographical sketch, 130; biology of human adaptation, 180; established "school" of physiological anthropology, 182; *Man in the Andes*, 181; photo, 133; research interests, 133–34

Baker, Thelma, 187; photo, 133

Barbour, George, 148

Barnicot, Nigel, worked weekends, 158

Basilius, Harold, on Wayne University Press board of editors, 98

Beals, Ralph L., 195; helped Humphrey, 39; offered access for study in Cheran, 118

Benedict, Ruth, 87

Bennett, Edward, 64

Bertram, James, 19; publication of *Democracy* in Peking, 21; interviews with Japanese leaders, 37

Bewley, Mary, 1; copybook, 2–3

Bielicki, Tadeusz, 194, 202

Biondi, Gianfranco, 204, 205; human genetics, 169

Birdsell, Joseph B., 209; background as engineer, 55; book on race, 149; on racial types, 93, 178; "P" genes, 179; studied anatomy, 61

213

Black, Davidson, anatomist, 28
Blair, Frank, *Big Science*, 182
Boas, Franz, bust of, 66; changes
  in racial types, ix, 172; migration
  model, 65; power analysis, 65;
  research methodology, 125, 187
Bogin, Barry, xii, 205; associate editor
  of *Human Biology*, 101; photo, 102;
  small size of Guatemalans due to
  chronic food shortages, 184
Boldsen, Jesper, 202, 206; biological
  history, 166; photo, 166
Bond, Carolyn Day, 73, 210
bone lab at Harvard, 45, 56
Borbolla, Daniel F. Rubin de la, 116,
  117
Bowles, Gordon T., 37, 209; physique
  of Harvard sons and daughters,
  52
Boyce, Anthony J., 152, 202; bursar
  of St. Johns College, Oxford, 139
Boyd, William C., 142; race concept,
  179
Brace, C. Loring, 56, 145, 209; photo,
  146; tooth dimensions, 146
Brede, Alex, editor of Wayne
  University Press books, 98
bribes, return of by Mexican officials,
  116
Broom, Robert, 147
Brothwell, Donald R., 195
Brozek, Josef, 98; board of editors
  of *Human Biology*, 99; partial
  starvation experiment, 171;
  resolution on race, 148
Brues, Alice M., background in
  genetics, 56; taught anatomy, 75
Buck, J. Loesing, 30, 209
Buenon, Gaston, on physical fitness,
  185
Buettner-Janusch, John, 142–44, 209
Burg Wartenstein, Austria, 73, 135

Buzzati Traverso, Adriano,
  population genetics, 168

Candela, P. B., blood typing of bone,
  142
Cannon, Walter, 61, 62
Carlson, David, associate editor of
  Human Biology, 101.
Carpenter, Charles Ray, 58
Carter, Edward C., founding of The
  Institute of Pacific Relations (IPR),
  5–6
Carter, Lindsay, somatotyping, 172
Cartmill, Matt, 75
Casillas, Leticia, 117
Castillo, Beatriz del, 118
Catholic workers movement, 70
Cavalli Sforza, L. L., study of
  surnames, 174
Cawley, L. P., 194
Centre for the Study of the History of
  Population and Social Structure,
  Cambridge, 162
Chang, Hsueh-liang, 21
Chapple, Eliot, 46–47, 51, 209;
  experiment with social behavior
  of mice, 44; introductory textbook,
  47; study of social interaction, xii,
  46
Chardin, Teilhard de, and Piltdown,
  179; belief in human evolution,
  179
Chiang, Kai-shek, 21, 34, 37
Chiarelli, Brunetto, 197, 198, 199,
  211; organizer of anthropology
  programs, 139; project in the
  Italian Alps, 167
Chin, Robert, psychologist, 65, 67
chiropractic, 87
Chou T'ung University, 20
Civilian Conservation Corps (CCC),
  15

Leslie, Charles M., 211
Lessa, William, 41, 42
Leue, William, 62
Lie, Trigvie, Secretary General of
  UN, 6
Lieberman, Leslie Sue, xii, 53
Lin, Yueh-hwa, 47, 58, 59; photo, 59
Linton, Ralph, 12, 13; gift to
  Herskovits, 87; knowledge of
  material culture, 149
Little, Michael A., xii, 58, 187, 209;
  helped establish "school" of
  physiological anthropology, 182;
  Man in the Andes, 181; photos, 76,
  188; with Baker in Peru, 134
Livingstone, Frank B., and
  hemoglobin variants and malaria,
  95, 146, 211
Lowie, Robert, 39
Lyman, Richard, 71

MacAleavy, Henry, 19, 31
MacBeth, Helen, 107
Macklin, Madge Thurlow, heredity
  in disease, 16
Mainland, Donald, 191
Maisel, Harry, 115
Malina, Robert, editor of *American
  Journal of Human Biology*, 104; on
  physical fitness, 185; photo, 104
Malinowski, Bronislaw, 49
Mallon, James, warder of Toynbee
  Hall, 8
Mandelbaum, David, 88, 194, 211
Mangin, William, 130–31
Mankind Quarterly, 51
Markee, Joseph E., 71
Marshall, Donald S., 196
Martin, R. *Lehrbuch der Anthropologie*,
  44, 211
Masali, Melchiorre, 168, 197
Mascie-Taylor, C. G. N., xii, 113, 153,
  200, 201, 202, 203, 204, 205, 206,

211; collaborated with Lasker,
  152; editor, 158; epidemiology
  of asthma, 113, 162; heavy work
  schedule, 164; on human fertility,
  107; on migration, 182; photo, 159
Mather, K., 191
McCarthy, Senator Joseph, 6, 22
McCorkle, Thomas, 87
McCown, Theodore D., 88, 96
Mead, Margaret, Stefansson's
  project on comparison of diets,
  59, 60; argued for attending
  racially segregated meeting, 150;
  nominated for president of AAAS,
  79
Meier, Robert, 42; photo, 146
Meiklejohn, Alexander, 11, 211
Menotti, Gian Carlo, opera
  Tamutamu, 90
Merton, Robert, review of Hooton's
  work on criminals, 170
Mexicans, spirit of enterprise of
  returned emigrants, 112
Michaels, Glenn, xi
Miller, H., 191
Mitchell, Jerald A., xii
Mitla, Oaxaca, 123–24
Montagu, M. F. Ashley, 75, 145,
  180, 191; criticism of Hooton,
  170; influence on wide audience,
  179; on mortality among tobacco
  smokers, 178; on race, 177; views
  attacked by Carlton Putnam, 148
Morton, Newton E., 38; study of
  surnames, 174, 175
Mueller, William H., 200

Nagasaki coaling ships, 36
Nankai University, economic and
  social institute, 16, 18
National Child Development Study
  (NCDS), 163